Socialism and Legal Hist

This book focuses on the way in which legal historians and legal scientists used the past to legitimize, challenge and explain the socialist legal orders, which were backed by dictatorial governments.

The volume studies legal historians and legal histories written in Eastern European countries during the socialist era after the Second World War. The book investigates whether there was a unified form of socialist legal historiography and, if so, what can be said of its common features. The individual chapters of this volume concentrate on the regimes that are situated between the Russian, and later Soviet, legal culture and the area covered by the German Civil Code. Hence, the geographical focus of the book is on East Germany, Russia, the Baltic states, Poland, and Hungary. The approach is transnational, focusing on the interaction and intertwinement of the then hegemonic communist ideology and the ideas of law and justice as they appeared in the writings of legal historians of the socialist legal orders. Such an angle enables concentration on the dynamics between politics and law as well as identities and legal history.

Studying the socialist interpretations of legal history reveals the ways in which legal scholars, situated between legal renewal and political guidance, gave legitimacy to, struggled to come to terms with, and sketched the future of the socialist legal orders.

The book will be a valuable resource for academics and researchers working in the areas of legal history, jurisprudence, philosophy of law and European Studies.

Ville Erkkilä is a Postdoctoral Researcher at the Center for European Studies, University of Helsinki, Finland.

Hans-Peter Haferkamp is Full Professor of Private Law and History of German Law. He is the Director of the Institute of Modern History of Private Law, German and Rhenish Legal History, University of Cologne, Germany.

Routledge Research in Legal History

The Royal Prerogative and Constitutional Law
A Search for the Quintessence of Executive Power
Noel Cox

Socialism and Legal History
The Histories and Historians of Law in Socialist East Central Europe
Edited by Ville Erkkilä and Hans-Peter Haferkamp

See more at https://www.routledge.com/Routledge-Research-in-Legal-History/book-series/RRLEGHIST

Socialism and Legal History

The Histories and Historians of Law in Socialist East Central Europe

Edited by
Ville Erkkilä and
Hans-Peter Haferkamp

Routledge
Taylor & Francis Group
LONDON AND NEW YORK

First published 2021
by Routledge
2 Park Square, Milton Park, Abingdon, Oxon OX14 4RN

and by Routledge
52 Vanderbilt Avenue, New York, NY 10017

Routledge is an imprint of the Taylor & Francis Group, an informa business

British Library Cataloguing-in-Publication Data
A catalogue record for this book is available from the British Library

Library of Congress Cataloging-in-Publication Data

Names: Erkkilä, Ville, 1978- editor. | Haferkamp, Hans-Peter, 1966- editor.
Title: Socialism and legal history : the histories and historians of law in socialist East Central Europe / edited by Ville Erkkilä and Hans-Peter Haferkamp.
Description: Milton Park, Abingdon, Oxon ; New York, NY: Routledge, 2021. | Series: Routledge research in legal history | Includes bibliographical references and index.
Identifiers: LCCN 2020027216 (print) | LCCN 2020027217 (ebook) | ISBN 9780367414757 (hardback) | ISBN 9780367814670 (ebook)
Subjects: LCSH: Law--Europe, Eastern--History. | Law--Europe, Central--History. | Socialism--Europe, Eastern--History. | Socialism--Europe, Central--History.
Classification: LCC KJC510 .S63 2021 (print) | LCC KJC510 (ebook) | DDC 349.4709/045--dc23
LC record available at https://lccn.loc.gov/2020027216
LC ebook record available at https://lccn.loc.gov/2020027217

ISBN: 978-0-367-41475-7 (hbk)
ISBN: 978-0 367-41983-7 (pbk)
ISBN: 978-0-367-81467-0 (ebk)

Typeset in Galliard
by MPS Limited, Dehradun

Contents

Contributors

Marta Bucholc is a professor of sociology at Käte Hamburger Kolleg 'Recht als Kultur' in Bonn and at the University of Warsaw. Her research fields are historical sociology, intellectual history, sociology of law and sociology of knowledge. Her recent publications include 'Law and Liberal Pedagogy in a Post-Socialist Society: The Case of Poland', *Journal of Modern European History*, 2020 (forthcoming); 'Schengen and the Rosary. Catholic religion and the postcolonial syndrome in Polish national habitus', *Historische Sozialforschung/Historical Social Research* (2020) 45:1, 153–181; 'Commemorative Lawmaking: Memory Frames of the Democratic Backsliding in Poland After 2015', *Hague Journal on the Rule of Law* (2019) 11, 85–110.

Ville Erkkilä is a post-doctoral researcher at the University of Helsinki. He works on the history of historiography, legal history of socialism and intellectual history of 20th century Europe. He is the author of the book *Conceptual Change of Conscience. Franz Wieacker and German Legal Historiography 1933–1968* (Tübingen 2019). His current project is about post-Second World War land reforms in North Eastern Europe.

András Földi is full professor of Roman law and comparative legal history at the Eötvös Loránd University of Budapest. He works mainly on Roman private law, including the continuity of Roman law tradition. He has published articles in German, Italian, English and French in journals of Roman law and legal history (e.g., *Fundamina*, *Index*, RIDA, SDHI, *SZ Rom. Abt.*, TR) as well as in a number of Festschriften and other collective volumes.

Adolfo Giuliani is a research fellow at the Max Planck Institute for European Legal History in Frankfurt. He works on historical epistemology (late-medieval and early modern judicial proof, interpretation and presumption), legal theory (20th century antiformalism) and the history of legal historiography. He is the author of two upcoming books: *The Age of Presumptions. A Study of Jacopo Menochio's De praesumptionibus (1587)* and *Changing Images of the Legal Past: Savigny, Kantorowicz and Glenn.*

Zara Luisa Gries (Ref. iur) and **Adrian Schmidt-Recla** (Prof. Dr. iur) are fellows of the Jena Research Centre for the Law of the German Democratic Republic of the Friedrich Schiller University in Jena. They examine the private law of the German Democratic Republic—its preconditions, structures, doctrines and history. Gries graduated from Jena (2020) and is working on a doctoral thesis on 'Mental Disorders in Socialist Law of the German Democratic Republic'. Schmidt-Recla graduated from Leipzig (1995), and he has focused on medieval and contemporary legal history, on medical law, on interferences and interfaces between medicine and law and on general German private law. His second book *Kalte und warme Hand. Verfügungen von Todes wegen in mittelalterlichen Referenzrechtsquellen* (Köln, Weimar, Wien, 2011) is regarded as a modern attempt to write a methodologically sound legal history of important and disputed institutions of German private law.

Éva Jakab is a professor of legal history and head of the department of Roman law at the University of Szeged. She has lectured and published extensively on Roman law and legal history of the ancient world. She is the author of several monographs on legal history, and her research interests include ancient Roman law, legal papyrology, ancient comparative law and legal humanism.

Marju Luts-Sootak is a professor of legal history at the University of Tartu. Her main research areas are history of law and legal scholarship in Estonia, in the former Baltic Sea provinces and in the Baltic Sea area, especially in Germany, Russia and the Nordic countries. Her teaching and research also concern the philosophy of law and the history of jurisprudence, as well as the theory and history of legal methodology. She has been a co-editor of the legal journal *Forum Historiae Iuris* (www.forhistiur.de) and is the editor-in-chief of the Estonian legal journals *Juridica* and *Juridica International* (www.juridicainternational.eu).

Sanita Osipova (Prof. Dr. iur.) is the vice president of the Constitutional Court of the Republic of Latvia and a professor at the Faculty of Law at the University of Latvia. Her research interests include legal history (history of family law, history of justice and court systems), legal sociology, state law and legal ethics. She has published extensively in international law journals and is the author of several notable monographs on Latvian and European legal history, e.g., *Eiropas tiesību priekšvēsture* (*Prehistory of the European Law*) (2017), *Nācija, valoda, tiesiska valsts: ceļā uz rītdienu* (*The Nation, language, rule of Law: on the way to tomorrow*) (2020).

Martin Otto is a post-doctoral researcher at the FernUniversität (Open University) of Hagen. He works on the history of family law, legal history of the GDR, church law, labour law and history of private law, biographies of legal scientists, mostly in 19th and 20th century Germany and Europe. He is the author of several books, e.g., *Von der Eigenkriche zum Volkseigenen Betrieb. Erwin Jacobi (1884–1965), Arbeits-, Staats- und Kirchenrecht zwischen Kaiserreich und DDR* (Tübingen 2008) and most recent '*Ein* *stiller Diplomat.' Ulrich E. Biel im Gespräch über die Berliner Nachkriegszeit* (Berlin 2017). His current project is on the legal history of family names in Germany.

Anton Rudokvas is a full professor at the Saint Petersburg State University. He works on the history of law, Roman law, civil law and comparative private law. He was a member of the authors team of the complete translation into Russian of the main monument of Roman law *Digesta Justiniani* (2002–2006) and the leader of the Russian team of the international research project 'Legal Cultures of Eastern Europe: Traditions and Transfers' (2004–2008) of the Max Planck Institute for European Legal History.

Preface

What kind of an impact did the academic discipline of legal history have on legal education and juridical self-understanding in the socialist regimes? Hitherto, these questions scarcely played any role in research on legal education in the socialist regimes.[1] Initially, with this project we aimed to address that dilemma.

At its inception lay the idea that legal history in particular is ideally suited to reveal the legal premises of socialism: on the one hand, the point of departure for historical materialism—already visible in the writings of Marx—was based on the unyielding ideological principle of assessing positive law as a result of the general historical development. We therefore assumed legal history to be characterised by a particularly close proximity to politics. On the other hand, it was also evident that as a mere superstructure (as per socialist theory), legal history was less important for the legitimation of socialism than, for example, the history of economy. Thus, it was also conceivable that it had merged with the subject of political economy and had thereby become nothing more than an irrelevant ancillary aspect of legal education. Finally, a third perspective was added to these conflicting assumptions: the idea of *ius commune* is an essential component of European legal history. Since the 19th century, however, it has been acknowledged that *ius commune*, with ancient Roman law at its core, was among the dominating factors responsible for the rise of capitalism. How did socialism deal with this heritage? To pursue these approaches forced us to constantly keep yet another aspect in mind: what was left of these traditions of legal education after 1989, and does it perhaps still shape the cultures of legal education of post-socialist states?

Against that background we organised a workshop, 'Socialist interpretations of legal history. The histories and historians of law and justice in the GDR, Poland and the Baltic states under the reign of communism', held on 22–23 March 2019 at the Institut für Neuere Privatrechtsgeschichte, Deutsche und Rheinische Rechtsgeschichte at the University of Cologne. Our aim was to collect different experiences of and views on the historically oriented legal science of the socialist regimes of East Central Europe, especially with regards to continuity from the preceding era, common narratives and cooperation between scholars. We wish to express our gratitude to the keynote speakers, the participants and the guests, as well as to Privatdozent Dr. Carsten Fischer, Katharina Happ, Jacqueline Weertz,

Eric Zakowski and Marianne Sandelin who all helped to facilitate an inspiring and successful workshop. The following contributions originate from this conference.

Several people have been of invaluable help during the process of turning a tentative idea into a book. First of all, our thanks go to Alison Kirk, who has been an incredibly patient and supportive publishing editor. Mark Shackleton's proofreading was the backbone of this project. Heta Björklund compiled the index, and Paul Behne assisted in translations and editing process. Iida Karjalainen's meticulous work in checking the individual contributions and compiling them into a manuscript, not to mention her work as a photo editor, was a priceless aid. Juhana Aunesluoma helped to conceptualise the multifaceted phenomenon of the politics of history; Kaius Tuori's comments were crucial in the writing progress. Salla Huikuri has been the best language editor, constructive critic and encouraging colleague during the whole time.

We wish to thank the people of the Centre of Excellence in Law, Identity and the European Narratives and the Centre for European Studies, situated at the University of Helsinki, and we are especially indebted to the hardworking members of the sub-project Law and the uses of the past (Paolo Amorosa, Jacob Giltaj, Saila Heinikoski, Ville Suuronen and Kaius Tuori)—your help and support during this project is very much appreciated. The research leading to these results has received funding from Academy of Finland funded Centre of Excellence in Law, Identity and the European Narratives, funding decision number 312154. Thett.

Ville V. Erkkilä, Helsinki
Hans-Peter Haferkamp, Köln

Note

1 See, for example, Bender, G., and Falk, U. (eds) (1999) *Recht im Sozialismus. Analysen zur Normdurchsetzung in osteuropäischen Nachkriegsgesellschaften (1944/45–1989), Vol. 2: Justizpolitik*, Frankfurt a. M.: Vittorio Klostermann, which offers a comparative view on legal education in Hungary, Czechoslovakia, Poland and the GDR.

Introduction

Socialist interpretations of legal history

Ville Erkkilä

This study of legal historians and legal histories written in Eastern European countries during the socialist era after the Second World War concentrates on a phenomenon of the recent past. Yet it speaks to the contemporary audience, who witnesses the challenging of the European ideal of the rule of law almost on a daily basis. Our book focuses on the way in which legal historians and legal scientists used the past to legitimise, challenge, and explain socialist legal orders that were backed by dictatorial governments.

The individual chapters of this volume concentrate on the regimes that are situated between the Russian (and later Soviet) legal culture and the area covered by the German Civil Code. Hence, the geographical focus of the book is on East Germany, Russia, the Baltic countries, Poland, and Hungary, but our approach is transnational. Instead of concentrating on the differences and distinct features of each national legal culture, we focus on the interaction and intertwinement of the then hegemonic socialist ideology and the ideas of law and justice as they appeared in the writings of legal historians and historically oriented legal scientists of socialist legal orders. Such an angle enables us to concentrate on the dynamics between politics and law as well as on identities and legal history.

Our aim is to study critically the presentations of legal history written under political guidance and to illuminate the ideological, academic, and biographical context of those presentations. Rather than reducing academic presentations on the history of law to mechanical extensions of the political order, the book perceives legal historiography as a form of the ever-ongoing dialogue between the political constitution of a society and the ideas of the rule of law and justice. Socialist legal histories were, nevertheless, attempts to reinterpret and give new meaning to the legal tradition after an abrupt change in the political and social context of law. Studying the temporal interpretations and representations of law of socialist countries enables us to provide a perspective on the more general problematic of law's embeddedness within societies.

It is clear that socialist interpretations of legal history were not written in an environment that followed the standards of the rule of law as described by present European convents and agreements. Due to that deviation, they also differentiated from their contemporary counterparts in the 'West'. The 'Eastern' and the 'Western' views diverged in their understanding of the limits of the executive power of the state and on the role of the legal order as an independent institute, but they also comprised two different regimes in using the past for redefining the relation between society and law.

After the Second World War in Western continental Europe, legal history was mobilised in the search for an untainted core of jurisprudence. Legal scholars attempted to locate the heart of legal principles that would not fall under totalitarian pursuits and could became a legal cornerstone for the slowly emerging coalition of the European nations. Legal historiography was dominated by the idea of the separate temporalities of law and general history (Koselleck, 1987; Wieacker, 1967). Jurisprudence was depicted as a system that could reinvent itself with the means of history, as a historically matured discourse which would enable a self-standing, self-regulating, and self-remedial matrix for mediating in disputes between the state and society (Liebrecht, 2018; Erkkilä, 2019).

The socialist regimes of East Central Europe perceived their societies according to a different concept of time. Marxism had revealed the underlying prior force of historical development, exposing the corrupted structures of thinking of the bourgeoisie, concurrently excluding other ways of conceptualising social activity. The establishment of the Soviet Union marked the beginning of a new era in which revolutionary ideas were put into practice. There was a singular, universal narrative of the historical development for society as a whole (Kolár, 2016, pp. 7–10; Schröder, 2016, pp. 64–65). The governments of the socialist bloc tried to control the idea of the separate temporality of socialist societies by 'rebooting' the revolution on a regular basis, sharpening the virtues of the true dogma and eliminating false interpretations of the revolution from the public sphere (Eckert, 1993; Poláčková and van Duin, 2019). A priority was also educating the people into dialectical materialist historical consciousness, in which the ruling communist parties invested a lot[1] (Connelly, 2000, pp. 208–225).

In the West, legal scientists were not impressed by the socialist concept of legal history. Notwithstanding its constant reference to the historicity of social structures, it seemed that socialist jurisprudence was not taking 'the past' seriously, which became especially apparent in the sidelining and neglecting of the academic disciplines of historical studies, legal history included (Stolleis, 2009, pp. 16–18; Schmidt-Hartmann, 1988). After the fall of the Berlin Wall, there was little use for the Eastern European concept of history in European academia (Lässig, 2007; Varga, 2016, p. 647). Indeed, the legal historiography of the socialist bloc took place within a system where law as whole was an instrument of the ruling elite in its task of guarding and reforming society. Legal nihilism that some of the foundational theories of socialist law manifested reduced the space of jurisprudential reflection to a minimum.

Nevertheless, not many legal cultures in world history can be situated in a context of *Rechtsstaat*, and yet studying different perceptions and uses of the past in constructing legal orders is important for the contemporary idea of the rule of law (Reimann, Zimmermann and Glenn, 2019, p. 438). Our contemporary idea is subject to constant reinterpretation, discussion, and flux. The legal orders of socialist East Central Europe were subordinated to politics, but the ruling parties had to express and portray themselves as bound to a legal procedure and to legality (cf. Skinner, 2019; Fraser, 2019, pp. 33–38). In order to understand socialist legality in a way that is relevant for contemporary discussion, we need to make an attempt to understand its own logic, its perception of law's embeddedness in society, and its use of the past.

This volume scrutinizes the place of legal historical presentations between the coercive state and the tradition of legal scholarly independence. It analyses the ways in which historical knowledge was applied in commenting on socialist law; rather than depicting socialist interpretations of legal history as a monolithic entity, it highlights the contradictions within the discourse, continuities with previous legal cultures, and different adaptations of the hegemonic dogma of Marxist-Leninism. With this approach, the book addresses the question of the relations between state pressure, personal and scholarly views, and Marxist-Leninism in (re)presentations of history. What was the impact of philosophical imperatives and the idea of a singular past on legal historiography? What kind of an effect did politically motivated structural changes in academia have on the production of legal historical knowledge? How were scholars able to find a space for the dissident use of the past within socialist jurisprudence?

In this introductory chapter, I will first give a brief overview of the political, ideological, and institutional context of socialist interpretations of legal history. This consists of discussing the concept of Sovietisation and outlining the effect that political socialism had on the legal orders, higher education, and legal cultures of the countries of East Central Europe. This is followed by a conceptualisation of the space of legal historical presentations within state socialism. My contribution ends with short descriptions of the individual chapters of this volume and the way they are thematised.

Sovietisation, socialism, and law

Here, Sovietisation means the tactics with which the Soviet Union attempted to rule the areas it had conquered during the Second World War—all aimed at stabilising the Soviet hegemony in the regions of East Central Europe and Baltic Countries and disseminating the revolutionary ideas on the state, politics, and the rule of law initially introduced by the Bolsheviks. It is not my intention to devalue the factual influence the Soviet Union imposed on the societies of East Central Europe but rather to question the one-sided idea of Sovietisation. After Stalin's ruthless use of unreserved terror, there was no supreme plan or even consensus among the commissariat for the means and subsistent goals for Sovietisation (Naimark, 2017; Kramer, 2017).

For Estonia and Latvia, there was no escaping their fate as fresh states in the Soviet Union. Their population was perceived with suspicion and given a 'precautionary procedure' (meaning, e.g., mass transportations to Siberia), and their short-lived national political and legal systems were replaced with Soviet ones (Kirby, 1994). Whereas the Baltic states were treated in a very similar fashion to the regions in the Caucasus and the Far East, which the Soviet Union assimilated

Figure 0.1 Polish war-hero, resistant fighter and spy for the Allied West Witold Pilecki at his show trial in Warsaw on March 3, 1948. Pilecki was executed two months later. At the picture Pilecki is sitting first on the left in the second row. In the first row are the solicitors.

during the interwar years, the protocol was not as lucid with regard to the countries in East Central Europe that fell under Soviet occupation from 1944 to 1945 (Naimark, 2017, pp. 63–65). Stalin himself, apparently lacking a preconceived and consistent blueprint for disseminating the communist revolution to East Germany, Czechoslovakia, Poland, and Hungary, announced the possibility of 'different paths' to communism (Naimark, 2017, pp. 65–70).

Such a stance seemed to emphasise the varying cultural and historical background of each region in their transformation process. Notwithstanding the comradely tenor in the 'soft' approach adopted by the Soviets and their cautious take on immediate implementation of major social reorganisations, such as sweeping collectivization, they did pay attention to the reorganisation of higher education and facilitated decisive attempts to convert the legal institutes of the regions they occupied to socialist institutions. Such an act of shaping the essence of domestic judicatures was carried out by replacing the judiciary with more 'class-conscious' lay judges and putting on display trials for the 'enemies of the working class' (Haferkamp and Wudtke, 1997; Kaluza, 1999; Boros, Gyulavári and Fleck 1999, pp. 147–151).

The protests of the 1950s and 1960s—both in the visible form of demonstrations and strikes and in the indiscernible moves to resist socialist reforms—laid down the ground for the later national character of each satellite state within the socialist bloc (Kramer, 2017). In East Germany, the political elite crushed the 1953 uprising with the help of the Red Army and succeeded in building a remarkably stable socialist system (Ostermann, 2001). The East German model was characterised by a tight grip of the state apparatus where there was little room for serious dissidence. In 1956 Poland and Hungary revolted. The Hungarian uprising was quashed by ruthless military intervention, but the Polish domestic leaders were able to convince Moscow that the use of brute force was unnecessary and inner-state measures were sufficient to keep Poland a loyal member of the flock (Kramer, 2017, pp. 148–154). In Poland, the national identity continued to play a significant role throughout the latter half of the 20th century, whereas in Hungary the memory of 1956 stood between many individual worldviews and the official jargon of socialism.

The socialist bloc was genuinely recreated in 1968. Crushing the dissident spirit of the 'Prague Spring' solidified the Brezhnev doctrine as a rule in defining the relations between the East Central European countries and Soviet Union on the one hand and between the satellite states themselves on the other (Kramer, 2017, pp. 159–164). Around and after the Helsinki Accord of 1975, when human rights became a worldwide lingua franca for evaluating political systems and efforts, socialist countries vocally defended their version of the rule of law and sharply criticised the 'Western world's' hypocritical advocation of subjective rights (Mälksoo, 2018; Kopeček, 2012). That paradigmatic change engaged many Eastern European legal scholars, but the broadened discussion at the same time inevitably revealed the inherent contradiction between the ideological principles and their practical implementation in state socialism.

Thus, the four-decade era of the Soviet influence in East Central Europe was characterised by a varying regional emphasis and temporal changes in the measures selected, not to mention the actual reception of the Soviet import of socialism. As John Connelly puts it:

> SED members may not have taken socialism seriously, but they and the East German population took the state very seriously [...] Czech comrades may not have taken the state very seriously but they did believe in their version of socialism [...] Poland's Party cadre took neither the state nor socialism very seriously. (Connelly, 2000, pp. 284–287)

Whereas Hungarian scholars were able to negotiate between their domestic tradition and Sovietisation, and the jurisprudential tradition of the Soviet Union was far from being a monolithic one, Baltic legal scholars had no choice but to take both the state and socialism very seriously.

All Soviet satellite states were, nevertheless, socialist countries, and their political and legal systems can be safely characterised as state socialist. According to Peter C. Caldwell, state socialism attempted to guarantee the proclaimed uber-democratic and anti-fascist essence of socialist societies—especially in comparison to Western countries and Western science—by giving the 'state plan' the final say with regard to politics, economy, and law (Caldwell, 2003). Yet by doing so, state socialism had to provide the state with a special position above the law and suppress some of the basic civil rights of its citizens; sacrifice legal certainty and equality in order to safeguard the alleged and necessary cohesion of society; and, by announcing that its politics merely implemented the will of the people (i.e. the 'working class'), had to surveil and uproot disobedient and potentially harmful ideas from the public sphere. In order to cope with the dilemma, the Marxist-Leninist dogma of the socialist bloc equated the will of the people with 'the state' and further concentrated the power of the state apparatus into the hands of a small elite, that is, the executive organs of the domestic communist parties (Schröder, 2016, pp. 61–62, 78).

The starting point for all socialist legal orders in 20th-century East Central Europe was the Soviet example—not their domestic and national traditions of socialism—and its concrete measures in reorganising the legal institutes as well as the political manifestations of Marxist-Leninism born out of and in the midst of that Bolshevik experiment (Markovits, 1968; Bender and Falk, 1999, pp. XIII–XIV). According to Lenin, the Soviet Union had taken the Marxist principles to a new, practical level with its concrete fighting, first visible in the October Revolution and further advanced in the actualisation of 'real socialism' (Zagladin, 1983, pp. 6–7).

The Marxist-Leninist dogma, which was a reinterpretation of the original Marxist thought, served as a wrapping in drafting, evaluating, and implementing law (Bender and Falk, 1999, pp. XI–XIII; Schröder, 2016, pp. 66–67). Intact in this dogma was the Marxist core of the foundational mission of the working class: dismantling the bourgeois society and its repressive structures via revolution and building a new socialist society, which would ultimately develop into communism. Such a process was to be achieved by cultivating the consciousness of the working class and fighting against the sabotage of the imperialistic enemies of the state and the socialist process (Zagladin, 1983, pp. 14–16).

The Marxist-Leninist dogma was translated to the national legal orders of the Soviet satellite states by the domestic communists approved by Moscow and the Soviet experts working in the countries in the socialist bloc (Connelly, 2000, pp. 68–69). The possible leeway for renewal, criticism, and new openings happened within this frame. Marxist-Leninist dogma—as steered and reinterpreted by the domestic communist parties—was the *ius commune* of the satellite states (Schröder, 2016, pp. 68–69). Furthermore, dissident voices were judged by their heresy with respect to the 'true meaning' of Marxist-Leninism, being judged as 'revisionism' or 'too formalistic.'

The national constitutions of the Soviet satellite states toed the line of the 1936 Constitution of the Soviet Union, which was assembled by Stalin's chief prosecutor, Andreii Vyshinski. The most prominent principles in the 1936 Constitution—and later in the Constitutions of the East Central Europe—were the democratisation of justice; the substitution of subjective rights with an assortment of social rights and civic duties of citizens; and, contrary to the Soviet Constitutions of 1918 and 1924, allotting the communist party an established position in coordinating and representing the will of the working class (Pomeranz, 2019, pp. 86–88). Although the state socialist governments later to a degree tried to distance their legal orders from Vyshinskian legality,' the above-mentioned basic principles remained (Stolleis, 2009, pp. 25–27; see also Richardson-Little, Dietz and Mark, 2019).

In principle, judges, lawyers, and legal scholars did not have the authority to interpret and further develop the law but to implement it (Schröder, 2016; Gizbert-Studnicki, Pleszka and Wolenski, 2016). This led to a 'hyper-positivist' reading of civil codes, with which judicature intended to secure their own position but also to make their case in such a way that there would be as little room as possible for questioning their arguments on political bases. Rather than being *Rechtsstaats*, the legal orders of the East Central Europe were 'norm-regimes' (*Normenstaats*) (Stolleis, 2009, p. 38).

The Soviet Union to a degree watched over the legal development of its satellite states. Sometimes in concrete administrative problems, the Soviet communist party expressed its 'opinion' on the preferable solution via the common networks of the socialist bloc or through diplomatic connections.[2] Especially important was to homogenise the legal concept of property, and socialist legal systems all, in one way or the other, adopted the idea of socialist property as defined by soviet legal theoristVenediktov (Raff and Taitslin, 2014). Nevertheless, soon after the end of the Second World War, in accordance with the 'different paths' doctrine, Stalin published his reinterpretation of Marxist-Leninist dogma, where he rearranged the relations between 'base' and 'superstructure' (Stalin, 1951). This enabled the domestic leaders of the socialist bloc to maintain their national civil codes, and rather than focusing on repealing the existing legal orders, the communist party elite could concentrate on controlling the interpretations of private law, in which legal history played an important role.

Higher education in socialism and national legal traditions

Education had a central position in the state socialist ideology of East Central Europe. That was due to Marx's emphasis on cultivating the consciousness of the working class as a prior task for the communist party but also to the aim of Leninism to distinguish the party cadre from the old institutions in establishing a new social elite (Lenin, 1977, pp. 23, 375). In the reality of post-Second World War Eastern Europe, it meant dismantling the prestige of the old academic bastions; replacing the university staff with a new, loyal one; and erecting new facilities of higher education aside from the universities.

Seizing the monopoly on education was vital in view of raising a new social elite from working class youth, but another, and in practice at least important, objective was the training of a new class of judges. The 'democratisation' of justice necessitated the replacement of the old judiciary with 'people's judges' whose education was situated—or at least that was the plan—outside the legal faculties (see, e.g., Schröder, 2016, p. 73; Boros, Gyulavári, and Fleck, 1999, pp. 344–359).

In general, state socialist governments determinedly diminished the societal significance of the traditional law faculties in favour of the natural sciences, new institutes of a technical character, or newly established academies for delicate disciplines like law or social studies (Stolleis, 2009, pp. 47–49, 121–122; Connelly, 2000, pp. 60–61, 67–70). The reforms for higher education were steered from offices and ministries of education under the leadership of the domestic communist parties and concentrated on recruiting students from working class backgrounds or people whose preliminary training consisted of courses in Marxist-Leninism. The aim of the educational means, such as regular revisions of the legal curricula, was to control the judiciary and legal scholarship in each of the satellite states (Haferkamp and Wudtke, 1997; Bena, 1999, pp. 377, 406).

In the Soviet Union, Bolsheviks had determinedly stripped the 'bourgeois traits' from universities. Already before the Second World War, social sciences had undergone a process of reorganisation in which the disciplines across the spectrum had been merged into a branch of 'new historical science'[3] (Fitzpatrick, 1979). In Soviet satellite states, the adaptation of the Stalinist view in the national cultures of higher education was, again, a more complex and dynamic thing. The universities within East Central Europe had all adhered to a Humboldtian ideal of free scholarship and could build on a prestigious past even though their individual national histories were very different. In addition, the universities had opted for different adaptation strategies in the face of the pre-Second World War National Socialist onslaught and had a varying relation to the middle and working classes of their respective nations (Connelly, 2000, pp. 2–16). Thus, the Sovietisation of the higher education in the Eastern bloc—despite considerable effort to produce homogeneous institutions in their aims and ethos—produced diverse results.

The Soviets considered the German professoriate thoroughly corrupted by fascist ideas, and, in accordance with the Western occupation zones, conducted a sweeping 'denazification' within the universities during 1945–1946 and ousted approximately 80% of the professors on the bases of their involvement in fascist policies and their memberships in the organisations of the National Socialist German Workers' Party (NSDAP). What made Soviet denazification different from the Western equivalent was its thoroughness and rigour. Although some of the removed staff were later able to return to a teaching position, there was no general amnesty for those who had been denazified (Stolleis, 2009, pp. 45–46).

Denazification paved the way for reintroducing German universities as reproducers of Marxist-Leninism, and, indeed, German professors and students seldom openly challenged the party policies but rather internalised their mission as a loyal instrument within state socialism (Markovits, 2018, pp. 44–48). As a state, the German Democratic Republic (GDR) was an anomaly in the socialist bloc. It was a model region among the Soviet satellite states despite its culture, history, and legal tradition that had just recently been forged into a totalitarian society and turned against the Soviet Union. The memory of a common past and legal culture with the Western neighbour never ceased to exist, and relations with the Federal Republic of Germany (FRG) and 'Germanness' very much overshadowed legal historiography, despite serious efforts to the contrary (Joseph, 1995, p. 584).

The main tenet in pre-Second World War jurisprudence in Hungary—unlike, for example, in Czechoslovakia (Bröstl, 2016)—was the dominance of the legal sociological stance and the rejection of the strict legal positivism of the Vienna School. It might have been the Hungarian legal scholars, nevertheless, who were able to cultivate the narrow Vyshinskian dogma furthest and into scientifically considerable legal theories, but naturally not outside the Marxist-Leninist frame (Varga, 2016). The coercive politics of state socialism also restricted the academic institutions in Hungary, and the shadow of the crushing of the 1956 uprising constantly hovered over civil society, reminding scholars of the limits of academic freedom.

It is not perhaps a coincidence that the first socialist Civil law code of the Soviet satellite states was promulgated in Hungary in 1959. Vilmos Peschka and Imre Szabó were renowned legal theorists in the socialist bloc, and their legal philosophical follow-up on Soviet 'revolutionary legality' was a starting point for a substantial body of socialist legal scholarship (Schröder, 2016, p. 80). In the discipline of legal history, the works of Hungarian scholars gained wide attention, and probably the most famous of them was the Roman law scholar Elemér Pólay. Pólay contributed significantly to the contemporary study of the history of Roman law and enjoyed wide appreciation in the West. Paradoxically, while in the West the narrative of Roman law was used to back up the freedom of private property, Pólay used the same narrative to outline the scientific standards of legal historiography in compliance with the Marxist understanding of historical development.

In Poland, Sovietisation measures failed to dismantle the traditional prestige of university professors. Moreover, the Polish national version of state socialism maintained and cultivated a strong notion of national identity and an idea of the special, historical path of Polish society and its structures (Connelly, 2000, pp. 127, 142–161, 283–284; Danyel and Behrends, 2019, p. 9). Among the countries in the socialist bloc, Poland's jurisprudential culture was the most pluralistic. The state did, however, control academic freedom and during internationally or domestically tense periods, the state's grip was tighter, e.g., in the form of censorship, than normally (Danyel and Behrends, 2019, p. 154).

After the Polish thaw (the 1956 revolt and its nonviolent ending), it was possible in Poland to portray oneself as a non-Marxist legal scholar, a combination of words that would not have been possible, for example, in the GDR. Polish legal scientists were entitled to a creative use of Marxism, but they were also aware of and discussed Western legal theories from Kelsen to Hart (Gizbert-Studnicki, Pleszka and Wolenski, 2016, p. 567). Poland's national legal culture was characterised by the heritage of Leon Petrazycki, whose remarkably wide learnedness and oeuvre benefited the whole field of Polish legal sciences and formed a basis for further innovative theorising in the latter half of the 20th century (Cotterrell, 2015).

Polish legal science was, however, careful not to cross the line and provoke the political sphere—a stance that might well represent Polish civil society in general during the 1960s and 1970s (Fijalkowski, 2016; Danyel and Behrends, 2019, pp. 150, 154). The authority to draft and further develop laws was the sole privilege of the state and the communist party. Lawyers or judges did not interpret the law in ways that would have resulted in precedents in further uses of the law. They studied the existing law and went no further. It was not possible, or at least not wise, to evaluate the existing law in the light of justice or fairness or any other criteria (Gizbert-Studnicki, Pleszka, and Wolenski, 2016, p. 581). But by means of legal history, it was nevertheless possible to indirectly challenge the existing legal order.

Mapping a space for socialist interpretations of legal history

The political frame of Sovietisation, the ideological language of socialism, and the concrete restrictions on the academic space of legal historians composed a framework for the legal historiography of the East Central European countries from the late 1940s to the final years of 1980s. In many cases, the academic careers of scholars depended on the level of loyalty they expressed towards the leadership of the communist party. Especially in the Baltic countries, the parallel state of the secret police watched over the teaching of academics, and its existence had to be taken into account in all scientific activity.

Concentrating on these boundaries, however, leaves scholars as mute reproducers of the hegemonic discourse and ignores their own identity and agency as citizens, scientists, and moral beings. In fact, the framework was not stagnant but historically situated. The context of Sovietisation in itself brought about constantly shifting circumstances within the fields of the domestic sciences. Both the state and legal historians had their opinions on the ways in which 'the past' could be mobilized in socialist societies on their historically determined journey to becoming communist.

Most of the legal historiography produced in the socialist bloc toed the official line and produced results that supported the self-justification of the socialist state. It presented socialist legality as a historically evolved model that, by adhering to the scientific principles of Marxist-Leninism, efficiently implemented the 'will of the people' in administration and legal institutes and as a system that was both equal for all and able to keep up with the pace of historical development. Consistently, by means of using the past, socialist legality was shown to be the ultimate answer to the perennial questions of justice, freedom, and democracy, while the Western idea of the rule of law appeared as its mere negation, 'imperialistic,' corrupted, and 'fascist' (Stolleis, 2009, pp. 27–31, 41; see, e.g., Tschernilowski, 1980, pp. 27–31).

Socialist legal historiography should not be perceived as a dysfunctional copy of the Western ideal, nor as a diluted application of the Bolshevik model of 'revolutionary legality' but as an autopoietic system that functioned according to

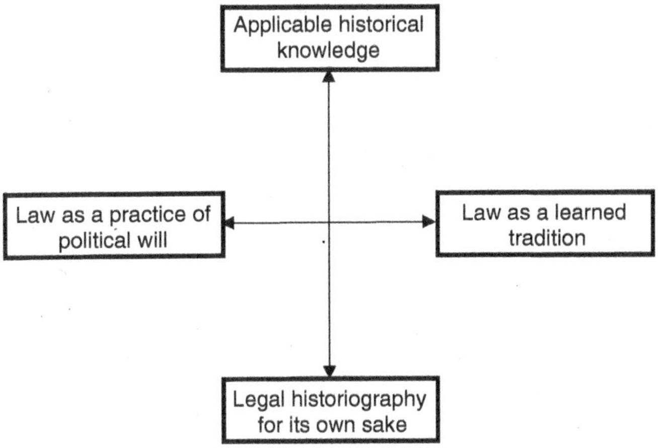

Figure 0.2

its own dynamics and rules, unavoidably connected to the past it shared with the 'Western' legal tradition (Luhmann, 1984). In what follows, my attempt is to describe the tension, on the one hand, between the state direction ('law as a practice of political will') and the autonomy of the legal historiographical discipline ('law as a learned tradition') and, on the other hand, between legal historical presentations whose primary aim is to comment on the phenomena of their contemporary society ('applicable historical knowledge') and histories that seek to exclude any direct relevance with their social-political context ('legal historiography for its own sake'). Associating these two axes in a scheme creates a model with which both the dynamic and historical nature of legal historiography can be analysed.[4] The socialist interpretations of legal history can be mapped within this space and between those polarities.

The tension in the horizontal axis between the ideas of law as a 'practice of political will' and 'learned tradition' did not lie in questions whether anti-fascism/anti-imperialism was a righteous norm for common identity or whether Marxist-Leninist dogma was an accurate matrix in steering society. The majority of scholars did not question, or had no choice but to accept, these principles. Furthermore, legal historiography in socialist countries did not challenge the instrumental essence of law in executing the 'state plan' of the domestic communist parties. The Marxist-Leninist methodology, as it displayed itself in legal historiography, can be described in a nutshell as follows:

The economic structure of society is the *base* from which the *superstructure* arises. The superstructure consists, for example, of the state as well as the religion, law, and philosophy of the given society. The various elements that make up the superstructure significantly influence the processes that take place at the base.[5] Also crucial is the way in which actual social events and developments are reflected in the minds of the participants and their political, legal, philosophical, and other views. Nevertheless, the state and law in the last instance are always determined by the economic conditions. *Class antagonism* creates the state and its legal system, and they can be conceptualized only in terms of class. Regardless of its multiple manifestations, the state is nothing more than the organised collective exercise of power of the propertied classes. Its law is an expression of the interests of the ruling class. These interests do not arise arbitrarily but are always dependent on the respective conditions of production, 'objectively' conditioned. With the help of law, the ruling class secures its control over the other classes and strata of societies (Tschernilowski, 1980, p. 26; also Sellnow, 1963).

The idea of 'law as a learned tradition' in implementing Marxist-Leninist dogma was not an *ideal* but a tacit *idea* that consisted of many different particles. Central was the romantic notion of law as a concrete manifestation of legal thinking (Schröder, 1980; Klenner, 1957, pp. 82, 84). Legal history was a narrative of the *relation* between law and society. It valued the past expressions and representations of law (in other words, the European legal tradition) as examples of a particular, legally oriented thinking, and learning from them was useful for contemporary socialism (Joseph, 1995, p. 584). The study of these past expressions had to respect the characteristics that distinguished legal thinking in the first place; in other words, one had to have a legally trained and conscious mindset in writing legal historiography (see, e.g,. Csizmadia, 1968, pp. 104, 114; Schöneburg, 1987, pp. 309–310, 319–320).

The idea of 'law as a learned tradition' bore some resistance to Sovietisation and implementations of 'socialist legality.' Especially in the Baltics, it was a concept that embedded the preservation and cultivation of national identity. Both history and legal history were spheres where the characteristics of different ethnic groups could be given a voice (Kolár, 2016, pp. 143–147). It did not comprise, however, a coherent ideological alternative for socialist legal science, and legal historians who advocated the idea did not perceive themselves as belonging to a particular school of thought. Especially in retrospect, many scholars claimed that their only goal within the state socialist society had been defending science (*Wissenschaft*) and the institutions that represented it, but on closer inspection, what they really might have defended were the privileges of the professoriate or the social status of the academic (Connelly, 2000, p. 283).

Neither of the ideas existed in their absolute form. It was not possible to retreat exclusively into a world of pure legal methods and scientific standards in a socialist science community. At least if one wanted to make a career. And yet a legal historical study that would have analysed law from an overtly orthodox starting point in which law was politics *per se* was not useful in legal education or in real administrative challenges. Even for an 'advanced socialist nation,' training judges capable of ruling on the basis of, and according to, the 'socialist consciousness,' or building a legal order where some legal certainty prevailed, without taking into account the jurisprudential tradition, was impossible.

The same requirement for adhering to and expressing 'socialist consciousness' also applied to legal scholars. State socialist governments attempted to bind scientific thinking to their political aims and harness it in building a communist society. The political instrumentality of law as expressed in legal curricula and in the announcements of the party assemblies also demanded 'responsibility' from legal historians, and their representations had to advance the cause of international revolution (Stolleis, 2009, p. 34; Joseph, 1995, p. 557):[6]

> While the bourgeois historian seeks to disguise his partisanship, the Marxist historian frankly takes the side of that class whose representative he is himself, openly advocating the positions of the working class, which is the only progressive social class. (Tschernilowski, 1980, p. 27)[7]

That sphere of 'socialist responsibility' was, nevertheless, not merely restrictive in nature. Many scholars genuinely believed in the anti-imperialism and anti-fascism of socialism, and even if they did not, especially the older generation of researchers had a vivid memory of the fascist totalitarianism of the 1930s and 1940s. To legal scholars in the latter half of the 20th century, it was equally clear that the idea of 'law as a learned tradition' had not been able to resist the National Socialist attack (Caldwell, 2003, pp. 71–73). Whether the West continued to be possessed by those traits was debatable, but the Eastern European media was quick to point out, for example, the faults in the West German denazification programme and the capitalist connections—real or alleged—in the scholarly culture of the Western world (Joseph, 1995).

Adhering to and expressing 'socialist consciousness' was a largely accepted state of affairs, although many privately grieved for the incomplete political execution of that ideal. Certainly, some legal historical studies had opportunistic intentions, and quite a few scholars adopted an indifferent attitude towards socialist ideology (Danyel and Behrends, 2019, pp. 207–230). Yet the 'emancipatory' ideal of socialism remained more than rhetoric to many scholars; thus, rearranging the relation between 'law as a practice of political will' and 'law as a learned tradition' was in some sense justified to them (Heuer, 1995).

In this space between the polarities, the communist governments regularly attempted to move the focus more towards the 'practice of political will.' They did this by rebooting legal curricula and by 'starting the revolution anew' on a regular basis in party assemblies (Markovits, 1968, pp. 14–15; Joseph, 1995; Danyel and Behrends, 2019, p. 214). In these events, the political guidelines and limitations for social sciences for the next few years were announced. Sometimes there was a public denouncement of legal scientists who had deviated from the implicit guidelines set by the party elite. Sometimes another scientist, stronger in his or her faith in the party, flayed the heretics and their indecent works in the pages of the few scientific journals (see, e.g., Otto 2008, pp. 375–382). Constant outcries about placing 'practice' over 'theory' in public statements were also expressions of the need of the communist parties to place legal science within the same revolutionary narrative than the rest of society (Haferkamp and Wudtke, 1997).

The vertical axis in the figure, between 'applicable historical knowledge' and 'legal historiography for its own sake,' stands for the tension between the polarising extremes in using the past. In the German legal science tradition—whose influence stretched far to the east and south beyond the actual borders of the German Empire—history had always had a special place. In the Central Eastern European legal systems that rested on a codification of law, arguments in interpreting and developing the law were derived from the classics of the legal tradition and preceding works on the national legal problematic. It was the task of jurisprudence to reinterpret its own tradition in order to come up with solutions in situations where the social need or new legislation was possibly in conflict with the letter of the law (Liebrecht, 2018). Thus, in East Central European societies in the early 20th century, legal historical knowledge, produced both in the past and in contemporary legal science, was highly relevant since it could be used to adjust the legal framework and to set the rules within which all other social activity took place.

In principle, admitting the historical nature of law and legal order as well as continuity in the legal sphere was a very difficult question for communist parties. On the one hand, the socialist revolution for Marx and Engels was based on historical necessity and the iron laws of historical materialism denoted the maturation process of societies towards communism. Socialism *was* history (Marx and Engels, 1970, pp. 36, 43, 45; Tschernilowski, 1980, p. 32). On the other hand, adhering to such an axiom opened the door for inconvenient questions concerning the existence of a bourgeois legacy within the legal orders of socialist societies. Had not Marx, Engels, and Lenin built their reasoning on previous philosophical and legal traditions? Should socialism also reject the concepts of Roman law, the ideals of natural law scholars, and the preceding bourgeois contribution in the fields of, e.g., contract and trade law?

However, attempts to historically contextualise the effectual legality of socialist societies did inevitably bring about larger dilemmas concerning the relation between an individual and the state, the nature and extent of universally valid and equal normative order, and the legitimation of the division of power (Joseph, 1995, p. 583). The critical dialectical materialist view on the past was not be extended all the way to contemporary state socialism:

> The basis for this development of law must be generally understood from the interests of the full application of [contemporary] norms. Hence, it does not mean that the exploration of the political and legal history of past epochs directly benefits the interpretation and application of Soviet law. That is impossible, and such a purpose cannot be seriously debated. (Tschernilowski, 1980, p. 33)[8]

That said, due to its historical self-justification and constant competition with the West, the communist parties needed legal historical research and 'critical' legal historical analysis. The countries of the socialist bloc had to prove that their system was able to produce a considerable scientific output and display an academic sphere that was capable of competing with their Western counterparts (Mälksoo, 2018).

With the model of the space of socialist interpretations of legal history, I have attempted to illuminate certain traits of continuity with regard to the 'bourgeois' or national tradition within the socialist legal historiography, and concurrently unfold the paradox that the communist parties both needed historical research to back their legitimacy and yet had to uproot vehemently some particular historical views. This was not a matter that concerned direct criticism of the party—such a thing did not belong to state socialism. Instead, a historical study of law that left the interconnections between law in the past and the contemporary socialist legality undone—even if the researcher represented the idea of the 'law as a learned tradition'—was from the party perspective harmless and, from time to time, useful as a façade (see, e.g., Sellnow, 1963, p. 16).

The communist parties to a degree encouraged theoretical explorations in legal science—advancement from 'revolutionary legality' was necessary in order to bring forth more sophisticated models. This offered some leeway for scholars to offer applicable historical knowledge without reducing law to a mere 'practice of political will.' Some employed 'the past' in their indirect criticism of the prevailing dogma and, by historically contextualising the discourse of Marxist-Leninism itself, distinguished between proper socialism and dogmatism (Sellnow, 1968, p. 40; Mamut, 1979; Klenner, 1985). The communist parties were determined in controlling their sole authority to reinterpret the dogma of Marxist-Leninism and attacked dissenting scholarly views as well as regularly narrowed the space for accepted legal science. Nevertheless, their status as oracles deteriorated over time. Thus, the last decades of the socialist bloc were characterised by an increased scholarly interest in Marx's thoughts outside the official canon (Varga, 2016).

Socialism and legal history

In concrete terms, this book traces the essence of socialist legal historiography on three levels—the legal culture, the academic structures and legal principles, and the biographical sides of socialist legal historiography. The first part of the book, *Framing the socialist legal historiography*, traces the tensions between the European legal tradition and socialist legal orders, and the ways in which these frictions were overcome or, alternatively, emphasised. The tensions became evident especially in relation to the preceding canon of legal historical works and to 'Western' legal historiography.

Some of the individual chapters in the first part of the book investigate the relation between legal historiography and socialist society in the context of legal academia concentrating on the demands that communist society placed on legal historians and the scholars' response to these challenges as a community in the context of e.g. teaching and research questions. Some chapters in the first part also analyse shifting meanings and the use of the fundamental building blocks of European legal science, such as open concepts or traditional legal virtues, in socialist legal historiography. An example of this kind of use of the legal tradition is the drafting of Hungarian Civil Code of 1959. András Földi illustrates the way in which fundamental concepts of *bona fides* and *boni mores* maintained their connection to their original historical framing in the text of the new code and, despite pressure from the political sphere and hard core Marxist-Leninists, remained as gateways for legal interpretation in reference to the jurisprudential tradition rather than vehicles of socialist state planning.

In his article, Martin Otto gives an overview of the development of legal historiography in the GDR between the pressure of Sovietisation and the attempt of legal scholars to retain their identity as members of a distinguished discipline within legal studies. The article follows the process of the reestablishment of the law faculties in East Germany, their afterlife in a society that guarded knowledge production via structural rearrangements in higher education, and also scrutinises the dominant research themes in the GDR as a result of ideological restriction and lopsided, yet existing, international contacts.

One might assume that Soviet legal historiography and its view of the European past provided a model example in implementing the idea of 'revolutionary legality.' Certainly, the discipline experienced the political and ideological steering of state socialism first-hand, but the same paradox of the indispensability of acknowledging the historical roots in socialist legal science remained. In their chapter, Anton Rudokvas and Ville Erkkilä present the long line of Roman law studies in the Soviet Union and both highlight the effect that politically originated shifts in the research stance imposed on the understanding of Roman law and show that the field remained a background for further historical and legal studies. Marju Luts-Sootak focuses on the Baltic experience within legal historical teaching in the Soviet Union. Although the state curriculum was designed to give students an orthodox illustration of the relation between law and material historical continuity from the viewpoint of the emerging socialist thought, teachers were able to deploy a vast historical time span and include national elements in their *de facto* teaching. The strict coercion of the state could be evaded in a subtle use of emphasis and hyperbole.

Like many other concepts dealing with Russia and legal science, the 'communist legal tradition' is a simplification of a very rich and diverse tradition whose geographical context and borders with respect to other legal traditions are hard to define. Adolfo Giuliani addresses in his chapter the struggle to give a comprehensive definition for the legal historical development taking place both in the 'East' and the 'West.' Although legal historians in the West have constant problems in placing 'the East' in their narratives of European law, the 'communist legal tradition' has prevailed as a convenient other for the 'European legal tradition.' This from its start has enabled the construction of the coherent entity of the 'Western legal thought' that has accommodated legal and political scientific works on the essence and origins of human rights.

The second part of the book, *Legal historians of socialist regimes*, concentrates on some significant individual legal historians in East Central Europe. Their biographies and professional choices within drastically altering post-Second World War societies witness the deep intertwinement of personal values and scholarly work in 20th century European legal science. In what ways did scholars 'start from scratch' after 1945, distinct from the 'bourgeois worldview' and previous historical narratives, and what stayed over from the inter-war period?

Of the countries in the socialist bloc, the GDR stands out as an example of the wide influence of the state in jurisprudence. Continuity with the national past was difficult because German scholarship in the 1930s and 1940s was used as an absolute antithesis to proper Marxist legal historiography. Some continuity, nevertheless, existed, and a few scholars who had started their careers in the pre-Second World War period remained active in the academia of the GDR. Adrian Schmidt-Recla and Zara Luisa Gries examine the works of legal historian Gerhard Buchda and the continuities and discontinuities within them. Further emphasis is paid to the possible impact that Buchda's scholarly identity had on the thoughts of his students and on the methodology of the theses he supervised.

In some regions in East Central Europe, the drastic changes in the political climate of the early 20th century, from hegemonic nationalism to authoritarian and finally to state socialist, were more temporally concentrated, clear-cut, and thorough than in others. In the Baltic countries, scholars witnessed not only the devastating occupation of their home countries by Nazi troops but also their ruthless assimilation into the Soviet Union and the totalitarian rule of the public sphere associated with such political ruptures. Sanita Osipova examines the career of the Latvian legal historian Valdemārs Kalniņš and shows that despite Kalniņš carefully excluding any elements from his texts that might have been interpreted as a nod towards the recent national past, he nevertheless succeeded in preserving the idea of Latvian national legal entity in his works. Marta Bucholc portrays a parallel contradiction between the official ideology and methodology and the scholar's identity in her article on Polish historian Juliusz Bardach. Bardach is a tragic example of how the Second World War not only changed structures and ideologies but also affected scholars on a personal level. Yet despite, or possibly because of, his personal experiences during and right after the war, Bardach was able to forge a remarkable scientific career and became an established figure in Polish academia.

With the collapse of the socialist bloc, dialectical materialism or the Marxist stance have become more or less marginalized in the field of legal historical study. For understandable reasons, these theories are still heavily associated with state socialism, although they were not responsible for the legal nihilism that state socialism in itself advocated. The works of Elemér Pólay are examples of the fact that it was indeed possible to produce self-standing research on the history of law applying Marxist methodology and in societies that devalued legal science. In her article on Pólay, Éva Jakab describes Pólay's academic oeuvre but also focuses on the difficult moral and ethical choices he faced while pursuing a career as a legal scholar and later when he became a renowned historian of Roman law.

The socialist regimes of East Central Europe announced their systems as ultimate answers to the perennial questions of democracy, the rule of law, and social justice and excluded other alternative explanations as 'imperialistic.' In practice, however, their political and legal orders embedded bureaucratic illegality, in which the frames of legal institutes produced coercion, intolerance, and oppression. This volume, however, does not concentrate on that framework, but on the self-justification of the legal orders of state socialism, and on the dynamics within this legality, to which the ruling elite portrayed themselves as bound. Concentrating on the mere framework would exclude the phenomenon of socialist legal historiography from the wider context of European history, leaving it nothing more than a temporary abnormality, without roots and further consequences. The socialist interpretations of legal history compose a nuanced and diverse discourse at the core of the socialist project of East Central Europe, which tells a lot about the interaction between law and society. Analysing that level is the aim of our book.

Notes

1 'It is the main task of the science of state and law in the German Democratic Republic to educate men [...] to think in terms of dialectical materialism in dealing with questions of state and law, and to propagate insight into the requirements for development of our state and law during the construction of socialism.' Editorial in the leading East German legal journal *Staat und Recht* in 1958, quoted in Markovits, 1968, p. 14.
2 See Földi in this volume.
3 See Rudokvas and Erkkilä in this volume.
4 The figure is an adaptation of Juhana Aunesluoma's scheme, which he presented in his talk 'Narratiivit vastakkain. Kylmän sodan päättymiseen liittyvät historiakiistat', in *Historiantutkimuksen päivät*-conference (October 25, 2019) at the University of Oulu, Finland.
5 This was the change that Stalin introduced into the original dogma of Marxist-Leninism (Stalin, 1951).
6 This was, of course, in line with the norm of the socialist states to evaluate not only the acts but also the intentions of its citizens and, if needed, to punish any dissident spirit (Stolleis, 2009).
7 'Während der bürgerliche Historiker seine Parteinahme zu verschleiern sucht, stellt sich der marxistische Historiker offen auf die Seite jener Klasse, deren Vertreter er selbst ist, vertritt er offen die Positionen der Arbeiterklasse, als einzig fortschrittlicher Gesellschaftklasse.'
8 'Die Gründe für diese Entwicklung des Rechts müssen im Interesse einer umfassenden Anwendung der Normen allgemeinverständlich sein. Daraus folgt nicht, dass dei Erforschung der Staats- und Rechtsgeschichte vergangener Epochen unmittelbar der Auslegung und Anwendung des sowjetischen Rechts zugute kommt. Das ist unmöglich, und ein solches Ziel kann nicht ernsthaft debattiert warden.'

References

Bena, J. (1999) 'Law Education in Czechoslovakia in the Years 1945–1989 with a special focus on the Comenius University Bratislava', in Bender, G. and Falk, U. (eds) *Recht im Sozialismus. Analysen zur Normdurchsetzung in osteuropäischen Nachkriegsgesellschaften (1944/45–1989). Band 2 Justizpolitik*, Frankfurt am Main: Vittorio Klostermann, 375–412.

Bender, G., and Falk, U. (1999) 'Einleitung', in Bender, G. and Falk, U. (eds) *Recht im Sozialismus. Analysen zur Normdurchsetzung in osteuropäischen Nachkriegsgesellschaften*

(1944/45–1989). Band 1 Enteignung, Frankfurt am Main: Vittorio Klostermann, VII–XVI.

Boros, L., Gyulavári, Á., and Fleck, Z. (1999) 'Die Beteiligung von Laien an der Rechtspflege im sozialistischen Ungarn', in Bender, G. and Falk, U. (eds) *Recht im Sozialismus. Analysen zur Normdurchsetzung in osteuropäischen Nachkriegsgesellschaften (1944/45–1989). Band 2 Justizpolitik*, Frankfurt am Main: Vittorio Klostermann, 147–200.

Boros, L., Gyulavári, Á., and Fleck, Z. (1999) 'Juristenausbildung und Rechtserziehung in Ungarn von 1945 bis 1990', in Bender G. and Falk U. (eds) *Recht im Sozialismus. Analysen zur Normdurchsetzung in osteuropäischen Nachkriegsgesellschaften (1944/45–1989). Band 2 Justizpolitik*, Frankfurt am Main: Vittorio Klostermann, 337–374.

Bröstl, A. (2016) '20th Century Legal Philosophy in Czechoslovakia, the Czech Republic, and the Slovak Republic', in Pattaro, E. and Corrado, R. (eds) *A Treatise of Legal Philosophy and General Jurisprudence: Volume 12, Legal Philosophy in the Twentieth Century: The Civil Law World*, Dordrecht: Springer, 613–634. DOI: 10.1007/978-94-007-1479-3_18.

Caldwell, P. C. (2003) *Dictatorship, State Planning, and Social Theory in the German Democratic Republic*, New York: Cambridge University Press.

Connelly, J. (2000) *Captive University. The Sovietization of East German, Czech, and Polish Higher Education, 1945–1956*, Chapel Hill and London: The University of North Carolina Press.

Cotterrell, R. (2015) 'Leon Petrażycki and contemporary socio-legal studies', *International Journal of Law in Context*, 11:1, 1–16. DOI: 10.1017/s1744552314000330.

Csizmadia, A. (1968) 'Über die Beziehung der Rechtsgeschichtswisssenschaft zur Geschichtswissenschaft, den Fachrechtszweigen und zur Praxis', in *Marxistische Beiträge zur Rechtsgeschichte*, Berlin: Wissenschaftliche Schriftenreihe der Humboldt-Universität zu Berlin, 102–115.

Danyel, J., and Behrends, J. C. (2019)*Grenzgänger und Brückenbauer. Zeitgeschichte durch den Eisernen Vorhang*, Göttingen: Wallstein Verlag.

Eckert, J. (ed) (1993) *Die Babelsberger Konferenz vom 2./3. April 1958. Rechtshistorisches Kolloquium 13.-16. Februar 1992 Christian-Albrechts-Universität zu Kiel*, Baden-Baden: Nomos Verlag.

Erkkilä, V. (2019) *The Conceptual Change of Conscience. Franz Wieacker and German Legal Historiography 1933–1968*, Tübingen: Mohr Siebeck. DOI: 10.1628/978-3-16-156692-9.

Fijalkowski, A. (2016) *From Old Times to New Europe. The Polish Struggle for Democracy and Constitutionalism*, London and New York: Routledge. DOI: 10.4324/9781315583464.

Fitzpatrick, S. (1979) *Education and Social Mobility in the Soviet Union, 1921–1934*, Cambridge: Cambridge University Press.

Fraser, D. (2019) 'Criminal law in Auschwitz: Positivism, Natural law and the Career of SS Lawyer Konrad Morgen', in Skinner S. (ed) *Ideology and Criminal Law Fascist, National Socialist and Authoritarian Regimes*, London: Bloomsbury, 33–58. DOI: 10.5040/9781509910847.ch-002.

Gizbert-Studnicki, T., Pleszka, K., and Wolenski, J. (2016) '20th-Century Legal Theory and Philosophy in Poland', in Pattaro, E. and Corrado, R. (eds) *A Treatise of Legal Philosophy and General Jurisprudence: Volume 12, Legal Philosophy in the Twentieth Century: The Civil Law World*, Dordrecht: Springer, 547–586. DOI: 10.1007/978-94-007-1479-3.

Haferkamp H. P., and Wudtke T. (1997) 'Richterausbildung in der DDR', in *forum historiae iuris*, https://forhistiur.de/1997-10-haferkamp-wudtke/ (accessed 15.3.2020).

Heuer, U.-J. (1995) 'Nachwort', in Heuer, U. J. (ed) *Die Rechtsordnung der DDR. Anspruch und Wirklichkeit*, Baden-Baden: Nomos Verlagsgesellschaft, 611–622.

Joseph, D. (1995) 'Rechtswissenschaft und SED', in Heuer, U. J. (ed) *Die Rechtsordnung der DDR. Anspruch und Wirklichkeit*, Baden-Baden: Nomos Verlagsgesellschaft, 549–610.

Kaluza, A., (1999) 'Politischer Gegner im Blickfeld der prärogativen Politik des polnischen Parteistaates 1944–1956', in Bender, G. and Falk, U. (eds) *Recht im Sozialismus. Analysen zur Normdurchsetzung in osteuropäischen Nachkriegsgesellschaften (1944/45–1989). Band 2 Justizpolitik*, Frankfurt am Main: Vittorio Klostermann, 1–28.

Kirby, D. (1994) 'Incorporation: the Molotov-Ribbentrop Pact', in Smith, G. (ed) *The Baltic States. The National Self-Determination of Estonia, Latvia and Lithuania*, London: Macmillan, 69–85.

Klenner, H. (1957) 'Zur ideologischen Natur des Rechts', in *Staat und Recht im Lichte Des Grossen Oktober: Festschrift zum 40. Jahrestage der Grossen Sozialistischen Revolution*, Berlin: VEB Deutschen Zentralverlag, 82–101.

Klenner, H. (1985) 'Gesellschaftsvertragstheorien vom 17. bis zum 20. Jahrhundert', in Klenner, H., and Müller, R. (ed) *Gesellschaftsvertragstheorien von der Antike bis zur Gegenwart*, Berlin: Akademie-Verlag, 31–75.

Kolár, P. (2016) *Der Poststalinismus. Ideologie und Utopie einer Epoche*, Köln, Weimar and Wien: Böhlau Verlag. DOI: 10.7788/9783412506490.

Kopeček, M. (2012) 'Human Rights Facing a National Past. Dissident "Civic Patriotism" and the Return of History in East Central Europe, 1968–1989', *Geschichte und Gesellschaft*, *38*:4, 573–602. DOI: 10.13109/gege.2012.38.4.573.

Koselleck, R. (1987) 'Geschichte, Recht und Gerechtigkeit', in Simon, D. (ed) *Akten des 26. Deutschen Rechtshistorikertages Frankfurt am Main, 22. bis 26. September 1986*, Frankfurt am Main: Vittorio Klosterman, 129–152.

Kramer, M. (2017) 'The Changing Pattern of Soviet–East European Relations 1953–1968', in Naimark, N., Pons, S., and Quinn-Judge, S., (eds) *The Cambridge History of Communism*, Cambridge: Cambridge University Press, 139–169. DOI: 10.1017/9781316459850.007.

Lenin, V. I. (1977) *Valitut teokset. Vol 9 (Collected works. Vol 9)*, Moscow: Kustannusliike Edistys.

Liebrecht, J. (2018) *Die junge Rechtsgeschichte. Kategorienwandel in der rechtshistorischen Germanistik der Zwischenkriegszeit*, Tübingen: Mohr Siebeck.

Luhmann, N. (1984) *Soziale Systeme. Grundriß einer allgemeinen Theorie*, Frankfurt am Main: Suhrkamp.

Lässig, S. (2007) 'Between Two Scholarly Cultures: Reflections on the Reorganization of the East German Historical Profession after 1990', *Central European History*, 40:3, 499–522. DOI: 10.1017/s0008938907000817.

Mamut, L. (1979) *Fragen der Staatstheorie im ideologischen Widerstreit*, Moscow: Progress Verlag.

Markovits, I. S. (1968) 'Civil Law in East Germany—Its Development and Relation to Soviet Legal History and Ideology', *Yale Law Journal*, 78:1, 1–51.

Markovits, I. S. (2018) 'Drei Geschichten einer Fakultät. Ostdeutsche Juraprofessoren im Sozialismus', in Haferkamp H. P., Thiessen, J., and Waldhoff, C. (eds) *Deutsche Diktatorische Rechtsgeschichten? Perspektiven auf die Rechtsgeschichte der DDR. Gedächtnissymposium für Rainer Schröder (1947–2016)*, Tübingen: Mohr Siebeck. 33–50. DOI: 10.1628/978-3-16-156696-7.

Marx, K., and Engels, F. (1970) *Kommunistisen puolueen manifesti*, Helsinki: Kansankulttuuri Oy.

Mälksoo, L. (2018) 'The Controversy over Human Rights, UN Covenants, and the dissolution of the Soviet Union', *Japanese Yearbook of International Law*, 61:1, 260–283.

Naimark, N. (2017) 'The Sovietization of East Central Europe 1945–1989', in Naimark, N., Pons, S., and Quinn-Judge S. (eds) *The Cambridge History of Communism*, Cambridge: Cambridge University Press, 63–86. DOI: 10.1017/9781316459850.004.

Ostermann, C. F. (2001) *Uprising in East Germany, 1953: The Cold War, the German Question, and the First Major Upheaval behind the Iron Curtain*, Budapest: CEU Press.

Otto, M. (2008) *Von der Eigenkirche zum Volkseigenen Betrieb: Erwin Jacobi (1884–1965)*, Tübingen: Mohr Siebeck.

Poláčková, Z., and van Duin, P. C. (2019) 'Gustáv Husák and the Foundations of 'Normalization': Slovak, Czechoslovak and Federative Perspectives 1968–197', *Slavonica*, 24:1–2, 36–51. DOI: 10.1080/13617427.2019.1623460.

Pomeranz, W. E. (2019) *Law and the Russian State: Russia's Legal Evolution from Peter the Great to Vladimir Putin*, London: Bloomsbury Academic. DOI: 10.5040/9781474224253.

Raff, M., and Taitslin, A. (2014) 'Property Rights under Socialist Civil Law: Looking Back to the Twentieth Century.' in Simons, W. B. (ed) *East European Faces of Law and Society: Values and Practices*, Leiden and Boston: Brill | Nijhoff, 251–306. DOI: 10.1163/9789004285224_009.

Reimann, M., Zimmermann, R., and Glenn, H. (2019) 'Comparative Legal Families and Comparative Legal Traditions,' in *The Oxford Handbook of Comparative Law*, London and New York: Oxford University Press, 423–440. DOI: 10.1093/oxfordhb/9780198810230.013.13.

Richardson-Little, N., Dietz, H., and Mark, J. (2019) 'New Perspectives on Socialism and Human Rights in East Central Europe since 1945. Introduction to the Thematic Issue', *East Central Europe*, 46:2–3, 169–187. DOI: 10.1163/18763308-04602004.

Schmidt-Hartmann, E. (1988) 'Forty Years of Historiography under Socialism in Czechoslovakia. Continuity and Change in Patterns of Thought', *Bohemia. Zeitschrift für Geschichte und Kultur der böhmischen Länder*, 29:2, 300–324.

Schröder, H. (1980) 'Vorwort des Herausgebers' in Tschernilowski, S. M., *Allgemeine Staats- und Rechtsgeschichte. Von der Entstehung des Staates bis zum Kapitalismus. Lehrbuch*, Berlin: Staatsverlag der Deutschen Demokratischen Republik, 25–34.

Schröder, J. (2016) *Rechtswissenschaft in Diktaturen. Die Juristische Methodenlehre im NS-Staat und in der DDR*, München: C. H. Beck.

Schöneburg, K. H. (1987) 'Aneignung der Wissenschaftsgeschichte als konstitutives Elemente der Wissenschaftlichkeit. Geschichte und Gegenwart der Staats- und Rechtstheorie', in Köhn, J. and Rode, B. (eds) *Eigentum. Beiträge zu seiner Entwicklung in politischen Gesellschaften. Werner Sellnow zum 70 Geburtstag*, Weimar: Hermann Böhlaus Nachfolger, 306–321.

Sellnow, W. (1963) *Gesellschaft - Staat - Recht. Zur Kritik der bürgerlichen Ideologien über die Entstehungen von Gesellschaft, Staat und Recht*, Berlin: Rütten & Loening.

Sellnow, W. (1968) 'Zum Problem der Rechtsgeschichte im System von Marx und Engels' in *Marxistische Beiträge zur Rechtsgeschichte*, Berlin: Wissenschaftliche Schriftenreihe der Humboldt-Universität zu Berlin, 40–71.

Skinner, S. (2019) 'Introduction: Glancing in the Mirror at Ideology and Criminal Law Under Fascist, National Socialist and Authoritarian Regimes', in Skinner, S. (ed) *Ideology and Criminal Law Fascist, National Socialist and Authoritarian Regimes*, London: Bloomsbury, 1–6. DOI: 10.5040/9781509910847.0006.

Stalin, J. (1951) *Marxism and Linguistics*, New York: International Publishers.

Stolleis, M. (2009) *Sozialistische Gesetzlichkeit. Staats- und Verwaltungsrechtswissenschaft in der DDR*, München: Verlag C. H. Beck.

Tschernilowski, S. M. (1980) *Allgemeine Staats- und Rechtsgeschichte. Von der Entstehung des Staates bis zum Kapitalismus. Lehrbuch*, Berlin: Staatsverlag der Deutschen Demokratischen Republik.

Varga, C. (2016) '20th-Century Legal Philosophy in Hungary', in Pattaro, E. and Corrado, R. (eds) *A Treatise of Legal Philosophy and General Jurisprudence: Volume 12, Legal Philosophy in the Twentieth Century: The Civil Law World*, Dordrecht: Springer, 635–651. DOI: 10.1007/978-94-007-1479-3_19.

Wieacker, F. (1967) *Privatrechtsgeschichte der Neuzeit. Unter besonderer Berücksichtigung der deutschen Entwicklung. 2., neubearbeitete Auflage*, Göttingen: Vandenhoeck & Ruprecht.

Zagladin, V. (1983) *Sosialistisen yhteiskunnan historiallinen tehtävä (Socialism: its role in history)*, Moscow: Kustannusliike Progress.

Part I

Framing the socialist legal historiography

1 The transformations of some classical principles in socialist Hungarian civil law

The metamorphosis of *bona fides* and *boni mores* in the Hungarian Civil Code of 1959

András Földi

On the historical background

As is well known, the concepts of *bona fides* and *boni mores* originate in Roman law. Before examining their fate in the socialist Hungarian civil law, it is necessary to refer briefly to the relationship between Hungary and the Roman law tradition. Until the middle of the 19th century, the Hungarian legal system did not belong to civil law jurisdictions. Apart from during the Roman times, Roman law has never been the law in effect in Hungary. In the Middle Ages as well as in the early modern period, Hungary had a conservative national customary law strongly characterised by feudalistic features. In these times, Roman law only had a limited impact on the development of Hungarian law (Bónis, 1964; Zlinszky, 1983, pp. 56ff; Hamza, 2009, pp. 366ff).

The modernisation of Hungarian law in terms of the reception of the Roman law tradition—I am speaking now about private law—began in the 19th century. Hungarian private law acquired a civilian (Roman law) character due to the introduction of the Austrian Civil Code (*Allgemeines bürgerliches Gesetzbuch*, ABGB) in 1853. Some years later, the ABGB was repealed but, as a matter of course, it was hardly possible to return to the old Hungarian private law. Judicature and other factors of legal development aimed for the creation of a modern Hungarian private law, mainly on the basis of German law (besides the impact of the Pandectists, it was in a certain period especially the Saxon Civil Code of 1863 which was regarded as a model code for developing the Hungarian private law), but the Austrian law and later (after the First World War) sometimes the Swiss law were taken into consideration as well.[1] At the end of the 19th century and in the first decades of the 20th century, several drafts of a Hungarian Civil Code were elaborated, even presented as bills to the Hungarian Parliament, but they were never adopted. Among these drafts, especially the last one, the Private Law Code of Hungary in 1928 is to be stressed, not only because of its high professional level, but also because of its considerable impact on the judicature, which tacitly recognised it as an effective source of law (cf. Zlinszky, 1983, p. 65; Földi, 1988, pp. 364ff; Képes, 2016, pp. 112f).

As far as the social-historical context of the development of Hungarian private law before the First World War is concerned, it is to be noted that this development took place within the framework of the Austro-Hungarian Monarchy. After the Compromise between Austria and Hungary was concluded in 1867, a golden age began for Hungary for some decades when both the economy and culture developed to a great extent (Rigó, 2017). These decades were dominated by the increasing influence of liberal ideas. In this context, it is important to refer to the emancipation of Jews in Hungary (Act No. XVII of 1867) and to their continuously growing role in the Hungarian economy and society. The Tiszaeszlár blood libel trial in 1882 and 1883 showed the presence of antisemitism in Hungary, but in spite of antisemitic agitation, the rule of law triumphed.

Unfortunately, the First World War did not only break the *belle époque*, it also led to the fall of the Austro-Hungarian Monarchy in 1918. It is not so much the emergence of new national states that is to be lamented in this respect but rather the loss of a number of high values, especially the devaluation of liberal ideas, not to mention socialist ones.

The definitive end of the liberal period of the former decades was marked by a short communist intermezzo that took place in 1919, namely, the formation of the first communist regime in Hungary on the March 21, 1919. The so-called 'Hungarian Soviet Republic' led by Béla Kun (1886–1938) had extremist ideas and applied terrorist means. It collapsed after 133 days. Since the majority of communist politicians leading the Soviet Republic of 1919 were of Jewish origin, albeit they were not members of the Jewish community, antisemitism in Hungary became stronger in the interwar period and it became a part of government policy as early as 1920 (Karady and Nagy, 2012).

The restoration of the Kingdom of Hungary in 1920 was possible in a territory reduced to two-thirds of its original size. Due to the Trianon Treaty of 1920, Hungary lost not only large and important territories, but also more than a quarter of native Hungarians suddenly found themselves outside of Hungarian borders, mainly in Romania, Czechoslovakia, and Yugoslavia. After such antecedents, from 1920 a national Christian course prevailed in Hungarian politics, characterised by strong anticommunism and increasing antisemitism as well as antiliberalism.

In the framework of the present study, I can refer only briefly to the tragic events of the Second World War and of the Holocaust that afflicted Hungary to a tragically great extent. The political and moral responsibility of the Hungarian governments and other influential political factors should not be underestimated in this respect. Between September 1944 and April 1945, the territory of Hungary was liberated or, as it turned out later, occupied by the Soviet Red Army. Soviet troops left the country only after the fall of communism in 1991. The Hungarian Communist Party took power in 1948 and in the same year the communist (called 'socialist') transformation of the Hungarian legal system began.

Creation of the first Hungarian Civil Code of 1959

In this transformation process, the greatest task was the creation of the first Civil Code of Hungary. The codification works began in 1953 and it was on July 30, 1959, that the Parliament adopted the Civil Code of the People's Republic of Hungary as Act No. IV of 1959. The Civil Code entered into force on May 1, 1960, and after several amendments remained in force until March 15, 2014, when the new Civil Code (Act No. V of 2013) entered into force.

Hungary in the 1950s as well as other socialist countries in Europe experienced a dark era characterised by massive brutality from the communist party, which made use of the state organs. On the other hand, there were a number of highly qualified jurists who had, fortunately, an important role in the gigantic project of civil law codification in Hungary. As we know from history, legal science (or at least the validity of private law) and a totalitarian regime do not necessarily exclude each other. The classical Roman jurists as well as the excellent jurists of Justinian worked in an autocratic empire (cf. Honoré, 1973–1974, p. 869).

As for the preparation of the first Hungarian Civil Code (Act No. IV of 1959), which began in 1953, its main drafters were Miklós Világhy (1916–1980), Gyula Eörsi (1922–1992), Endre Nizsalovszky (1894–1976), Elemér Pólay (1915–1988), and Béla Kemenes (1928–2000). Nizsalovszky was perhaps the greatest Hungarian private lawyer of his time. From 1938 he was the Professor of Civil Procedure Law at the University of Budapest, and from 1943 he was also Professor of Private Law there. He was a member of the Hungarian Academy of Sciences from 1939. He is mentioned in third place in the list given above because as a non-communist, he could have only a limited influence on the actual codification.

It was in fact remarkable in those times that Nizsalovszky was invited to the codification committee at all. Many of his colleagues, having been labelled 'bourgeois scholars,' were forced to retire between 1945 and 1950; if they had been members of the Academy of Sciences, as a rule they lost their membership. Nizsalovszky, however, was an extremely renowned legal scholar, and he was, moreover, politically more liberal than conservative being by no means hostile towards progressive ideas prior to the Second World War.[2]

The leading members of the codification committee were Világhy and Eörsi. Formerly as law students they had been Nizsalovszky's pupils. A semi-official letter written by Nizsalovszky to Eörsi in 1954 attests that the esteemed professor treated his young colleague as a good friend (see Bodzási, 2018, fol. 16, pp. 1146ff). In spite of their 'bourgeois' family background, both Világhy and Eörsi as persons open to new ideas—Eörsi being in addition a Holocaust survivor—became convinced communists after 1945. They were appointed Professors of Civil Law at the University of Budapest in 1953 and later also became members of the Hungarian Academy of Sciences. The fact that the Civil Code of 1959, despite some socialist institutions, remained a Romanistic one is especially due to Világhy and Eörsi who, possessing a certain political influence, could successfully insist that a number of classical traditions of private law be preserved.

At this point, the Soviet jurists to some extent controlled to what extent socialist principles were present in the new Hungarian Civil Code. A well-known Soviet jurist, Anatolii Venediktov (1887–1959), professor at Leningrad State University and member of the Soviet Academy of Sciences (cf. Benevolenskaya, 2013, pp. 173ff), sent a letter containing general observations on the draft of the new Hungarian Civil Code in December 1957. Venediktov welcomed the fact that the new Hungarian Civil Code as the first socialist civil code would not contain a general part (cf. Baldus and Dajczak, 2013).[3] Venediktov adds, however, that just that is why the preliminary provisions should be more detailed than in a civil code having also a general part. Lacking a Russian translation, Venediktov, as he himself observed, was not in a position to ascertain whether the preliminary provisions in the Hungarian draft contained to a satisfactory extent the principles of socialist civil law, even if taking into account the current lower stage of the development of socialism in Hungary.[4] A less rigorous and at the same time a less detailed letter was sent by the Institute of Legal Sciences of the Soviet Academy of Sciences (Antimonov, Bratus, Sadikov) to Gyula Eörsi in May 1958 (Bodzási, 2018, fol. 8, pp. 567ff).

As highly qualified jurists, although hardly being convinced communists, Pólay and Kemenes had important roles in the codification. They were appointed professors at the University of Szeged in 1951 and 1961, respectively. Pólay was especially renowned as a scholar of Roman law.[5]

As for the preparatory materials of the Civil Code of 1959, it is an advantageous recent development that on the basis of a mandate given by the Minister of Justice of Hungary these materials stored in the National Archives of Hungary were digitalised in 2015 and 2016 (Verebics, 2017, p. 12). These materials, amounting to 16,000 pages, were rendered accessible online in 2018 (Bodzási, 2018). A part of these documents was published in printed form in 2017, and the corresponding volumes are also accessible online.[6]

The materials mentioned above—typically typed, sometimes written with a pen, and sometimes printed—attest that the preparation of the Hungarian Civil Code of 1959 was carried out at a highly professional level. Excellent jurists who had been educated during the previous era took part in the work and clearly did their best. It is characteristic of the high professional standards that both a former project of the famous Professor of Roman law, Géza Marton (1880–1957),[7] and a study written by Ferenc Mádl (1931–2012)[8] were taken into account with regard to civil liability regulations.

The coming into being of the socialist equivalent of *bona fides*

In the framework of the present study, I will deal with the socialist transformation of two classical principles of private law, namely, that of 'good faith and fair dealing' (*bona fides*) and that concerning the prohibition of contracts 'contrary to good morals' (*contra bonos mores*).

The Bill of a Private Law Code for Hungary, published in 1928 mentioned above, contained, similar to the Swiss Civil Code (para. 1 of art. 2), the principle of 'good faith and honesty' (section 2) and also contained, like the French 'Civil code' (*Code civil*) (old art. 1133), the prohibition of contracts 'contrary to good morals and public policy' (section 973). From 1949 these concepts were regarded in Hungary as being incompatible with socialist civil law. These notions were regarded as expressions of the relationships of capitalism. This evaluation was reflected not only in the Hungarian legal literature of the 1950s but also in the subsequent decades.

Eörsi laid down in his monograph on the development of ownership published in 1951 that the principle of good faith applied in the traffic of goods, i.e., 'good faith and fair dealing' (*Treu und Glauben*) served as an instrument to moderate the impoverishment ('proletarisation') of small capitalists and to prevent anarchy. He regarded this principle as a reflection of the impotence and class character of the imperialist patrimonial law (Eörsi, 1951, II, 65, 388). In a later monograph published in 1965, Eörsi ascertained that 'good faith and fair dealing' had been inserted into the German and Swiss civil codes as an 'alien body' since these codes reflected the cold business mentality of capitalism. Eörsi added that the principle of good faith was a 'rubber rule' that generated legal uncertainty (Eörsi, 1965, p. 72).

In 1965 a monograph of Imre Sárándi was published about the abuse of rights. Sárándi explains that good morals, the habits of an honest man, and good faith and fair dealing are bourgeois principles, the content of which is always being established in accordance with the current class interests of monopoly capitalists (Sárándi, 1965, p. 69). In the following year, a monograph by László Asztalos was published on sanctions in civil law. Being a highly qualified jurist, Asztalos was an expert on both civil law and legal history. He also considered the principle of 'good faith and fair dealing' to be a symptom of the crisis of monopoly capitalism (Asztalos, 1966, p. 153; see similarly Szabó, 1964, p. 99).

In his comprehensive book on comparative private law published in Hungarian in 1975 and also in English in 1979, sometimes called the 'socialist Zweigert/Kötz,' Eörsi regarded 'good faith and fair dealing' to be the most efficient instrument of monopoly capitalist law that served as a 'Jack of all trades' (*Mädchen für alles*) (Eörsi, 1975, pp. 452ff; idem, 1979, pp. 476ff). In 1981 Eörsi evaluated the principle of good faith in a more positive manner, at least as regards the *United Nations Convention on Contracts for the International Sale* of 1980, otherwise known as the Vienna Convention. Eörsi welcomed the weakening of the former *rigor commercialis* and expressed his hope that the principle of good faith would play a greater role during the actual application of the Convention rather than being a compromise merely worked out on paper among the representatives of the United Nations member states (Eörsi, 1981, pp. 19f).

References to the capitalist character of 'good faith applied in the traffic of goods' can also be found in the preparatory documents of the Civil Code of 1959. In a document written by Gyula Eörsi and Béla Csánk in 1951, it is emphasised that the good faith applied in the traffic of goods is a product of the constant crisis of capitalism that had to alleviate the antagonistic conflicts especially in favour of the small capitalists so that they would not become proletarians. The authors ascertained that such conflicts would not arise in people's democracies (Bodzási, 2018, fol. 4, p. 831).[9]

Since the principle of 'good faith and honesty' laid down in the Bill of 1928 was considered a bourgeois concept, it was replaced by new principles in section 4 of the new Civil Code. The text of paragraph 1 was published in the following form: 'In the course of exercising their rights and fulfilling their duties the parties in civil law relations shall display such a conduct that enforcement of their interests shall be in harmony with the interest of society.'

The coming into being of this passage can be observed very well in the light of the preparatory documents. In some versions up to December 1958, the reference was not made to the interests of 'society' but to those of the 'community.'[10] Moreover, in the first drafts up until 1957, the expression 'interest of the public' applied.[11] The reference to 'society' was in this way the third stage in a development during which the drafters were always looking for a better expression. I think that the word 'society' was finally preferred because as a rather abstract notion, it could serve as a milder means regarding the limitation of private autonomy.

Paragraph 2 of section 4 in its published form laid down that '[i]n civil law relations [the parties] shall cooperate mutually and act in compliance with the requirements of socialist coexistence. Cooperation shall be realised by the exact fulfilment of duties and by such an enforcement of rights which is in compliance with their [social] destination.' This formulation appeared already in the first Draft of 1955. Later only small corrections of a stylistic nature took place.

The duty of mutual cooperation laid down in this passage can be regarded as a progressive idea that spread from the 1950s in Western legal cultures and is present also in art. III. 1:104 of the *Draft Common Frame of Reference* (Bar et al., 2009, I, pp. 685ff). The reference to the requirements of socialist coexistence is of ideological nature, but it is not to be regarded as a limitation on private autonomy but much more as a principle requiring consideration of the interests of other persons and in this way it constitutes continuity with the classic principles of good faith and honesty.[12]

The next phrase contains strict rules concerning both parties of the civil law relations. The requirement of exact fulfilment of duties is in a way contrary to the classical principle of good faith, which sometimes renders possible a milder treatment of the debtor's duties (cf. Brox, 2000, p. 149; idem, 1984, p. 91; Medicus, 1999, p. 113). It is to be noted that the vision of a negligent debtor could have a role when drafting this rule, against whom the legislator had to protect the other party. The reference to the exercise of rights is a sign of a significant extension of the prohibition of chicane in socialist civil law, which is more thoroughly explained in section 5 treating the abuse of rights.

In the first versions of the Draft, a third paragraph in section 4 laid down that '[t]he socialist organisations exercise their rights in order to fulfil their duties based upon the plan of the people's economy' (see the Draft of 1955 in Bodzási,

2018, fol. 16, p. 233). This paragraph, however, was deleted at the end of 1956 or somewhat later and was not included in the final text.[13] The deletion of this paragraph is a sign that the socialist character of the draft of the Civil Code was moderated.[14]

In the first Drafts, such provisions in section 4 were substituted for the former principle of good faith and honesty. One similarity to para. 2 section 2 of the Bill of 1928 is that section 4 of all versions of the draft was followed by a section 5 containing the prohibition of the abuse of rights, albeit the effectiveness of the prohibition was significantly extended.

Neither the expression 'good faith' nor the word 'honesty' appeared in the various versions of section 4. 'Fair dealing' is not mentioned in these texts, either. It is still more remarkable that not even the first versions of the rationale contain any reference to the fact that section 4 was substituted for the former principle of good faith and honesty.[15]

As referred to briefly above, these classical notions were omitted since they were regarded as reflections of capitalism. On the contrary, emphasis was laid on collective aspects, namely on the interests of society, and on the relationships between parties, especially on their duty of cooperation. At the same time, only the expression 'socialist coexistence' has an explicit ideological connotation in these provisions.

During the preparation of the Civil Code, proposals were made suggesting preserving some reference to good faith. Among the preparatory materials, a voluminous study amounting to 100 pages can be found that was presented in November 1957 by judge Kornél Berndt. This study contained an explicit proposal to insert into the Civil Code the principle of good faith and honesty with reference to a similar provision in the Bill of 1928 (Bodzási, 2018, fol. 16, p. 72).[16] It is not surprising that this proposal was rejected. It is in fact more remarkable that the Bill of 1928 could be referred to as a model. In this era, the entire old Hungarian law was regarded by a number of influential communist jurists to be an obsolete reflection of capitalism with some surviving elements of feudalism. Indeed, in the 1950s, the interwar period was often referred to as the era of Horthy fascism.[17]

In the beginning of 1959, the Hungarian minister of foreign affairs, Endre Sík (1891–1978), proposed that the presumption of good faith should be inserted into the Preliminary provisions of the Civil Code, similar to section 3 of the Bill of 1928. This proposal was rejected with the explanation that the new code would have a more severe regulation and, in some cases, even the presumption of bad faith had to apply. Such an inverse presumption of bad faith could be feasible, in particular, if 'capitalist elements' were concerned who were, however, slowly disappearing from Hungarian society (see Bodzási, 2018, fol. 8, p. 107).

Even if such conservative efforts failed, they had still some consequences, namely, some surrogates for the missing classical principle of good faith and honesty were finally inserted into the Civil Code. At the end of 1957 or somewhat later, somebody noted the Latin word *nemo* written in pen in a copy of the Draft published in printed form in the autumn of 1957, in the rationale of section 4 (see Bodzási, 2018, fol. 11, p. 701). This was obviously a reference to the maxim 'no one alleging his own turpitude is to be heard' (*nemo suam turpitudinem allegans auditur*). As a consequence, in the Draft of December 1958, a third paragraph appeared in the text of section 4, laying down that '[n]obody can rely on their own misfeasance in order to acquire an advantage. [...]' (See Bodzási, 2018, fol. 14, p. 4.)

A further supplement concerning good faith and honesty appeared in the Draft published in the autumn of 1957. It is in the third paragraph inserted into section 5, which deals with the abuse of rights. The new provision laid down that '[t]he court may obligate to full or partial reparation the person whose intentional behaviour has induced another person in good faith to such an action whereby the latter has suffered a damage through no fault of his own.' This paragraph became in the Draft of December 1958 the separate section 6 (see Bodzási, 2018, fol. 14, p. 4). This state of affairs is known as 'implicit conduct,' and it preserved its position and wording also in the published version.[18] The text of the provision as well as the rationale to the (final) section 6 attest that the 'implicit conduct' was really a surrogate for the lack of good faith. The text of the provision contains an explicit reference to the 'good faith' of the possible plaintiff and the rationale refers several times to the importance of 'confidence in good faith.'

Can we say that the classical principle of good faith and honesty could survive in a way in the Civil Code of 1959 due to the provision on implicit conduct? I am afraid that the answer to this question has to be negative since the good faith referred to hereby is the so-called subjective good faith (in German *guter Glaube*), while the classical principle of good faith and honesty is connected with the objective good faith (in German *Treu und Glauben*).[19]

A further impact of the conservative proposals mentioned above can be verified in the ministerial rationale to the Bill of 1959 which was later published together with the norm text of the Civil Code. While the former drafts of the rationale did not refer to this problem at all, the rationale in its final form observes that the Bill does not lay down the presumption of good faith, although such a presumption can be found in the Bill of 1928, in many bourgeois civil codes and also in article 5 of the 'Polish General Part' of 1950 (of a Polish civil code being that time scheduled only). The further explication treating 'good faith and fair dealing' as well as the good faith of the possessor without any distinction shows that the drafter of the rationale was unable to distinguish between the subjective and the objective meanings of good faith (Hungarian Civil Code of 1959, hereinafter HCC, 1959, p. 25).

Even if considering the confusion of the meanings of good faith in the rationale, it was advantageous that the norm text of the Hungarian Civil Code of 1959 emphasised some objective standards instead of laying down the principle of good faith and honesty. Thanks to this solution, in the subsequent decades, there was no Hungarian jurist who would have confused the objective and the subjective senses of good faith, at least not within Hungarian civil law. The terminology applied by the Civil Code of 1959 guaranteed that good faith meant only (or overwhelmingly) the subjective state of mind, while the principle of objective good faith (and honesty) had an entirely different terminology. The advantage of the solution preferred in the Hungarian Civil Code of 1959 is obvious if we compare it with para. 3 of art. 1134 of the French *Code civil* of 1804 (abrogated in 2016) that laid down that 'the contracts shall be performed bona fide' ([e]*lles* [viz. les conventions—A. F.] *doivent être exécutées de bonne foi*). This provision, namely the ambiguous term *bonne foi,* constituted one source of confusion concerning subjective and objective good faith in French civil law (cf. Tallon, 1994, p. 12).

Developments since the Novel of 1977

As far as the subsequent fate of section 4 is concerned, during the preparation of the Novel of 1977, László Asztalos proposed that the prohibition of unfair business activity and unfair profit making be inserted into the preliminary provisions (Asztalos, 1976, p. 120). A more radical proposal was made by Imre Sárándi, who suggested laying down the principle of exercising rights and duties in compliance with their destination and in good faith (Sárándi, 1977, pp. 35ff). Asztalos's proposal was accepted to some extent and the Novel (Act No. IV of 1977) laid down the prohibition of unfair business activity in para. 2 of section 4. Sárándi's proposal including the restoration of the principle of good faith could not be accepted at that time.[20]

As far as the background of the Novel of 1977 is concerned, in 1968 a significant modification of the regulation of the economy took place in Hungary, namely, the so-called 'new economic mechanism' was introduced that was aimed at diminishing the role of central planning and at increasing the role of market relations.

It was only Act XIV of 1991 that later restored the classical principle of good faith and honesty overwriting para. 1 of section 4. Since 'good faith' meant in Hungarian civil law for some decades (between 1960 and 1991) an exclusively subjective notion, the restoration of the classical principle caused considerable misunderstandings. Most jurists did not remember the principle of 'good faith and honesty' as being formerly fixed by the Bill of 1928 (Földi, 2003, pp. 82ff). An amendment, namely Act No. III of 2006, was required to make matters less ambiguous, both by means of some slight corrections of the relating terminology and through the relating rationale, namely that in Hungarian civil law objective and subjective good faith are to be distinguished (Földi, 2007, pp. 53ff). In the new Hungarian Civil Code (Act. No. V of 2013), the same terminology applies (para. 1 of section 1:3; cf. Földi, 2016, pp. 173ff).

The coming into being of the socialist equivalent of *boni mores*

The Bill of 1928, mentioned several times above, contained not only the principle of good faith and honesty (its section 3, being similar to art. 2 of the Swiss Civil Code) but also, similar to the French civil code (*Code civil*) (old art. 1133),[21] the prohibition of contracts 'contrary to good morals and public policy' (section 973). Just as the principle of good faith and honesty was not compatible with socialist ideas, so, too, this was the case with regard to *boni mores.* That is why a new provision was substituted for *boni mores* in para. 2 of section 200 of the Civil Code of 1959 with the following wording: 'Any contract contrary to legal rules or made to elude the legal rules is rendered null and void unless a legal rule attaches different legal consequences to it. A contract is likewise null and void when it is evidently contrary to the interests of the working people or to the requirements of socialist coexistence.'

This ruling came into being as a result of a development that had several stages. In the first draft of the law of obligations made in July 1953,[22] there was a shorter formulation according to which '[a] contract is null and void if it is contrary to legal rules or made to elude the legal rules or is not in the interests of the working people in some other way.' (See Bodzási, 2018, fol. 19, p. 8.)

In the draft of the law of obligations of October 1954 signed by Nizsalovszky, Világhy, and Eörsi, three further states of affairs were added to the first version of the new rule. One of them was a reference to the contracts contrary to the planned tasks of both parties. A further type of nullity was constituted by contracts contrary to the requirements of socialist coexistence, and a third case was constituted by the contracts aimed to damage the state (see Bodzási, 2018, fol. 19, p. 74).

The reference to the interests of the working people was modified in the version in question by inserting the adverb 'evidently.' This addition could have been inspired by art. 2 of the Swiss Civil Code,[23] and it obviously served to increase the certainty of the law. This modification is a little sign of the political changes after Stalin's death in 1953.

Moreover, the codification commission wished for a reference to 'socialist morals' to be added to the wording of the law (see Bodzási, 2018, fol. 19, p. 74). This proposal does not seem to have any echo in the later materials. It is strange that the word 'morals' was not acceptable even though accompanied by the word 'socialist.'

It was Gyula Eörsi who inserted (in ink) the word 'determined' before the words 'planned tasks' in a copy of the September 1955 Draft. At the same time, Eörsi also added (again in ink) that the reference to damaging the state should be discussed (for both corrections by Eörsi see Bodzási, 2018, fol. 19, p. 174). These proposals were also aimed to increase the certainty of the law that Eörsi felt was being endangered by such general clauses.

In a later version of the Draft probably at the end of 1955, the reference to the conflict with planned tasks was struck out in ink but the reference to damaging the state was left untouched (see Bodzási, 2018, fol. 17, p. 1). In a somewhat later version of the Draft, which no longer contained a reference to the planned tasks, the reference to damaging the state was also struck out in ink (see Bodzási, 2018, fol. 19, p. 218).

In spite of the corrections aimed to increase the legal certainty, critical observations were made that the reference to 'fraudulent intention to evade the law' (*in fraudem legis agere*) was not exact enough.[24] According to another, more radical criticism, the reference to the conflict with the interests of working people and the requirements of socialist coexistence would be superfluous since the corresponding cases were covered by the prohibition of contracts contrary to legal rules as well as contracts made 'in circumvention of the rules of law' (*in fraudem legis*). Furthermore, according to this criticism, these general clauses were dangerous as they made it possible to pass arbitrary sentences.[25]

These concerns, which can sometimes appear nowadays, did not have any impact on the legislation. The text formulated in the Draft of September 1956 (para. 2 of section 181 [later 200], see Bodzási, 2018, fol. 11, p. 59) was also preserved in the later versions and if compared with the final enacted version reveals only minor modifications of a stylistic character.

The ministerial rationale of the Bill of 1959, published together with the norm text of the Civil Code, referred explicitly to the fact that the reference to the conflict with the interests of the working people and with the requirements of socialist coexistence was substituted for the former prohibition of contracts contrary to good morals (HCC, 1959, p. 154).

Developments since the Novel of 1977

In the Novel of 1977, a more timely reference was substituted for the 'working people,' namely, 'society.' It was only the Novel of 1991 mentioned above in which the prohibition of contracts 'against good morals' (*contra bonos mores*) was substituted for the modified socialist formula in section 200, preserving, however, from the socialist definition the restrictive adverb 'evidently.' At the same time, the former reference to the 'public order' known in the respective provision of the Bill of 1928 was omitted by the Novel of 1991. Therefore, the Novel in question did not restore the formula of the Bill of 1928 completely. The new Hungarian Civil Code (Act No. V of 2013) has preserved the provision introduced in 1991 (section 6:96; cf. Földi, 2016, pp. 183f).

The judicature dealt thoroughly with the problem, in which cases an evident conflict with the interests of society or with the requirements of social coexistence could be verified. The selling of real estates of the state at a low price in bad faith was a typical case of violation of the interests of society. Violation of the requirements of socialist coexistence was verified when a person who was aware of the grave illness and bad medical prognosis of the other party concluded with him or her a contract for support (maintenance) or for life annuity in order to acquire the other party's apartment at a low cost.[26]

Conclusions

Drawing some general conclusions, we can ascertain that the socialist transformation of some classical principles of civil law in Hungary did not cause extremely grave damage. The contents of *bona fides* as well as that of *boni mores* were translated into a new and sometimes surprising language, but the changes can also be seen as a kind of modernisation. The details of application of these general clauses of ancient origin sometimes became more understandable. Moreover, in the case of *bona fides,* the transformation was useful, namely, in order to avoid the confusion of the subjective and objective meanings of good faith. It should be noted that the traditional technical term 'good faith' itself is very problematical and has constituted a source of misunderstandings for many centuries (Juenger, 1995, p. 1253; Földi, 2007, pp. 53ff). It is less understandable why in socialist Hungarian civil law the notion of 'morals' could not apply even with the attribute 'socialist' either, despite such proposals attested by the preparatory materials.

As for the background of the low level of 'communist distortions' appearing in the codification of the HCC of 1959, several advantageous circumstances can be mentioned. The members of the codification commission were jurists qualified at a very high professional level in the period before the Second World War. They often represented a higher professional level than many of the jurists trained later in the socialist era, having to create the new 'capitalist' private law of Hungary after 1990. This inverse development of the recent past has not been less paradoxical than the former situation was in the 1950s.

Most of the members of the codification commission of the HCC of 1959 were not engaged communists or at least not before 1945. Some of them assumed the task because of opportunism. It has to be added, however, that the former regime known as Horthy era (1920–1944) became odious not only because of the tragic events that happened during the last years of the war. With regard to the adverse antecedents, the communist regime did not seem so much unacceptable in the time of its emergence as it seems nowadays.

As far as the preparatory materials allow us to judge it, the Soviet Union controlled the process of codification in an absolutely soft way. No detailed translations of the drafts were sent to Soviet jurists. There are only a very few direct references to the Soviet law in the preparatory materials. The more remarkable is that a number of references to the Bill of 1928 can be found in the same documents. These references are not always negative. As attested by the preparatory materials, the socialist features of the draft were moderated both after Stalin's death (1953) and after the revolution of 1956.

Naturally there were strict limits determining the socialist character of the codification. As referred to above, neither the notion of good faith and fair dealing nor that of the good morals could be mentioned in the norm text of the HCC until 1991. They might be referred to only in the rationale. These 'bourgeois' notions could not be admitted in the Novel of 1977 either, in spite of repeated proposals, albeit also this Novel reduced a bit the socialist character of some of the provisions in question. There was a slow, by no means a continuous, but in any case a long process of erosion of socialist character of the provisions limiting the private autonomy.

Finally, it was fortunate that the codification of the Hungarian Civil Code of 1959 was led by two highly qualified jurists, M. Világhy and Gy. Eörsi. Having become communists despite their 'bourgeois' roots, they had the political influence to retain a great many elements of the civil law tradition in Hungary.

Notes

1 Commercial law was regulated in Hungary by the independent Commercial Code of 1875, cf. Zlinszky, 1985, p. 435, p. 441.

2 On the basis of political considerations the communist regime distinguished a number of 'strata' of 'bourgeois' scholars and applied different treatment towards them. Some older professors like Endre Nizsalovszky (private law), Géza Marton (Roman law), or Ferenc Eckhart (legal history) could keep their chairs; Nizsalovszky and Marton could also keep their membership in the Academy of Sciences. Other professors appointed before 1944, e.g., Sándor Kornél Tury (Professor of Commercial Law in Budapest), were sent to the Institute of Administrative and Legal Sciences of the Hungarian Academy of Sciences so that they would not disturb the ideological development of the students. Tury had the opportunity to make observations on the drafts of the new Civil Code; see, e.g., Bodzási, 2018 [http://impp.mhk.hu/document/view/id=17], p. 192 (as for the following references to the Preparatory Materials, the number of the corresponding folder and that of the electronic page will only be given). The case of István Szászy (Professor of Private Law and Private International Law in Budapest, known also as Étienne de Szászy) was peculiar because he was forced to retire in 1951 but he did not lose his membership in the Academy of Sciences. In the 1950s, he could earn money as a translator. From the 1960s, a number of his monographs were published in Hungary in English. See Burián, 2001, pp. 147ff.

3 The role or even the raison d'être of the general part was discussed in Soviet legal literature as well as in some other socialist countries. A letter sent by the Secretary of State of the East German (GDR) Ministry of Justice, Dr. Toeplitz, to the Hungarian Minister of Justice in February 1959 seems to be sceptical as regards the rejection of the general part. Dr. Toeplitz was curious about the arguments for this solution being discussed in the GDR, see the original letter in Bodzási, 2018, fol. 8, pp. 781ff. A head of department, István Timár answered that the system of the civil code did not have to be identical with the scientific system of civil law and the latter necessarily contained a general part. See Timár's letter sent in April 1959 in Bodzási, 2018, fol. 8, p. 785ff.

4 I did not find the original text of Venediktov's letter. Among the preparatory materials published recently a Hungarian translation can be found, see Bodzási, 2018, fol. 8, pp. 570ff. This document does not contain any reference to whom the letter was sent.

5 For the scientific oeuvre of Pólay, see Éva Jakab's study in this volume. A folder of the preparatory materials of the Civil Code of 1959 contains Elemér Pólay's offprint from the *Acta Antiqua Academiae Scientiarum Hungaricae* (vol. 5 [1957]; this is a study entitled *Die Blütezeit des römischen Wirtschaftslebens und die klassiche Zeit des römischen Rechts*) dedicated to Béla Kemenes on the February 15, 1958 (see Bodzási, 2018, fol. 23, p. 704). It is, however, not probable that this study could be used during the codification work, and Pólay's study can be regarded here as a kind of 'textus fugitivus.' The preparatory materials attest that Pólay made several proposals in order to preserve as many classical institutions as possible in the new Civil Code, see, e.g., Bodzási, 2018, fol. 19, p. 963.

6 See http://impp.mhk.hu/document/view/id=49.

7 See G. Marton, *Tervezet egy polgári törvénykönyv kártérítési fejezetéhez* (A draft of the chapter on damages of a new Civil Code) in Bodzási, 2018, fol. 17, pp. 257–329. Marton's draft was first published (in a different version) in his posthumous monograph: Marton, 1992, pp. 298–327. For more on Géza Marton himself, see Szabó, 2001, pp. 424f.; Hamza, 2009, pp. 398f.

8 See F. Mádl, *Az objektív felelősségi rendszer történelmi kialakulása* (Historical formation of the system of strict liability) in Bodzási, 2018, fol. 23, pp. 640–703.

Ferenc Mádl was a professor at the Eötvös Loránd University (Budapest); a member of the Hungarian Academy of Sciences; and, between 2000 and 2005, President of the Republic of Hungary.

9 This document was written for the professional and political training of jurists in the framework of a conference organised by the Department of Codification of the Ministry of Justice; see the cover on p. 822 (Bodzási, 2018, fol. 4).

10 So still in the Draft of December 12, 1958 in Bodzási, 2018, fol. 14, p. 4. In this copy, however, the word 'community' is crossed out in pencil and the word 'society' is substituted. In another copy, the same correction was made with a pen, see ibid. p. 498.

11 See a copy of the Draft of 1955 with corrections made in both pen and pencil. Bodzási, 2018, fol. 16, p. 351. This correction was made prior to July 27, 1957, cf. ibid. p. 374.

12 Gy. Eörsi in Eörsi and Gellért, 1981, I, 49 observes that the socialist character of the cooperation laid down in section 4 means that the parties shall not be only neutral or peaceful as regards the other party's interests (as is the case in bourgeois legal systems) but they shall carry out activity as well if it is necessary in the given case. As an example, Eörsi refers to a judgment passed in 1970 according to which a special (remedial) recreation home, if being specialised also for receiving motor-disabled guests, should put carpets on the floor so that walking is made safer.

13 A section crossed out with red pencil can be found in a copy of the Draft of September 1956 (see Bodzási, 2018, fol. 11, p. 247). In the Draft published in autumn 1957 this provision is already omitted (see ibid. p. 699). 'Enterprises ha[d] to report on the state of plan fulfilment of the annual plan every quarter or even at shorter intervals,' see Földi, 1992, II, p. 582.

14 The Novel of 1977 inserted a new provision into section 4 in which the idea of the planned economy reappeared. This modification was, however, in connection with the liberalisation of the economy.

15 See the Draft Rationale of Spring 1957 in Bodzási, 2018, fol. 12, pp. 15f; similarly in the (printed) Draft Rationale of August 1957 in fol. 2, p. 113 as well as in the (printed) Draft Rationale of Autumn of 1957 in fol. 11, p. 701, p. 974.

16 Berndt also made further conservative proposals, e.g., to receive sections 4–7 of the Bill of 1928 as well as to include also family law in the Civil Code; see ibid. fol. 16, p. 44.

17 A prominent representative of this course was also the internationally well-known legal philosopher and comparatist Imre Szabó (1912–1991), Director of the Institute of Administrative and Legal Sciences of the Hungarian Academy of Sciences. In 1955 Szabó published a controversial monograph radically condemning the older Hungarian legal philosophy. Szabó stated in a conference on the civil law codification in his Institute on February 14, 1957, that the Draft Rationale contained too many historical elements while the earlier Hungarian private law should be forgotten and the new Civil Code as a tabula rasa should not be interpreted on the basis of the former judicature but on its own basis, in accordance with the principles of the people's democracy (see Bodzási, 2018, fol. 21, p. 1360).

18 Currently, in the new Hungarian Civil Code adopted as Act V of 2013, the implicit conduct is no longer regulated in the Preliminary provisions but in the chapter entitled 'Further facts generating an obligation,' and specifically in section 6:587. Such a transplant was earlier suggested in 1958 by the Supreme Court (see Bodzási, 2018, fol. 8, p. 491) as well as by Endre Nizsalovszky, with reference to the *variae causarum figurae* of Roman law (see Bodzási, 2018, fol. 9, p. 116). Nizsalovszky ascertained, however, that the implicit conduct does not belong to the conducts causing damage.

19 At this point it is necessary to refer to the problem of the different interpretations of good faith in various legal cultures. A number of jurisdictions firmly differentiate between (1) subjective good faith characterised by belief in the lawfulness of one's possession, etc. (in German *guter Glaube*) and (2) objective good faith and fair dealing (in German *Treu und Glauben*). The dualist interpretation derives from the older *ius commune*, but it gained importance only as a consequence of a monograph by Wächter, 1871. Since then the dualist interpretation has been embraced the world over. For a detailed treatment, see Földi, 2007, pp. 53ff; idem, SZ Rom. Abt. 124 (2007), pp. 603ff; idem, 2010, pp. 483ff; idem, 2014, pp. 312ff. See also, e.g., Martins-Costa 2015, pp. 40ff; Novaretti, 2010, pp. 953ff. Before the global spread of a dualist interpretation, a kind of 'subjective monism' prevailed which regards good faith always as a subjective state of mind. Besides these interpretations a kind of 'objective monism' is also known, which is dominant in Austrian law in which good faith is called *Redlichkeit*. As for the future, it cannot be ruled out that a pluralist interpretation will become predominant, which acknowledges various meanings of good faith. Cf. Zimmermann and Whittaker, 2000, pp. 690ff. Cardilli, Dajczak, Fiori, Stolfi and Zannini warn of the dangers of a dualist interpretation, see Garofalo 2003, and cf., with detailed bibliographic data, Földi, SZ Rom. Abt. 124 (2007), pp. 603ff, idem, 2007, pp. 53ff.

20 The Novel of 1977 inserted into para. 1 of section 4 a second phrase, which laid down that '[e]conomic organisations shall act in their civil law relations in compliance with the requirements of the planned and proportional development of the people's economy.' The same Novel inserted into para. 4 of section 4 a first phrase, according to which '[un]less this Act provides a stricter requirement, one has to proceed in civil law relations as it may generally be expected in the given situation.'

21 As is generally known, in 2016 an important reform of the French Code civil in some places deleted references to *bonnes mœurs*.

22 As observed in the preliminary remarks, the Department of Codification thought that it was feasible to create a draft of the law of obligation, i.e. not in the framework of a civil code, see Bodzási, 2018, fol. 19, p. 2. See also Eörsi's note in the same sense in a copy of a draft of 1953 (written in ink), ibid. p. 39.

23 See para. 2 of section 2 of the Swiss ZGB: 'Der offenbare Missbrauch eines Rechtes findet keinen Rechtsschutz.' The official translation is: 'The manifest abuse of a right is not protected by law.' It is to be noted that the corresponding provision in the Bill of 1928 (para. 2 of section 2) inspired otherwise by the Swiss Civil Code, did not contain the attribute 'manifest.'

24 This observation was made by the Legal Department of the Hungarian National Bank in February 1955, see Bodzási, 2018, fol. 19, p. 1166. It is remarkable that the most Western civil codes do not declare the prohibition of in *fraudem legis agere*, except the Italian Codice civile of 1942 in its art. 1344 (*contratto in frode alla legge*). This prohibition can be traced back to Roman law, see Paul. D. 1.3.29.

25 This criticism was made by an attorney called László Sarlós at an official conference held in Szekszárd in January 1958, moderated by Professor Lóránt Rudolf (University of Pécs), see Bodzási, 2018, fol. 19, p. 1261. A similar criticism was presented by a public prosecutor named Gyula Zoltay at another official conference held in Győr in January 1958, moderated by the Vice President of the Supreme Court, László Sztodolnik, see ibid. p. 1268.

26 See K. Benedek in Eörsi and Gellért, 1981, I, p. 920 for data on related judgements. See more recently Menyhárd, 2004, pp. 31f; Deli, 2014, pp. 11ff.

References

Asztalos, L. (1966) *A polgári jogi szankció (Sanction in civil law)*, Budapest: Akadémiai Kiadó.

Asztalos, L. (1976) 'Az érdekegység és az együttműködés tartalmi változásainak kifejezésre juttatása a Ptk. alapelveiben (Asserting changes in the unity of interests and in cooperation in the general principles of the Civil Code)', *Jogtudományi Közlöny*, 31, 111.

Baldus, Ch. and Dajczak, W. (eds) (2013) *Der allgemeine Teil des Privatrechts*, Frankfurt am Main: Peter Lang. DOI: 10.3726/978-3-653-03070-9.

Bar, Ch. von et al. (2009) *Principles, Definitions and Model Rules of European Private Law. Draft Common Frame of Reference. Full Edition*, I, Munich: Sellier. DOI: 10.1515/9783866537279.

Benevolenskaya, Z. (2013) 'Celebrating a star in the legal firmament of Russia: The CXXV anniversary of the birth of academician A.V. Venediktov', *Review of Central and East European Law*, 38:2, 172–189. DOI: 10.1163/092598812x13274154887466.

Bodzási, B. (2018) *Preparatory Materials to the Civil Code of 1959 published online by the Ministry of Justice of Hungary* [Az 1952. évi Pp., az 1959. évi Ptk. és az 1977. évi Ptk. Novella előkészítő iratai, http://impp.mhk.hu (accessed 30.9.2019)], Budapest: Magyar Közlöny Lap- és Könyvkiadó Kft.

Bónis, Gy. (1964) *Einflüsse des römischen Rechts in Ungarn (IRMAE, V, 10)*. Mediolani: Giuffrè.

Brox, H. (1984) *Allgemeines Schuldrecht*, München: Beck.

Brox, H. (2000) *Allgemeiner Teil des BGB*, Köln, Berlin, Bonn, München: Heymann.

Burián, L. (2001) 'Szászy István (1899–1976)', in Hamza, G. (ed) *Magyar jogtudósok (Hungarian legal scholars)*, II, Budapest: Professzorok Háza, 148–168.

Deli, G. (2014) 'How did good morals become a general clause?' in Barbero, F. R. (ed.) *Principios generales del derecho: Antecedentes históricos y horizonte actual*, Madrid: Dykinson, 11–30.

Eörsi, Gy. (1951) *A tulajdonjog fejlődése (The evolution of ownership)*, I–II, Budapest: Jogi és Államigazgatási Könyv- és Folyóiratkiadó.

Eörsi, Gy. (1965) *A szocialista polgári jog alapproblémái (Fundamental problems of socialist civil law)*, Budapest: Akadémiai Kiadó.

Eörsi, Gy. (1975) *Összehasonlító polgári jog (Comparative civil law)*, Budapest: Akadémiai Kiadó.

Eörsi, Gy. (1979) *Comparative civil (private) law*, Budapest: Akadémiai Kiadó.

Eörsi, Gy. (1981) 'Az 1980. évi bécsi nemzetközi adásvételi Konvenció margójára és ürügyén (On the margin and the occasion of the Vienna Convention of 1980)', *Állam- és Jogtudomány*, 24:1, 3–28.

Eörsi, Gy. and Gellért, Gy. (eds) (1981) *A Polgári Törvénykönyv magyarázata (A commentary to the Civil Code)*, I, Budapest: Közgazdasági és Jogi Kiadó.

Földi, A. (1988) 'Living institutions of Roman law in Hungarian civil law', *Helikon* [Messina], 28, 363–380.

Földi, A. (2003) 'Rinascita del principio della buona fede oggettiva in Ungheria', in Garofalo L. (ed) *Il ruolo della buona fede oggettiva nell'esperienza giuridica storica e contemporanea. Atti del Convegno internazionale di studi in onore di Alberto Burdese*, Vol. II, Padova: Cedam, 59–98.

Földi, A. (2007) 'Remarks on the notion of 'bona fides'', *Annales Universitatis Scientiarum Budapestinensis de Rolando Eötvös nominatae*, 48, 53–72.

Földi, A. (2010) '*Osservazioni intorno al cd. dualismo della 'bona fides''*, in *Studi Antonino Metro*, II, Milano: Giuffrè, 483ff.

Földi, A. (2014) 'Traces of the dualist interpretation of good faith in '*ius commune*' until the end of the 16th century', *Fundamina*, 20:1, 312–321.

Földi, A. (2016) 'Appunti sugli elementi romanistici nel nuovo Codice civile ungherese', in Urbanik J. et al. (eds) *Mater familias. Scritti romanistici per Maria Zabłocka*, Warsaw: University of Warsaw, 161–190.

Földi, T. (ed) (1992) *Market economy and planned economy: An encyclopaedic dictionary*, I–II. München, London, New York, Paris: Saur.

Garofalo, L. (ed) (2003) *Il ruolo della buona fede oggettiva nell'esperienza giuridica storica e contemporanea. Atti del Convegno internazionale di studi in onore di Alberto Burdese*, I–IV, Padova: Cedam.

Hamza, G. (2009) *Entstehung und Entwicklung der modernen Privatrechtsordnungen und die römischrechtliche Tradition*, Budapest: ELTE Eötvös Kiadó.

HCC (1959) *A Magyar Népköztársaság Polgári Törvénykönyve (Civil Code of the People's Republic of Hungary)*, Budapest: Közgazdasági és Jogi Kiadó.

Honoré, A. M. (1973–1974) 'The Background to Justinian's Codification', *Tulane Law Review*, 48, 859–893.

Karady, V. and Nagy, P. T. (eds) (2012), *The numerus clausus in Hungary. Studies on the first Anti-Jewish Law and academic antisemitism in modern Central Europe*, Budapest: Central European University.

Képes, Gy. (2016) 'Birth and youth of the modern Hungarian private law', *Journal on European History of Law*, 7:2, 102–113.

Martins-Costa, J. (2015) *A boa fé no direito privado*, São Paulo: Marcial Pons.

Marton, G. (1992) *A polgári jogi felelősség (Civil law liability)*, in Zlinszky, J. (ed), Budapest: Triorg.

Medicus, D. (1999) *Schuldrecht. Allgemeiner Teil*, 11, Aufl. München: Beck.

Menyhárd, A. (2004) *A jóerkölcsbe ütköző szerződések (Contracts contrary to good morals)*, Budapest: Gondolat.

Novaretti, S. (2010) 'General clauses and practice: The use of the principle of good faith in the decisions of Chinese courts', *European Review of Private Law*, 18, 953–981.

Rigó, B. (2017) '1867 as the year of constitutional changes around the world', *ELTE Law Journal*, 2, 39–63.

Sárándi, I. (1965) *Visszaélés a joggal (The abuse of rights)*, Budapest: Akadémiai Kiadó.

Sárándi, I. (1977) 'A magyar polgári jog alapelvei (On the general principles of Hungarian civil law)', *Acta Fac. Pol.-Iur. Univ. Budapest*, 19, 3.

Szabó, B. (2001) 'Géza Marton', in Stolleis, M. (ed) *Juristen. Ein biographisches Lexikon*, München: Beck.

Szabó, I. (1964) *Társadalom és jog (Society and law)*, Budapest: Akadémiai Kiadó.

Tallon, D. (1994) *Le concept de bonne foi en droit français du contrat*, Roma: Centro di studi e ricerche di diritto comparato e straniero.

Verebics, J. (2017) 'Előtanulmány a magyar polgári jogi kodifikáció 1953–1962 közötti történetével kapcsolatos igazságügyminisztériumi iratanyaghoz (A preliminary study of the materials of the Ministry of Justice concerning the history of Hungarian civil law codification between 1953 and 1962)', in *Az Igazságügyminisztérium iratanyaga az 1959-es Polgári Törvénykönyv előkészítésével és hatályba léptetésével kapcsolatban (Materials of the Ministry of Justice concerning the preparation and entering into force of the Civil Code of 1959), ed. Bodzási, B.*, vol. I, Budapest: Magyar Közlöny Lap- és Könyvkiadó Kft.

Wächter, C. G. von (1871) *Die bona fides insbesondere bei der Ersitzung des Eigenthums*, Leipzig: Edelmann.

Zimmermann, R. and Whittaker, S. (2000) 'Coming to terms with good faith', in Zimmermann, R. and Whittaker, S. (eds), *Good Faith in European Contract Law*, Cambridge: Cambridge University Press, 653–701.

Zlinszky, J. (1983) 'Die Rolle der Gerichtsbarkeit in der Gestaltung des ungarischen Privatrechts vom 16. bis zum 20. Jahrhundert', *Ius commune,* 10, 49.

Zlinszky, J. (1985) 'Die historische Rechtsschule und die Gestaltung des ungarischen Privatrechts im 19. Jahrhundert', *Acta Jur. et Pol. Szeged*, 33, 433.

2 We few, we happy few? Legal history in the GDR

Martin Otto

Introduction: The very beginning

By May 1945, Germany was totally defeated. Total reversal replaced total war. Universities had been closed during the last months of the war, and many of their buildings were destroyed or out of use. During wartime the number of students was already small, and with the peace and after political deliberation, legal lectures and teaching of legal history ceased to exist. But 1945 was not a 'Point of Zero': when the universities reopened in the following years, the National Socialist past was present. The official point of reference in all education was 'before 1933.' Yet courses in the 'History of Private Law' (*Privatrechtsgeschichte*) were not integrated into the official part of the legal studies until 1935 (Haferkamp, 2010), and taking up an older tradition of legal history seemed impossible. Some legal historians even considered abolishing the lines between German, Roman and Canonic legal history for a genuine new beginning.[1] By the same token, the whole history of universities in the German Democratic Republic (GDR) had to face a vast number of contradictions.

On the one hand, the GDR defined itself as completely new—a renunciation of the evil German tradition, the first workers' and peasants' state. Only the 'good' parts of German heritage like Humanism, Enlightenment or 'progressive' culture were adopted. On the other hand, even the Communists knew that a total restart was impossible. Hence, a general tension between the remaining 'bourgeois' and the upcoming, new generation of Marxist scholars was accepted, and as long as the German reunification was the official aim of Soviet politics, ties between the universities in the East and the West were generally maintained and tolerated by the government. An idea of the common past with the Western neighbour and even a continuity in the 'good' parts of history were supported—as long as the leading role of the SED (Sozialistische Einheitspartei Deutschlands; Socialist Unity Party of Germany; "unity" refers to the merge of Communists and Social Democrats) was not disputed.

In legal sciences, there was at first sight less continuity. But as, for example, most non-socialist lawyers left the GDR by 1949, some traits that dated back to the pre-war years did exist. Most notable of them was the German civil code BGB (*Bürgerliches Gesetzbuch*) that was still in effect in both German states. In many cases there was no real alternative in referring to the old scholars and tradition. German universities were mostly conservative, and the left-wing (not to speak of communist) scientists had composed a small minority already in the Weimar Republic. For the large part, academics were conservative and a considerable number of the university professors of the GDR had been in office already before 1945.

Typical for German legal science since 19th century was the definition of jurisprudence as a historic discipline, resulting in a strong role of the legal historical studies as part of the university training. Likewise, the GDR could not offer legal studies without legal history, so legal historians were needed, and because there was no Marxist legal history before 1945, the continuity among legal historians was even bigger than in other legal disciplines. For the legal science of the GDR, the presence of the 'other' German state (and the jurisprudential research carried out within it) was self-evident, yet all the initiatives and research results from the 'West' were categorically rebuked. For the legal historiography of the GDR, the fact that it did not represent the stance of the 'whole German jurisprudence' was even more awkward since it did share a common national past—which often was the object of legal historical studies—with the 'Western' German legal historical writing. The research results derived from that common past and understanding of the essence of the common tradition were nevertheless in many places very different from the Western equivalent.

Where have all the universities gone?

During the first post-war years, the difference between 'Zones of Occupation' (*Besatzungszonen*) was small. Allied forces mostly kept politically quiet. Everywhere a lack of professors and scholarly literature was remarkable (Rückert, 1995). A genuine new beginning was intended, but in reality this was hopelessly impracticable, especially for the universities in the Soviet area of occupation.

Friedrich-Schiller-University Jena (originally founded in 1558) was reopened in October 1945 by the Soviet military government (Steiger, 1980). Like most parts of Thuringia, Jena was originally occupied by the US army. Under American rule, Thuringia seemed to be returning to the German 'rule of law' (*Rechtsstaat*) (Wahl, 1999). But American occupation lasted only one summer—and it had no effect on the university. Although Americans made plans to re-open Jena University, this only became reality under Soviet rule, and the university was faced with a marked 'brain drain' to West Germany, the Faculty of Law especially (Stolleis, 2009, pp. 100–109). When in October 1946, Hermann Schultze von Lasaulx finally left Jena, there were no remaining legal historians—and it was not until 1949 that Gerhad Buchda returned from Halle to fill his place (Lingelbach, 2008).

Rostock University (originally founded 1419) was reopened in January 1946 (Lieberwirth, 1988, p. 195). The famous legal historian Heinrich Mitteis was a member of the Faculty of Law, but he left for Berlin in 1947, and legal history and church law were lectured by the enigmatic Hans Gotthilf Strasser (Mechow, 1970, p. 278 and Soldwisch, 2007, p. 225), a former journalist and member of the liberal political party LDPD (*Liberal-Demokratische Partei Deutschlands*). Strasser was also the Minister of Finance in Mecklenburg from 1946 to 1948 (Handschuck, 2003). The Rostock Faculty of Law was closed down for political reasons in 1951.

Leipzig University (originally founded 1409) was reopened in autumn 1945 (Lieberwirth, 1988, p. 194). Leipzig as well was first occupied by the Americans. The famous 'Jurist Faculty' (*Juristenfakultät*) began lecturing in January 1946. The Supreme German Court (*Reichsgericht*) was no longer in operation. The faculty of law boasted an impressive number of names from the old days, including Alfred Schultze in German legal history and Heinrich Siber in Roman legal history, both old-aged. Senior faculty member and long-term Dean was Erwin Jacobi, a former friend of Carl Schmitt and one of the leading public lawyers in the Weimar Republic with merits in labour law and church law. During the first post-war years, Leipzig was considered the most 'bourgeois' law faculty in the Soviet area of occupation (Stolleis, 2009, pp. 109–121).

In 1946 in Leipzig, the first post-war habilitation thesis in legal history (Lieberwirth, 1986) was passed by Gertrud Schubart-Fikentscher, a student of Alfred Schultze (Lieberwirth, 2010, pp. 1–26). The year 1947 saw the installation of the 'Social Science Faculty' or GEWIFA (*Gesellschaftswissenschaftliche Fakultät*, a Marxist faculty) and the 'Worker and Peasant Faculty' (*Arbeiter-und-Bauern-Fakultät*) in the 'socialist redesign' of the university. Another brain drain to West Germany began, concerning nearly all the lawyers with the exception of Jacobi (Otto, 2004), who in 1950 was the only non-socialist left. The teaching of legal history nearly disappeared completely, although this was not the intention of the politicians. When Jacobi died in 1965, the Leipzig faculty specialised in socialist economic law without covering legal history.

The traditional Prussian university, Martin-Luther-University Halle-Wittenberg (Wittenberg University was founded in 1502 Halle University in 1694), was reopened in February 1946 (Stolleis, 2009, pp. 93–99) with the returned POW Gerhard Buchda as the 'surviving' legal historian. Buchda, however, was soon dismissed for political reasons. The 78-year-old Rudolf Joerges, although specialised in economic law, went back to his scientific roots, and gave preliminary lectures in Roman law. In 1948, Gertrud Schubart-Fikentscher, now a member of the socialist SED, became the chair of legal history, the first female German professor of law (Lieberwirth, 2000). Schubart-Fikentscher made Halle into a hub of legal history in the GDR.

The world-famous Friedrich-Wilhelms University Berlin (founded 1809) reopened in January 1946. It was situated in the Soviet sector of Berlin, which eventually came completely under Communist rule (Will, 2010). After 1947, legal history was represented by Heinrich Mitteis, who left for Munich in the same year (Brun, 1991). Lectures by Gerhard Buchda, who soon left for Jena, were only given for a short time (Stolleis, 2009, p. 84). In 1949 the university was renamed Humboldt University.

Ernst-Moritz-Arndt-Universität Greifswald (originally founded in 1456) was reopened in February 1946, though this coincided with the Faculty of Law closing down. The legal historians Bernhard Rehfeldt and Heinrich Molitor moved to West Germany. In 1958 small attempts to establish Marxist constitutional history were made by Karl-Heinz Schönherr in his position as 'Rubenow Chair for State Law,' although these attempts ended with his sudden death in 1961 (Otto, 2009, p. 319).

'Polak versus Mitteis'

In the first years of the GDR the illusion that traditional approaches and Marxist science could coexist was still alive. Heinrich Mitteis and Karl Polak clearly revealed their differing views on legal history in the leading journal *Neue Justiz* (Mitteis, 1947 and Polak, 1947), but it was a debate that never was (Schröder, 2001). The orthodox Marxist Polak became the GDR's most influential lawyer and was a member of the official 'Council of State' (*Staatsrat*). With no chance of succeeding in the GDR, Mitteis decided to go to Munich University (Ogorek, 1994, pp. 34–36). Ironically, the consequence of this mock-debate was not the total withdrawal of 'bourgeois' legal history.

The GDR had no interest in losing all its non-socialist scientists, and in other fields, such as medicine, there was a real need for skilled professionals. From 1949 to 1957, about 1.5 million people left the GDR, among them a large number of academics, and maintaining a proper academic sector caused an increasing need for manpower. Some parts of the GDR wooed non-communist scientists, even in the humanities. East German playwright Heiner Müller ironically called it a kind of socialist 'Popular Front Policy' (*Volksfront*) (Müller, 1992, p. 122):

> [T]o the cultural 'Popular Front' concept of the GDR belonged of course an alliance with the bourgeois, traditional and conservative university people. One was not allowed to criticise them.[2]

Müller's opinion was an extra-legal interjection, but especially fitting for legal history. Nevertheless the 'Popular Front Policy' had no effect on the continuing decline of legal history in the GDR. Even scholars sympathetic to the socialist state claimed that there was continuing discrimination and defamation of their field of study. Horst Schröder—who might have expressed his opinion as a disappointed Marxist—wrote: 'From the beginning until the end of the GDR, legal history was a politically defamed and theoretically discredited discipline.' (Schröder, 2001, p. 5).[3]

Mostly no Marxists: Centres of legal history research in GDR

Most legal historians were not Marxists. The GDR claimed to be the first German 'Worker and Peasant State,' but legal historians obviously did not care

Figure 2.1 Heinrich Mitteis in 1937 as Dean of Vienna Legal Faculty. (Archiv der Universität Wien – Bildarchiv Signatur: 106.I.2986)

about this. In any case, they formed a minority among the comparatively small number of legal scientists, the 'happy few.'[4] They worked in a small niche and for political reasons they concentrated mostly on the German Middle Ages, the early modern age and the Enlightenment. Legal history was concerned with local issues, but it was also more conservative and traditional than in West Germany. Even the third GDR 'university reform' (*Dritte Hochschulreform*) in 1968 had in fact no effect on legal history. The 'old school' of GDR legal history consisted of two chairs *pari passu*. In 1951 the GDR government gave an order for university courses in legal history (Lieberwirth, 1988, pp. 196–197). They were initially intended to take place in each legal faculty in a to-be-founded 'Institute for Constitutional and Legal History' (*Institut für*

Staats- und Rechtsgeschichte). In Leipzig such lessons were not arranged from above and the institute failed, more by chance than by intention. The neighbouring institute of Marxist legal philosophy in Berlin played a special role here, as will be discussed later. The most powerful places of traditional legal history in the GDR were at Jena and Halle.

The Jena chair

Jena chair was initially held by Gerhard Buchda (Lieberwirth, 1988, p. 198; see also the article of Adrian Schmidt-Recla and Zara Luisa Gries in this book). Born 1901 in Stadtroda (Sachsen-Altenburg, Thuringia), Buchda attended Jena University in 1923 and became a member of a conservative student fraternity. In 1929 Buchda wrote his thesis on the legal philosophy of natural law and Immanuel Kant under the supervision of the Romanist lawyer Hans Albert Fischer (Tilitzki, 2002, p. 179). In 1934 Buchda passed his habilitation in German private law and legal history on 'joint ownership' (*Gesamthand*) under the supervision of Rudolf Hübner und Arwed Blomeyer in Jena. After 1934 Buchda worked as a judge in Thuringia, where the NSDAP already played an important role in public service before Hitler came to power.

In 1937 Buchda joined the *Sturmabteilung* (SA) and accepted the chair of legal history at Prussian Halle in the following year (Lieberwirth 1996, pp. 30–31). He joined the NSDAP in 1939. His research interests covered traditional areas of German legal history (*Hirtenschutt,* i.e., 'shepherd's wages'), mostly history of procedural law, but also made innovative attempts in history of economic law (Buchda, 1938) according to Justus Wilhelm Hedemann. In 1943, Buchda joined the armed forces of Nazi Germany (*Wehrmacht*) but remained only a private during the war. Buchda lost his chair as did nearly all the former members of the NSDAP in the Soviet Occupation Zone; he was dismissed very early in 1945, but in 1949 he regained the chair of legal history and commercial law at Jena. In 1946 Buchda, a Lutheran, became a member of the liberal party LDPD, a political reservoir of the remaining 'bourgeois' on the way to a nearly no-ruling but legal 'Blockpartei' closely tied to the Socialist Unity Party of Germany or SED (*Sozialistische Einheitspartei Deutschlands*). Buchda focused on medieval and early modern legal history, especially 'juror chair' (*Schöffenstuhl*) in Thuringia and Saxony. He made an edition of judgements from Pößneck court (Buchda, 1954–1962). Other publications concerned the German zoologist Alfred Edmund Brehm (Buchda, 1976). In 1958 Buchda became a member of the endangered Saxon Academy of Science in Leipzig and always kept in touch with colleagues in West Germany and abroad. From 1971 onwards he wrote many entries for the West German legal encyclopedia *Handwörterbuch zur Deutschen Rechtsgeschichte.*[5] He served for a long time as the dean of the legal faculty, defending scientific standards against the gathering Marxism (Lenski, 2017, p. 112). He retired from the university in 1967. His role as a member of the NSDAP was never revealed (Waibel, 2011, p. 56); probably it wasn't even known. He died 1977 in his hometown of Stadtroda, aged 76.

The Halle Chair

The Halle Chair, probably the most important chair in the GDR, was initially given to Gertrud Schubart-Fikentscher. Born Gerturd Fikentscher in 1896 in Zwickau (Saxony), she grew up in a wealthy family that had for generations been industrialists and artists; her grandfather was founder of a chemical factory in Zwickau (Lauterbach, 2013). In 1916 she became a 'social engineer' (*Fürsorgerin*) and worked for a long time in Berlin. Confronted with the legal problems of juvenile delinquents, she attended Berlin University to improve her legal knowledge. In 1928 she married papyrologist Werner Schubart (1873–1960; Fikentscher, 2014). After passing the Prussian legal 'state examination,' she studied under Berlin legal historian Ernst Heymann and became one of the first female researchers in legal history. She wrote her thesis on German marriage law in the town Brünn in Moravia, continued research during National Socialism collaborating with *Monumenta Germaniae Historica,* and also taught at Leipzig University. In 1945 she became a member of the Social Democratic Party of Germany (*Sozialdemokratische Partei Deutschlands,* SPD) in Halle, the SPD being taken over by the SED in 1946. In 1948 she became the first German female legal professor, holding the chair of legal history at Halle. She continued in medieval German 'city law' (*Stadtrechte*; Schubart-Fikentscher, 1950) but mostly specialised in the history of natural law at Halle (Schubart-Fikentscher, 1960, and Schubart-Fikentscher, 1967) and she also served as the dean of the Halle Faculty of Law. In 1951 she left the SED without consequences and retired from the University in 1957. In 1959 Schubart-Fikentscher became a member of the Saxon Academy of Science in Leipzig. She still maintained ties to West Germany as a member of *Monumenta Germaniae Historica* in Munich and since 1971 as an author of many entries for *Handwörterbuch zur Deutschen Rechtsgechichte.*[6] By the time of her death, she was one of the last survivors of the German pre-war academia. When she was born in 1896, Queen Victoria had still four years to live; when she died in 1985, Gorbachev was already the chairman of the Soviet Union Communist Party.

And now for something completely different: The Babelsberg Conference 1958

The Babelsberg Conference on April 2–3, 1958, represented a real fracture in East German legal science. Opened by Walter Ulbricht with a keynote speech written by Karl Polak, it marked a great rift with what remained of traditional jurisprudence (Eckert, 1993). 'Babelsberg' ended the illusion of at least a semi-autonomous legal science in the GDR. Attempts to construct a discipline of 'Marxist' legal history ceased to exist after the Babelsberg Conference, and subsequent efforts to re-establish legal history were small. The *festschrift* for Erwin Jacobi also in 1957 was a case in point as it contained little reference to legal history (but see Brehme, 1957).[7] By this time, traditional legal historians were a real minority, and everyone knew that legal history would never regain a major role in the GDR universities even in a Marxist sense.

During the GDR years, legal history had no confirmed place in the regular legal studies. It was a 'marginalised science,' a discipline of scientific bystanders, isolated but international. It would have been easy to abolish legal history, but there was an official desire for a kind of reservation for remaining scientists, rated strange but harmless. In this reservation, personal continuity was high. Gerturd Schubart-Fikentscher was followed in 1957 by her first student Rolf Lieberwirth (1920–2019),[8] who held the chair until 1986. The Lutheran Lieberwirth was, like Buchda, a member of the LDPD, and was called by Karl Kroeschell 'the last stronghold of civic legal history in the GDR,' and this hit the target exactly. (Stolleis, 2009, p. 94; Lieberwirth, 2005; Cordes, 2007). Lieberwirth focused on *Sachsenspiegel*-research and had strong collaboration with the Saxon Academy of Science. A related area of research with ties to East European legal history was 'Madgeburg Town Law' (*Magdeburger Recht*), which concerned areas in the socialist 'brother countries' (*Bruderländer*) Poland and the Soviet Union. Both areas of research also had special roots before 1949 (Lieberwirth, 1982; Lieberwirth, 1986a; Lück, 1999).

In Halle, local and specific field of research was natural law, and especially Christian Thomasius (Lieberwirth, 1955). This continued an old Halle tradition of research, begun by Max Fleischmann in 1928. Lieberwirth, who published a lot in 'non-socialist countries abroad' (*Nichtsozialistisches Ausland*[9]), retired in 1986 and was gradually replaced by his former student Heiner Lück (born 1954).[10] In Jena, the long-time vacant chair was given in 1988 to Gerhard Lingelbach (born 1948), originally a student of Gerhard Haney.[11] Lück and Lingelbach formed together with Lieberwirth scholar Bernd Schildt (born 1948)[12] the last generation of the GDR legal history outside Berlin. However, the few happy scholars were more international than many GDR scientists and seemed more a part of the Western scientific community. Also, the *Savigny-Zeitschrift*, the leading German-speaking periodical for legal history, was published in the GDR town of Weimar.

On the other hand, East German legal historians were methodologically more conservative than their Western colleagues. The link with a worldwide community of researchers was gone with the extinction of Roman law, which in GDR only played a marginalised role in classical history (Härtel and Pólay, 1987). GDR legal history was very national, and the focus on German legal history was becoming old-fashioned in Western Germany. Academic life after 'Babelsberg' was largely quiet. The 'third university reform' (*3. Studienreform*) of 1967 closed down university institutes and also 'Academies for State and Law' that had played a large role in the reforms of the higher education in the early years of the GDR. At the level of university administration, however, significant efforts for saving the institutes were made—the institutes were simply changed into research 'areas' (*Bereiche*). There was no '1968' in the GDR, no 'New Universities,' no increased number of students, no 'university for the masses' (*Massenuniversität*), and no methodological controversies.

Legal historians remained careful, and even informal get-togethers between the minorities of legal historians and the very few students opposing the state were not remarkable at all. Legal historians in the socialist provinces lived in an academic bubble of *Sachsenspiegel*, town law and Enlightenment. This formed a restricted area of research between 'refuge and political justification' (Lück, 1998), very regionally based, and fitting for a Marxist 'historic heritage.' The objects of legal historical research included the famous law book *Sachsenspiegel* (i.e., literally 'Saxon Mirror'), early courts of appeal like the 'jury stool' (*Schöppenstuhl*) in Thuringia and Saxony or the Wismar 'supreme court' (*Obertribunal*) (Wernicke, 1984)[13] of the Baltic area. Natural law and the Enlightenment were the main focuses of research at Halle University. A remarkable 'long-term seller' was a small book on 'Latin in Law' written by Rolf Lieberwirth in 1986 (Lieberwirth, 1986c; second edition 1988).

Topics concerning modern phenomena, for example, the history of labour law (see Zierholz, 1985) or welfare legislation, never played a big role. Hence, Günther Baranowski in Berlin carried out research on Pufendorf (Baranowski, 1982) and Lieselotte Jelowik in Halle on the political struggle against criminal punishment for abortion ('§ 218 StGB') in Weimar Republic (Jelowik, 1984). A legal history on the class struggle remained outside the possibilities of the minority. This was reserved for reliable Marxists like Polak and his successors (Schöneburg, 1975).

Marxist Island: Berlin

The West German trials of Uwe Wesel and others for 'legal historical materialism' (*Materialistische Rechtsgeschichte*) (Wesel, 1974), a Marxist approach, had no effect on the legal historiography written in the GDR. Legal historians accepted their role of not interfering with the official Marxist interpretation of law. Only Berlin played a special role with a more political legal history promoted by Horst Schröder (born 1930)[14] and Marxist bystanders like Hermann Klenner (born 1926). Werner Sellnow (born 1913)[15] approached legal history from a very Marxist point of view (Sellnow, 1968) but also in the secrecy of conferences abroad published on non-socialist lawyers like Hugo Preuss (Sellnow, 1972). A similar legal historian with a focus on the 19th and 20th centuries was Horst Kuntschke.[16] Schröder first started as a lecturer in 1968 and obtained a chair in 1971 (Stolleis, 2009, p. 84). But these scholars, mostly members of the SED, acted mainly as legal philosophers (see Schröder, 1971). They formed a Marxist Wing of GDR legal history in the capital, close to the power and endangered (Lieberwirth, 1988, p. 199). Research on Prussian civil code 'General Land Law' (*Allgemeines Landrecht*) (Heuer, 1960) and Friedrich Carl von Savigny (Schröder, 1984) took place mostly in Berlin with its special circumstances and special challenges.

Publishing and academia

Important parts of legal history like Roman law, canon law or constitutional history did not exist at GDR universities. Some parts of research only took place at the 'Academies of Science.' However, some research groups in the GDR were internationally recognised. Such groups worked at the Academies of Science in Berlin and in Leipzig. The former concentrated on Byzantine Law (Winkelmann, 2002), the latter on *Sachsenspiegel* (Jelowik, 1998) and Magdeburg Law (Lieberwirth, 1986a). Ties to legal historians of Western Germany, Austria,

Switzerland and Scandinavia remained relatively strong during the whole GDR, and *Savigny-Zeitschrift*, the most important German-speaking journal of legal history, was also published in the GDR (Ogris, 2008).

Legal history trickling down

A part of the short-lived GDR legal history dealt with a small but secure cultural position. Some results of research 'trickled down' (Liebrecht 2018, p. 299) from academia. A lavish book called *Unser Deutschland*, introduced in 1957 as an official present for the socialist coming-of-age ritual called 'youth consecration' (*Jugendweihe*), interpreted German history as more national than socialist, noting the merits of famous Germans like Luther, Goethe (see Schubart-Fikentscher, 1977), Schiller (see Lingelbach, 1984), Lessing and related heroes. German Enlightenment was also represented by the lawyer Christian Thomasius (*Zentralausschuss für Jugendweihe*, 1957, p. 35):

> Christian Thomasius (1655–1728) was a professor, solicitor and philosopher in Halle, who successfully stood up for the use of the German language in teaching instead of Latin at the university.[17]

Thomasius was mentioned more as an impassioned advocate of the German language than as a lawyer (though in this tradition, see Lieberwirth, 1987). This was another version of socialist 'Popular Front' (*Volksfront*), but Thomasius had to share his humble place in the book with the Communists Ernst Thälmann and Wilhelm Pieck. Mentioning Thomasius meant offering an intellectual homeland to non-socialist citizens. *Unser Deutschland* was inspired by the more intellectual Marxist scientist Paul Wandel (Neubert, 1997, p. 119) and it was replaced again in 1958 by its 1954 precursor, the more communistic and atheistic 'Space-Earth-Man' (*Weltall-Erde-Mensch*), and so the references to the enlightened lawyer Thomasius disappeared.

Scholarly without a doubt was the 1973 publication of 'Atlas of History' (*Atlas zur Geschichte*), which continued a special German tradition (Wolf, 1977) begun in 1886 by Gustav Droysen, that was also observed in West Germany even in the conservative newspaper *Frankfurter Allgemeine Zeitung* in 1974. The versatile 'atlas' offered legal history a small place on the map, seeing the spread of 'Magdeburg Law' in Eastern Europe. This spread was interpreted from a Marxist perspective as a part of the history of feudalism (*Zentralinstitut für Geschichte*, 1973, p. 32): 'The Feudal German eastward expansion' (*Die feudale deutsche Ostexpansion* (10.–14. Jh.)

The Luther Jubilee in 1983 meant an opportunity to present the GDR as a culturally and religiously free state. This also gave room for 'Legal History's Contribution' written by Gerhard Lingelbach (Lingelbach, 1983) and Hermann Klenner (Klenner, 1983). In practice this was more a surviving strategy for an endangered species than the real desire of a very secure GDR at the climax of its international recognition. The jubilee of the revolutionary theologian Thomas Müntzer in 1989 had even less of an impact for legal history (but see Lück, 1989).

The last bid

Continuing the mode of the Luther Jubilee, the newly introduced history calendar in the official periodical *Staat und Recht* (Mohnhaupt, 1984) represented the last concerted effort to maintain GDR legal history. In the last years of the GDR, the jubilees were initiated by Gerhard Lingelbach. In 1989 he remembered the birthdays of Montesquieu, Max Weber and even the 70th anniversary of the Weimar Constitution, the 'most progressive German constitution in power at that time' (Lingelbach, 1989, pp. 69, 71, 74). When Lingelbach wrote his history calendar for 1990, German reunification in 1990 was not yet predicted. As worthwhile Jubilees Lingelbach picks the 100th anniversary of the abolishment of Bismarck's anti-socialist law (*Sozialistengesetz*), the 150th anniversary of August Bebel, and the 50th anniversary of the death of Hermann Kantorowicz (Lingelbach, 1990, p. 82–83). The 175th birthday of Bismarck, praised for his 'modest realism' (*Realitätssinn mit Augenmaß*) in foreign politics, was mentioned equal to the 30th anniversary of the death of Communist GDR President and 'popular statesman' (*volkstümlicher Staatsmann*) Wilhelm Pieck (Lingelbach, 1990, pp. 85, 91). Lingelbach ended his calendar with the putative 800th birthday of Eike von Repgow (Lingelbach, 1990, p. 95). So GDR legal history ended with an outmoded date, as seen from a contemporary Western point of view, but it also showed impressive Janus-faced discipline.

Conclusion

In its first years the GDR had to face an enormous brain drain to the West, and jurisprudence was heavily affected as well. Despite all 'antifascist' and revolutionary rhetoric, it was not in the interests of the GDR and its leading party SED to burn all the bridges behind. The SED could not dismiss the importance of universities in its socialist project, and as a result the need for academics was real. As far as the legal studies in the German tradition were concerned, legal historians and the GDR government shared a common goal of maintaining legal historical studies in the remaining universities with legal faculties. Legal historians like Gerhard Buchda and Gertrud Schubart-Fikentscher were fully integrated members of the early GDR academia—with strong but quiet roots in the years before 1945. Their 'bourgeois' approach to legal history was not a problem as long as the research themes were specific and dealt with distant times. The presence of non-socialist scientists, and not only in legal history, was mostly welcome. It seemed to prove that recognised scientists, too, could find a place in the GDR, but in reality, that place was narrow and endangered.

Already during the first years of the GDR, the teaching of and research on legal history was heavily diminished in comparison to the pre-war universities. The 'Babelsberg conference' was a turning point for legal science in the GDR. It marked a change to a more applicative and political legal science, but legal history as discipline was hardly affected. The discipline continued to play an insignificant role inside and outside academia, but its international recognition was indispensable. Thus, the discipline was allowed to encapsulate to its own research dimension. This was the reason for the relatively conservative GDR approach to legal history. Legal history was parochial, knotted with the 'province,' or with the neighbouring universities of Halle and Jena. The areas of research emphasised 'regional' items like the *Sachsenspiegel* and Halle Enlightenment. From the point of view of the SED, this was harmless.

In the academic sphere of Berlin, legal history played a special role in the vicinity of legal philosophy. There historically oriented legal scholars—like Horst Schröder—were Marxists and mostly members of the SED. They had to face a stronger supervision by the SED and were more at odds with the official ideas of proper legal science. Conflicts were numerous. Legal history did not, however, lose its jurisprudential prestige and significance to legal philosophy. In fact, legal philosophers were even more endangered, at risk of unwanted party attention and consequent sanctions—of which the fate of Hermann Klenner is a good example. Yet, many legal historians, like Gerhard Lingelbach, had roots in legal philosophy.

Classical legal history was written outside the capital. The GDR legal historians, except for a small number of Marxists, formed a kind of scientific cloister throughout these years—a refuge that was sometimes called upon by their Marxist colleagues when 'historical background' was required. German reunification ended the GDR, but some scholars got an opportunity to continue and succeed in the new unified Germany and abroad. The end of the GDR was followed by the end of the scientific sanctuary of distant and specific research topics for the few GDR legal historians. The challenge to explain why as modern lawyers we need to know about *Sachsenspiegel* is still a valid issue in all parts of Germany.

Notes

1 Erwin Jacobi in a letter to Eugen Rosenstock-Huessy, 'Leipzig p. 3, November 8, 1946: In Berlin however prevails a conservatism that would preferably fall back on the course catalog of 1912.' (Leipzig S 3, am 8. November 1946. In Berlin allerdings herrscht ein Konservatismus, der am liebsten auf die Vorlesungsverzeichnisse von 1912 zurückgreifen möchte); quoted in Otto (2008), p. 276–277.

2 'Und so wie damals gehörte nun zum Volksfront-Konzept in der DDR im Bereich der Kultur natürlich die Allianz mit den bürgerlichen, traditionellen, konservativen Universitätsleuten. Sie durften nicht kritisiert werden.'

3 'Bei der Rechtsgeschichte handelte es sich um einen in der DDR vom Beginn bis zum Ende ihrer Existenz politisch diffamierten und theoretisch diskreditierten Wissenschaftszweig.'

4 William Shakespeare, Henry V., IV, 3: 'We few, we happy few, we band of brothers [...].'

5 Buchda's articles include 'Altmärkische Glosse zum Sachsenspiegel,' 'Aktenversendung,' 'Anklage,' 'Anwalt,' 'Appellation,' 'Appellationsprivilegien,' 'Artikelprozeß,' 'Berufung,' 'Beschlagnahme,' 'Beweisinterlokut,' 'Büttel,' 'Cautelarjurisprudenz,' 'Contumacia,' 'Delegation,' 'Einlassung,' 'Fallrecht,' 'Freischöffe,' 'Freistuhl,' 'Fronbote,' 'Fronung,' 'Gebundene Tage,' 'Gelehrte Richter,' 'Gelöbnis,' 'Gemeines Sachsenrecht,' 'Gerichtsgefälle,' 'Gerichtsverfahren,'

'Gerichtsverfassung,' 'Gerüfte,' 'Gesamthand, gesamte Hand,' 'Görlitzer Rechtsbuch,' 'Heimbürge,' 'Hermann von Oesfeld,' 'Jus evocandi,' 'Klage,' 'Kursächsische Konstitutionen,' 'Kummer,' 'Läuterung,' 'Landfriedensgericht,' 'Landgemeinde,' 'Landrechtsbücher,' 'Landrechtsglosse,' 'Laten,' 'Leipzig' and 'Magdeburger Recht.'

6 Schubart-Fikentscher's articles include 'Johannes Althusius,' 'Karl von Amira,' 'Matthias Berlichius,' 'Georg Beseler,' 'Just Henning Böhmer,' 'Sebastian Brant,' 'Heinrich Brunner,' 'Benedict Carpzov,' 'Emil Goldmann' and 'Johannes Friedrich Harpprecht' (all 1971). For Neue Deutsche Biographie she wrote articles on Wilhelm von Brünneck, Dietrich II. bishop of Naumburg, Max Fleischmann, Christian Gottlieb Haubold, Ernst Heymann and Carl Gustav Homeyer (1955–1972).

7 For contemporary Marxist criticism see Otto (2008), pp. 366–381.

8 PhD thesis: Die gesetzlichen Pfandrechte zur Zeit der Aufklärung unter besonderer Berücksichtigung der Halle-Wittenberger Juristen Augustin Leyser und Samuel Stryk, Halle 1952.

9 For Handwörterbuch zur Deutschen Rechtsgeschichte Lieberwirth wrote during the GDR period (all 1971) the articles 'Amtsvergehen (Amtsverbrechen)' 'Angstmann,' 'Armesünder,' 'Auslieferung von Missetätern,' 'Ausstäupen,' 'Beleidigung,' 'Bigamie (Doppelehe),' 'Carolina,' 'Crimen laesae maiestatis (Majestätsverbrechen),' 'Diebstahl,' 'Ehebruch,' 'Entführung (crimen raptus),' 'Entmannung,' 'Ertränken,' 'Feldfrevel,' 'Folter,' 'Freiheitsstrafe,' 'Frevel,' 'Friedebann,' 'Gefangene, Gefängnis,' 'Glücksspiel,' 'Gotteslästerung,' 'Gundling, Nicolaus Hieronymus,' 'Haftstrafe,' 'Halsgerichtsordnungen' and 'Halslösung'; for Lexikon des Mittelalters the article 'Eike von Repgow' (1985), for Neue Deutsche Biographie (1961–1971) articles on August Finger, Ernst von Globig, Nicolaus Gundling, Gottlieb Heineccius and Karl Ferdinand Hommel, for Kindlers Literaturlexikon (1971) an article on Thomasius, De Crimine Magiae.

10 PhD thesis: Die Spruchtätigkeit der Wittenberger Juristenfakultät, Halle 1982; 'Habilitation': Die kursächsische Gerichtsverfassung von 1423 bis zur Mitte des 16. Jahrhunderts unter besonderer Berücksichtigung der landesherrlichen Gerichtsorganisation, Halle 1988.

11 PhD thesis: Das Verhältnis der deutschen Rechtswissenschaft, insbesondere der Juristenfakultät der Universität Jena, zur Französischen Revolution zwischen 1789 und 1820, Jena 1978; 'Habilitation': Änderungen der Beschuldigtenstellung bei der Überwindung des feudalen Inquisitionsprozesses im Spiegel der deutschen Rechtswissenschaft, Jena 1985.

12 PhD thesis: Die Spruchtätigkeit der Halleschen Juristenfakultät nach dem Wiener Kongress, Halle 1980; 'Habilitation': Verfassung und Wirtschaftsrecht der spätfeudalen Landgemeinde im Spiegel thüringischer Dorfordnungen, Halle 1988.

13 The courts of 'Hanse' were part of common history and so increased after 1989.

14 PhD thesis: Die antidemokratische und antinationale Politik der rechten SPD-Führung in den Jahren 1945–1952, Berlin 1961. 'Habilitation' (1976): Schröder, 1984.

15 PhD thesis: Gesellschaft—Staat—Recht. Zur Kritik der bürgerlichen Ideologien über die Entstehung von Gesellschaft, Staat und Recht von der bürgerlichen Aufklärung bis zum deutschen Positivismus des 19. Jahrhunderts, Berlin 1963; 'Habilitation': Zum Problem der Rechtsgeschichte im Werk von Marx und Engels, Berlin 1968.

16 PhD thesis: Die geschichtliche Stellung des Reichsgerichts im Deutschen Kaiserreich von 1871 und seine Rechtsprechung zu den demokratischen Freiheiten gegenüber der Arbeiterklasse, Berlin 1964.

17 Christian Thomasius (1655–1728) war Professor, Jurist und Philosoph in Halle und trat mit Erfolg für den Gebrauch der deutschen Sprache an Stelle der lateinischen im Lehrbetrieb der Universität ein.'

References

Baranowski, G. (1982) 'Samuel Pufendorf—ein Vorkämpfer der bürgerlichen Staats- und Rechtslehre. Zum 350. Geburtstag', *Staat und Recht*, 31, 58–64.

Brehme, G. (1957) 'Die Verstaatlichung der Kohlebergbaurechte in Sachsen und die Novemberrevolution von 1918', in Bönninger, K., Such, H. and Arzinger, R. (eds), *Festschrift Erwin Jacobi*, Berlin: Deutscher Zentralverlag, 164–196.

Brun, G. (1991) *Leben und Werk des Rechtshistorikers Heinrich Mitteis unter besonderer Berücksichtigung seines Verhältnisses zum Nationalsozialismus*, Frankfurt am Main: Peter Lang.

Buchda, G. (1938) 'Wirtschaftsrecht in jüngeren thüringischen Landesordnungen', in Freisler, R., Löning, G. A. and Nipperdey, H. C. (eds), *Festschrift Justus Wilhelm Hedemann zum sechzigsten Geburtstag am 24. April 1938*, Jena: Frommann, 34–50.

Buchda, G. (1954–1962) *Die Schöffenspruchsammlung der Stadt Pößneck*, 4 vol., Weimar: Böhlau.

Buchda, G. (1976) 'Testament und Nachlaß des Naturforschers Alfred Edmund Brehm', in Becker, H.-J. (ed), *Rechtsgeschichte als Kulturgeschichte. Festschrift für Adalbert Erler zum 70, Geburtstag*, Aalen: Scientia, 591–610.

Cordes, A. (2007) Interview mit Prof. Dr. Rolf Lieberwirth am 12. September 2007 in Halle (21. December 2007) *forum historiae iuris*, https://forhistiur.de/2007-12-cordes/ (accessed 20.12.2019).

Eckert, J. (ed) (1993) *Die Babelsberger Konferenz vom 2./3. April 1958*, Baden-Baden: Nomos.

Fikentscher, R. (2014) *Liebe, Arbeit, Einsamkeit. Wilhelm Schubart, Papyrologe. Gertrud Schubart-Fikentscher, Rechtshistorikerin. Ein Gelehrtenpaar in zwei Diktaturen*, Halle (Saale): Mitteldeutscher Verlag.

Härtel, G. and Pólay, E. (1987) *Römisches Recht und römische Rechtsgeschichte, Eine Einführung*, Weimar: Böhlau.

Haferkamp, H.-P. (2010) 'Wege der Historiographie zur Privatrechtsgeschichte der Neuzeit', *Zeitschrift für Neuere Rechtsgeschichte*, 32, 61–81.

Handschuck, M. (2003) *Auf dem Weg zur sozialistischen Hochschule. Die Universität Rostock in den Jahren 1945 bis 1955*, Bremen: Edition Temmen.

Heuer, U.-J. (1960) *Allgemeines Landrecht und Klassenkampf. Die Auseinandersetzungen um die Prinzipien des allgemeinen Landrechts Ende des 18. Jahrhunderts als Ausdruck der Krise des Feudalsystems in Preußen*, Berlin: Deutscher Zentralverlag.

Jelowik, L. (1984) 'Der Kampf der KPD gegen § 218', *Staat und Recht*, 33, 671–675.

Jelowik, L. (1998) 'Der Sachsenspiegel als Gegenstand des akademischen Unterrichts an der halleschen Juristenfakultät im 19. und 20. Jahrhundert', in Lieberwirth, R. (ed), *Rechtsgeschichte in Halle*, Köln, Berlin, Bonn and München: Carl Heymanns, 69–80.

Klenner, H. (1983) 'Recht wider Recht bei Martin Luther', *Staat und Recht*, 32, 867–873.

Lauterbach, I. R. (2013) *Friedrich Christian Fikentscher (1799–1864), ein früher Chemiefabrikant. Unter Berücksichtigung seiner Briefe aus den Jahren 1823, 1824 und 1830*, Stuttgart: Wissenschaftliche Verlagsgesellschaft.

Lenski, K. (2017) *Geheime Kommunikationsräume? Die Staatssicherheit an der Friedrich-Schiller-Universität Jena*, Frankfurt am Main and New York: Campus.

Lieberwirth, R. (1955) *Christian Thomasius. Sein wissenschaftliches Lebenswerk. Eine Bibliographie*, Weimar: Böhlau.

Lieberwirth, R. (1982) *Eike von Repchow und der Sachsenspiegel*, Berlin: Akademie.

Lieberwirth, R. (1986a) *Das sächsisch-magdeburgische Recht als Quelle osteuropäischer Rechtsordnungen*, Berlin: Akademie.

Lieberwirth, R. (1986b) 'Die Rechtshistoriker an der Leipziger Juristenfakultät in der ersten Hälfte des 20. Jahrhunderts', in Kroeschell, K. (ed) *Festschrift für Hans Thieme zu seinem 80. Geburtstag*, Sigmaringen: Thorbecke, 391–402.

Lieberwirth, R. (1986c) *Latein im Recht*, Berlin: Staatsverlag der DDR (simultaneously Heidelberg: C. F. Müller).

Lieberwirth, R. (1987) 'Christian Thomasius und die deutsche Sprache im Universitätsbetrieb', *Staat und Recht*, 36, 768–770.

Lieberwirth, R. (1988) 'Die Rechtsgeschichte in der DDR', *Zeitschrift für Neuere Rechtsgeschichte*, 10, 194–205.

Lieberwirth, R. (2000) 'Der erste weibliche Professor ordinarius an einer Juristenfakultät im deutschsprachigen Raum', *Rechtshistorisches Journal*, 19, 619–623.

Lieberwirth, R. (2005) 'Meine erste Begegnung mit dem Rechtswissenschaftlichen Seminar bei der Hallischen Juristenfakultät', in Lück, H. (ed) *150 Jahre Juristisches Seminar der Martin-Luther-Universität Halle-Wittenberg*, Halle (Saale): Stekovics, 59–63.

Lieberwirth, R. (2010) *Geschichte der Juristischen Fakultät der Universität Halle-Wittenberg nach 1945. Fakten und Erinnerungen*, Halle (Saale): Universitäts-Verlag Halle-Wittenberg.

Liebrecht, J. (2018) *Die junge Rechtsgeschichte. Kategorienwechsel in der rechtshistorischen Germanistik der Zwischenkriegszeit*, Tübingen: Mohr Siebeck.

Lingelbach, G. (1983) ''Yhe weniger Gesetz, yhe besser Recht'. Zu den Auffassungen von Martin Luther zum spätfeudalen Recht', *Staat und Recht*, 32, 851–859.

Lingelbach, G. (1984) 'Friedrich Schiller und sein Staatsverständnis. Zum 225. Geburtstag des Dichters am 10. November 1984', *Staat und Recht*, 33, 842–847.

Lingelbach, G. (1989) 'Kalendarium zur Geschichte von Staat und Recht und seiner Wissenschaft für das Jahr 1989', *Staat und Recht*, 38, 69–79.

Lingelbach, G. (1990) 'Kalendarium zur Geschichte von Staat und Recht und seiner Wissenschaft und seiner Wissenschaft für das Jahr 1990', *Staat und Recht*, 39, 82–95.

Lingelbach, G. (2008) 'Gerhard Buchda (1901–1977)', in Cordes, A., Haferkamp, H.-P., Lück, H. and Werkmüller, D. (eds) *Handwörterbuch zur Deutschen Rechtsgeschichte*, vol. 1, Berlin: Erich Schmidt, 698–699.

Lück, H. (1989) 'Beobachtungen zu Zehnt, Zins und anderen Abgaben in den Urkunden des Klosters Kaltenborn', in Gesellschaft für Heimatgeschichte im Kulturbund der DDR, Bezirksfachausschuss Numismatik (ed) *Thomas Müntzer und die frühbürgerliche Revolution. Thomas-Müntzer-Ehrung der DDR 1989. Münzausstellung, 30. April bis 11. Juni 1989 in Bad Frankenhausen*, Halle (Saale): Gesellschaft für Heimatgeschichte, 24–34.

Lück, H. (1998) 'Zwischen Refugium und Systemrechtfertigung. Rechtsgeschichte in der DDR', in Lück, H. (ed) *Recht und Rechtswissenschaft im mitteldeutschen Raum. Symposium für Rolf Lieberwirth zu seinem 75. Geburtstag*, Köln, Wien and Weimar: Böhlau, 165–176.

Lück, H. (1999) ''Der Deutsche kommt also im Osten in kein Neuland...' Das Institut zur Erforschung des Magdeburger Stadtrechts (1940–1945)', in Lück, H. and Freitag, W. (eds) *Historische Forschung in Sachsen-Anhalt. Ein Kolloquium anläßlich des 65. Geburtstages von Walter Zöllner*, Stuttgart and Leipzig: Hirzel, 125–145.

Mechow, M. (1970) *Namhafte CCer. Kurzbiographien verstorbener Landsmannschafter und Turnerschafter*, Stuttgart-Möhringen: Verband Alter Herren des Coburger Covents, 277–278.

Mitteis, H. (1947) 'Rechtsgeschichte und Gegenwart', *Neue Justiz*, 1, 27–29.

Mohnhaupt, H. (1984) 'Beobachtungen zur Rechtsgeschichte der DDR im Spiegel der Zeitschrift 'Staat und Recht'', *Ius Commune*, XII, 253–285.

Müller, H. (1992) *Krieg ohne Schlacht. Leben in zwei Diktaturen*, Köln: Kiepenheuer & Witsch.

Neubert, E. (1997) *Geschichte der Opposition in der DDR. 1949–1989*, Berlin: Christoph Links.

Ogorek, R. (1994) 'Rechtsgeschichte in der Bundesrepublik Deutschland 1945–1990', in Simon, D. (ed) *Rechtswissenschaft in der Berliner Republik. Studien zur Wissenschaftsgeschichte der Jurisprudenz*, Frankfurt am Main: Suhrkamp, 12–99.

Ogris, W. (2008) 'Zum Erscheinen von Band 125 der Zeitschrift der Savigny-Stiftung für Rechtsgeschichte', *Zeitschrift der Savigny-Stiftung für Rechtsgeschichte (Germanistische Abteilung)*, 125, XXXI–XLVIII.

Otto, M. (2004) 'Werner Weber—ein Opfer der politischen Säuberung nach 1945', *Sächsische Verwaltungsblätter*, 12, 201–205.

Otto, M. (2008) *Von der Eigenkirche zum Volkseigegen Betrieb: Erwin Jacobi (1884–1965). Arbeits-, Staats- und Kirchenrecht zwischen Kaiserreich und DDR*, Tübingen: Mohr Siebeck.

Otto, M. (2009) 'Öffentliches Recht und Arbeitsrecht: Erwin Jacobi (1884–1965)', in Lege, J. (ed) *Greifswald—Spiegel der deutschen Rechtswissenschaft 1815 bis 1945*, Tübingen: Mohr Siebeck, 303–321.

Polak, K. (1947) 'Wesen und Wert der Rechtsgeschichte', *Neue Justiz 1947*, 1, 54–58.

Rückert, J. (1995) 'Abbau und Aufbau der Rechtswissenschaft nach 1945', *Neue Juristische Wochenschrift*, 48, 1251–1259.

Schöneburg, K.-H. (1975) '*Wissenschaft von der Geschichte der Staats- und Rechtstheorie: Notwendigkeit, Konzeption, Aufgabe. Zum 70. Geburtstag von Karl Polak*', *Staat und Recht*, 24, 1457–1466.

Schröder, H. (1984) *Friedrich Karl von Savigny. Geschichte und Rechtsdenken beim Übergang vom Feudalismus zum Kapitalismus in Deutschland*, Frankfurt am Main: Peter Lang.

Schröder, H. (1971) *Eduard Gans, Philosophische Schriften. Herausgegeben und eingeleitet von Horst Schröder*, Berlin: Akademie.

Schröder, H. (2001) 'Polak versus Mitteis', in Schröder, H. and Simon, D. (eds) *Rechtsgeschichtswissenschaft in Deutschland 1945–1952*, Frankfurt am Main: Vittorio Klostermann, 5–18.

Schubart-Fikentscher, G. (1950) *Quellen zur deutschen Privatrechtsgeschichte vor der Rezeption*, Weimar: Böhlau.

Schubart-Fikentscher, G. (1960) *Hallesche Spruchpraxis. Consiliensammlung Hallescher Gelehrter aus dem Anfang des 18. Jahrhunderts*, Weimar: Böhlau.

Schubart-Fikentscher, G. (1967) *Die Unehelichen-Frage in der Frühzeit der Aufklärung*, Berlin: Akademie.

Schubart-Fikentscher, G. (1977) *Goethes amtliche Schriften. Eine rechtsgeschichtliche Untersuchung*, Berlin: Akademie.

Sellnow,Werner (1968). *Zum Problem der Rechtsgeschichte im Werk von Marx und Engels*, Berlin.

Sellnow, W. (1972) 'Hugo Preuss, ein Verwaltungsrechtler im Kampf mit dem preußischen Verwaltungsrecht', in Csizmadia, A. (ed) *Entwicklungsfragen der Verwaltung in Mitteleuropa. Aus Materialien der Internationalen Konferenz über Verwaltungsgeschichte in Pécs-Siklós 18.-20. Mai 1972*, Pécs: Pécsi Tudományegyetem Állam- és Jogtudmányi Kara, 229–252.

Soldwisch, I. (2007) *'...etwas für das ganze Volk zu leisten und nicht nur den Zielen einer Partei dienen'. Geschichte der Liberal-Demokratischen Partei in Mecklenburg 1946–1952*, Berlin and Münster (Westf.): Lit.

Steiger, G. (1980) *Ich würde doch nach Jena gehen. Geschichte und Geschichten, Bilder, Denkmale und Dokumente aus 4 Jahrhunderten Universität Jena*, Weimar: Böhlau.

Stolleis, M. (2009) *Sozialistische Gesetzlichkeit. Staats- und Verwaltungsrechtswissenschaft in der DDR*, München: C. H. Beck.

Tilitzki, C. (2002) *Die deutsche Universitätsphilosophie in der Weimarer Republik und im Dritten Reich*, vol. 1, Berlin: Akademie.

Wahl, V. (1999) 'Erweiterung und Neuaufbau 1945', in Post, B. and Wahl, V. (eds) *Thüringen-Handbuch. Territorium, Verfassung, Parlament, Regierung und Verwaltung in Thüringen 1920 bis 1995*, Weimar: Böhlau, 41–51.

Waibel, H. (2011) *Diener vieler Herren. Ehemalige NS-Funktionäre in der SBZ/DDR*, Frankfurt am Main, Berlin, New York and Paris: Peter Lang.

Wernicke, H. (1984) *Studien zum Verhältnis der Städtehanse zum norddeutschen Fürstentum und zum Reich*, Thesis (B) Greifswald University.

Wesel, U. (1974) 'Zur Methode der Rechtsgeschichte', *Kritische Justiz*, 7:4, 337–368.

Will, R. (2010) 'Die Juristische Fakultät in der DDR', in Grundmann, S. (ed) *Festschrift 200 Jahre Juristische Fakultät der Humboldt-Universität zu Berlin. Geschichte, Gegenwart und Zukunft*, Berlin und New York: Walter de Gruyter, 797–848.

Winkelmann, F. (2002) 'Als Kirchenhistoriker in der Berliner Akademie der Wissenschaften', in Meyer, D. (ed) *Kirchengeschichte als Autobiographie. Ein Blick in die Werkstatt zeitgenössischer Kirchenhistoriker*, vol. 2, Köln: Rheinland, 367–407.

Zentraler Ausschuss für Jugendweihe (1957) (ed.) *Unser Deutschland. Ein Buch für alle, die es lieben*, Berlin: Neues Leben.

Zentralinstitut für Geschichte der Akademie der Wissenschaften der DDR (ed) (1973) *Atlas zur Geschichte, vol. 1: Von den Anfängen der menschlichen Gesellschaft bis zum Vorabend der Großen Sozialistischen Oktoberrevolution*, Gotha and Leipzig: Hermann Haack.

Zierholz, H.-P. (1985) *Arbeiterschaft und Recht in Brandenburg-Preußen. 1648–1800*, Weimar: Böhlau.

3 Roman law studies in the USSR

An abiding debate on slaves, economy and the process of history

Anton Rudokvas and Ville Erkkilä[1]

Introduction

In pre-revolutionary Russia, both lawyers and historians studied Roman law intensively. In accordance with their colleagues in Continental Europe, Russian lawyers considered Roman private law to be the foundation of civil law doctrine in the modern legal system. Developing and applying that legal doctrine necessitated an understanding of Roman law in its ancient context as well as its significance in the construction process of the legal doctrine of Russian Empire.

In the Soviet Union, the situation, however, changed for the worse. The teaching of Roman law vanished for almost three decades, and although the faculties of law at the main universities of the USSR included Roman private law courses in their curricula again in 1948, they were unable to produce any considerable research on Roman law (see, e.g. Rudokvas, 2017, pp. 261–288). Hence, in this chapter we will focus on the study of the history of Roman law in general (that is, both public law and private law) by Soviet historians. These scholars were specialists in the history of Ancient Rome and dealt with issues related to Roman law in the context of their works on the wider development of ancient societies.

In the academic field of humanities in the socialist bloc, the historiography produced in the Soviet Union was surrounded by an aureole of prestige. The Soviet Union was displayed as a model regime also with regard to its scientific achievements. Any ambitious and comprehensive study in law, history or sociology had to at least refer to Soviet research.[2] That was done either in order to show that the author had comprehended correctly the wider (socialist) aim that all study was supposed to advance or for the purpose of demonstrating that the study at hand was well aware of the previous, ideologically appropriate takes on history. Hence, the Soviet historiography of antiquity was an important point of reference for all legal historical works on ancient law produced in the socialist East Central Europe.

Soviet historians aimed at an all-encompassing elaboration of the socio-economic and political history of Ancient Rome. They studied Roman law as an important element, but only as one element among others, in the political and social history of classical antiquity. Therefore, and in order to provide an overview of the study of Roman law in the USSR, in what follows we will describe the evolution of Soviet historiography on Ancient Rome and the ideological and intellectual historical context of its presentations.

Soviet historiography in the first decade after the Revolution of 1917

After the revolution, the traditional structures of educational and scientific institutions in Russia broke down. The Bolshevik regime took decisive actions in order to recreate science as a social institution and practice. One part of the project was to replace the existing university staff with a new class of professors and researchers imbued with the spirit of Marxist-Leninism. This meant that virtually all faculties of law and history were abolished during the first decade after the Revolution of 1917 (see, e.g. Connelly, 2000, pp. 22–30).

Historical, legal, sociological and other similar studies were assimilated into newly established and artificial 'Faculties of Social Sciences' (Fitzpatrick, 1979, p. 71). The ideological justification for the rearrangement came on one hand from the will to generate a synthesized (socialist) human knowledge and demolish the harmful divisions between separate special sciences and on the other from the conviction that law will 'wither away' during the imminent social development to communism (Engels, 1970, p. 147). The Bolshevik reformers' enthusiastic pursuit of the ideal of the universality of human knowledge in practice abolished the teaching of general history courses from both universities and secondary schools.

The utter abandonment of specialization in the field of humanities was an obvious utopia. In the academy, considerable historical research (including the ancient world) was carried out in the *Russian Academy of History of Material Culture* established in 1919. After the creation of the USSR, it was in 1926 renamed *The State Academy of History of Material Culture* (see, e.g. Alexeev-Popov, 1936, pp. 193–194; Dlužnevskaja, 2006, pp. 128–138; Ivanova, 1968; *Narodnyj Komissariat Prosveŝeniâ RSFSR*, 1935).

In addition, special research institutes, in particular historical institutes, were established within the new faculties of social sciences and within the academy. These institutes sometimes further founded sections for the study of the history of antiquity, medieval history, modern history and Russian history. The researchers affiliated with these organizations often held on to the pre-revolutionary stance on historical research and continued their scientific activities using their usual methodology.

The Soviet government, however, was persistent in its renewal project and insisted on creating a new historical science. For this purpose, in 1924 all research institutes of social and economic sciences were merged under the umbrella of the *Russian Association of Research Institutes of Social Sciences*, led by the ideologist of the new Marxist historical science, Michail Pokrovskij. From May 1918 to the end of his life in 1932, Pokrovskij was Deputy People's Commissar of Education for the Russian Soviet Federal Socialist Republic and was referred to as 'historian number one' in Communist Russia (Brandenberger, 2006, p. 202).

Pokrovskij himself studied the history of Russia, but his associates tried to apply Marxist methodological techniques of 'historical materialism' also in other areas of historical science. Characteristic for the research of the 'Pokrovskij school' was an attempt to depict the historical reality of the past with modern concepts and principles of contemporary society. In particular, Pokrovskij himself introduced the concept of 'trade capitalism' for describing the socioeconomic realities of the preindustrial era (Pokrovskij, 1915–1918). However, in their struggle with the 'idealistic bourgeois historiography' of the pre-revolutionary school, on whose flaws and features Pokrovskij's supporters elaborated meticulously and in a laborious manner, they themselves gradually moved further away from Marxism.

As a result, instead of Marxism's idea of the progressive movement of social progress from more primitive stages to more developed forms of social and economic order, the Pokrovskij school began to deviate from the main line of the theoretical teaching of historical materialism in the direction of long-held ideas about the 'cyclicity' of the historical process. For the Pokrovskij school, various historical periods appeared as alternating combinations of different economic structures, rigidly defining the social and political structures of society. Clearly, this approach easily justified the direct extrapolation of modern phenomena into the past and the use of modern concepts to describe the social processes of past eras (Kuziŝin, 1980, p. 328).

The new regime favoured and emphasized the importance of publishing literature suitable for teaching material in higher education. The Bolsheviks wanted to ensure that the teaching of social sciences in higher education, necessary for training personnel for new ideological positions in society, was carried out in a proper socialist manner. The sociological approach to history, directed against the more traditional and antiquarian historiography and affected by the modernization process of society, had nevertheless started long before the Revolution of 1917 (see, e.g. Frolov, 1999, pp. 312–397).

Hence, one can say that the stance of the Pokrovskij school represented a continuation of the older methodology in the post-revolutionary period in a new ideological wrapping. In this respect, the Marxist historical science of the first years of the Soviet regime actually offered nothing fundamentally new.

The most notable Pokrovskij school historians of classical antiquity were Alexander Tûmenev, Vladimir Serĝeev and Serĝey Kovalev. Tûmenev was the first to apply the Marxist concept of the slave-owning formation to the history of ancient Greece. However, he considered the societies of the Ancient East and the societies of Ancient Greece and Rome to be two different types of slave societies. His main contribution to the socioeconomic historiography of antiquity was *Did Capitalism Exist in Ancient Greece?: On the Genesis of Capitalism: The Experience of Comparative Historical Research*, which was published in Petrograd in 1923. Both the topic and the long title were characteristic of the works of the Pokrovskij school.

If Tûmenev mainly engaged in the research of the Ancient East and Ancient Greece, his associates Serǵeev and Kovalev paid more attention to Ancient Rome. During the first decade of the Soviet regime, Serǵeev published two textbooks on the history of slave societies of Ancient Greece and Rome (Serǵeev, 1922; Serǵeev, 1925), and Kovalev contributed with a two-volume *Course of Universal History,* published in Petrograd in 1923–1925. Both authors shared Pokrovskij's ideas about the coexistence of slavery with feudalism and 'trade capitalism' in antiquity (see, e.g. Serǵeev, 1926). In particular, Kovalev's texts show his commitment to the cyclic theory of the development of the historical process and the tendency to operate with the concepts of 'capitalism', 'feudalism', 'the proletariat' and 'the peasant revolution' in the description of the history of societies of classical antiquity (Frolov, 1999, pp. 433–434).

The modernizing ideas of the Pokrovskij school and its commitment to the idea of cyclical world history were clearly heretic with respect to orthodox Marxist-Leninism, which was based on the principle of linear progressive development. Paradoxically, in this sense, some historians representing more traditional views on history appeared more Marxist than their 'progressive' colleagues. One of them was Professor Dmitry Petruševskij from Moscow University, who, among other topics, was engaged in the research of the problems of transition from Late Antiquity to the Middle Ages.

In 1925, Petruševskij edited the Russian translation of Max Weber's book *The Agrarian History of the Ancient World.*[3] This book stood in clear opposition to the ideas of the new historical school of Pokrovskij, since Max Weber, as we know, perceived ancient society as a primitive counterpart of the modern world, whereas Pokrovskij and his disciples attempted to describe ancient history using modern concepts. However, in 1928, following the publication of the Russian translation of Weber, Professor Petruševskij published his own book *Essays on the Economic History of Medieval Europe*, which also demonstrated a clear deviation from the Marxist canon. Petruševskij now portrayed feudalism as an exclusively political institution, not associated with certain forms of economic life. As a result, he denied the existence of any free community of citizens in medieval society, insisted on the eternity of private ownership and emphasized social inequality among the ancient Germans. For these reasons, he is usually characterized in the literature as a neo-Kantian (Kuziŝin, 1980, p. 332).

Only a few historians in the first years of the Soviet Union clearly opposed the ideological principles of the new rulers. Nevertheless, the efforts of both the ideological supporters and the 'fellow travellers' of the Bolshevik regime already then began the entropic process of socialist state ideology. Such an inherent contradiction was emblematic in the specific provisions that the state conditioned to particular spheres of social sciences and in the more or less successful attempts of the scholars to fulfil these provisions. Probably it was not so difficult because the classics of Marxism-Leninism wrote so much on various occasions that in their works it was easy to find a justification for any diametrically opposed points of view.

Obviously, under the screen of ideological uniformity in the first decade of Soviet Russia's existence, there was a plurality of different opinions and their clashes, which corresponded to the plurality of the factional struggle in the Communist Party of this period. Hence, in an analogous manner to the process of Christian faith becoming the dominant religion in the Late Roman Empire, the ideological consolidation of the new regime necessitated the institution of the one and only true doctrine. Such an undisputed foundation was needed for determining the goals and methods of further development, not only of science but of society as a whole.

For this purpose, by 1927 the first twenty-volume canonical edition of the complete works of Lenin was published. After 1928, volumes of the canonical collection of works by Marx and Engels in the Russian translation began to appear. For the Soviet Marxist historical science, the publication of Lenin's lecture entitled 'On the State' (*O gosudarstve*) in the newspaper *Pravda*, N 15, 18.01.1929, was a particularly important and ground-breaking moment. For the emerging ideology of Marxist-Leninism in Russia, the collected works constituted a specially selected body of 'Holy Scriptures', and therefore endowed with absolute authority, a collection of texts from the founders of the new secular religion.

If described using theological terms, the advent of the scriptures was inevitably followed by the formation of a sacred tradition, i.e. the canonical interpretation of sacred texts. The years subsequent to the institution of the ideological foundation of the new secular religion of Marxist-Leninism were characterized by a struggle to define the proper reading and application of the doctrinal texts. The theoretical debate that had real-life consequences included detecting and excluding the heretical deviations associated with the use of non-traditional methods of interpreting the canonical works and attempts to supplement the scriptures with noncanonical statements of the founders.

The official intervention and the eradication of the Pokrovskian view

The processes of ideological consolidation in the early 1930s ended the existence of factions in the Communist Party. They also led to the revision of the new historical science formed in the previous decade. The political leadership of the USSR began to bring down the predominant view of the Pokrovskij school with the decree *On teaching civil history in schools of the USSR* by the Central Committee of the Communist Party and the Council of People's Commissars of the USSR on May 16th, 1934, published in issue 113 of the News of The Central Executive Committee of the USSR and the all-Russian Central Executive Committee.

The decree ordered the introduction of a systematic course of history in higher and secondary schools and for this purpose demanded the production of comprehensive history textbooks. According to the decree, since September 1, 1934, the Communist government restored history faculties in Moscow and Leningrad universities, and the reopened faculties were designated to teach all sections of world and Russian history. Following this decision, on June 9th, 1934, the Central Committee of the Communist Party adopted a resolution *On the introduction of an elementary course of general history and history of the USSR in primary and lower secondary school.* In the wake of the Party decisions, during 1935 and 1936 several history faculties were opened in universities and pedagogical institutes of the Soviet Union (Kuzišin, 1980, p. 336). With the decree *On the history textbooks* on January 26, 1936, the Central Committee of the Communist Party and the Council of People's Commissars of the USSR announced a contest for the best history textbook.[4]

However, the ideological consolidation also took a more concrete form. The open persecution of the historical school of Pokrovskij, and the scholars associated with it, began in January 27th, 1936, with the publication of the official report on the decision of the Central Committee of the Communist Party and the Council of People's Commissars of the USSR (*On the situation in historical science and history teaching*). In page 4 the report stated:

> [A]mong some of our historians, especially historians of the USSR, [there are] rooted anti-Marxist, anti-Lenin, in fact liquidator, anti-scientific views on historical science. The Council of People's Commissars and the Central Committee of the CPSU(b) emphasize that these harmful trends and attempts to eliminate history as a science are primarily associated with the spread among some of our historians of erroneous historical views inherent in the so-called 'historical school of Pokrovskij'.[5]

At the same time, Joseph Stalin and some other figures of the Soviet political leadership commented critically on the history textbooks of the USSR and the 'new history' for higher education. The above-mentioned Party and state documents manifested the need for a deep combination of Marxist-Leninist theory with a thorough analysis of historical sources, the need to create a full-fledged world history and the rejection of schematism and dogmatism in historical research (Brandenberger, 2006, pp. 204–205).

In the context of historiographical methodology, the shifting tide of politics turned the scale in favour of the traditional and moderate opponents of the Pokrovskij school. The substitution of specific studies of historical sources with retrospective sociological speculation was no longer welcomed by the political authorities, and therefore such a speculation had to give way to a more balanced approach, which was naturally advocated by pupils of the old pre-revolutionary school.

Accordingly, the eradication of theoretical constructions of the Pokrovskij school in the field of historical materialism began. Cyclic theory of history was dismissed as incompatible with Marxist-Leninism. The only accepted approach comprised the concept of a single world-historical process of development of human society that passed from primitive to slave, then to feudal and finally to capitalist formations and moved after 1917 to the Communist formation. At the same time, each subsequent formation represented a higher stage of social development than the preceding formation (Kuzišin, 1980, p. 337).

Professors Serǵeev and Kovalev recognized the change in the ideological atmosphere and took an active part in the scholarly discussions concerning the reorientation of historical science. They noted that their previous views on the essence of the social and economic nature of the ancient world were incompatible with what the political leadership regarded as a correct understanding of historical development. In short, their previous views were now erroneous. As a result, they started to emphasize and endorse the concept of the slave-owning formation and the specific ancient mode of production corresponding to it (see, e.g. Tolz, 2014, pp. 80–81).

In their subsequent writings, they paid much attention to the ancient economy and slave revolts in antiquity, clearly avoiding paying special attention to the obvious diversity of this economy as well as the fact that slaves in their social position in the community could play completely different roles. Furthermore, it is obvious that the social position of the slave working on a plantation or in a mine was strikingly different from the position of a slave who was a city police officer (see, e.g. Frolov, 2004, pp. 200–220) or the manager operating a commercial enterprise belonging to his owner (see, e.g. Cerami and Petrucci, 2010, pp. 36–67, pp. 166–171).

Despite these flaws, scientific research focusing on the economic circumstances of the phenomenon of slavery and slave revolts as crucial social turning points made a significant contribution to the historiography of the ancient world. The kind of Marxist approach that emphasized the tensions between the owners and the slaves and the economic narrative to which that inherent inequality connected has provided knowledge on the provisions of Roman law corresponding to the legal regulation of slave relations and on the general economic relations in antiquity (Frolov, 1999, pp. 429–430; Kuziŝin, 1980, p. 338, pp. 349–350).

The governmental intervention resulted in the rearrangement of the institutional base of teaching and researching history as well as producing the desired scientific contributions. In the recreated historical departments, a systematic course in ancient history was introduced and departments of the history of the ancient world were set up. In 1936, the Institute of History of the USSR Academy of Sciences was established, including a sector on Ancient History. The *Journal of Ancient History* has been published continuously since 1937. Responding to the call of the Communist Party and the USSR government, Professor Serǵeev published in 1939 a textbook *Essays on the History of Ancient Rome.* Two years earlier than this, Professor Kovalev had published a course of lectures consisting of two volumes: *The History of Ancient Slave Societies, Part 1–Greece* and *Part 2–Hellenism and Rome* (1937). Ten years later in 1948, he saw the publication of his major work, *The History of Rome.*

Stalinism and the legal historiography of the Roman world

The histories of the classical ancient world produced during Stalin's reign were in general characterized by a consolidated approach to present the history of classical antiquity as the history of passing stages of socioeconomic formation. Moreover, the slave-owning method of production was conceived as the socioeconomic base of ancient societies. Historians saw the driving force of ancient society in the class struggle of two main class antagonists: the class of slaves and the class of slave owners. The history of ancient societies was considered to be a progressive process of slave-owning relations, their subsequent flourishing and final disintegration. Scholars focused on social relations that emerged from this decomposition and, after the fall of the ancient world, became the basis of a new, higher feudal formation.

The active involvement of the political elite in historiographical issues put an end to the sociological experimentalism of the Pokrovskij school, but the representatives of the old pre-revolutionary school were also forced to demonstrate their loyalty to the new approach. The ideological consolidation of the Soviet Union and the obvious, real-life consequences for dissident views on the past framed the space of historical interpretation. The historians of antiquity had to respect the requirements provided by the political elite, and yet totally abandoning or ignoring one's previous scholarly views while writing politically correct historiography was often complicated, to say the least.

One peculiar aspect of the 1930s research on the ancient past is that the leading Soviet historians of classical antiquity turned to the study of the formation of Imperial power in Rome. Many studies focused on the legal embodiment of Imperial rule and the social essence of Caesarism as a political phenomenon. This interest clearly correlates with the strengthening of Joseph Stalin's regime of personal power in the USSR.

During these years, Professor Serǵeev wrote a lot about the dictatorships of Sulla and Julius Caesar, as well as about the Roman emperors of the period of the regime of the Principate—Augustus, Tiberius, Claudius, the Antonin dynasty and the Severian dynasty (Serǵeev, 1938). Another fundamental textbook on the history of ancient Rome (*The History of Ancient Rome*) was reissued three times (1947, 1949 and 1956) by Professor Nikolai Maškin of Moscow State University. In his research, Maškin studied the problems of transition from Republic to Empire as well as the relationship of the provinces with Rome, the culture of Rome and Roman Africa. His work *The Principate of August* (1949), published shortly before the author's death, became a classic in Soviet science. It was translated into Hungarian, Italian, German and Romanian. In this work, Maškin investigated the Principate as a form of statehood, its genesis, ideology and social essence. In 1951 Professor Maškin was awarded (posthumously) the Stalin Prize second degree for *The Principate of August.*

The case of Serǵei Žebelëv gives an illustrative example of the incorporation of the contemporary doctrines of historical development to traditional scholarly views. Žebelëv made his academic career in Imperial Russia and in 1927 became an academician of the USSR Academy of Sciences (Kozlov, 2011, p. 376). He was a well-known expert in classical philology and ancient history, who spent his life studying the history of Ancient Greece. Fear of persecution and possible repressions forced him first in 1932 to make biased conclusions about the so called 'discovery' of a previously unknown slave rebellion in the Bosporan Kingdom in the second century BC (Žebelev, 1932).

Žebelev based his whole presentation on a tendentious interpretation of one Greek term from the text of ancient inscription found on the Northern shore of the Black Sea. Then he, together with Professor Kovalev in 1934, turned to the study of the slave revolts in Sicily in the Roman period and the Spartacus movement (Žebelëv and Kovalev, 1934, pp. 139–180). Thus, paying tribute to the official ideology, he bought indulgence for the continuation of his favourite activities, namely epigraphy and classical philology.

The new direction of research of ancient history in the Stalinist USSR is especially eminent in the studies concentrating on the 'slave revolts' of the Roman world. A good illustration of the body of scholarly works focusing on the theme is the monograph *Spartacus Uprising* by Alexander Mišulin, Professor at Moscow University, which appeared in 1936. The author interpreted Spartacus revolt as the culmination of many years of slave struggle for freedom, the highest point of the contradictions in Roman slave society. All other social conflicts of ancient Rome, including movements of the ruined free peasantry, he considered to be minor, accompanying the main conflict of the main antagonistic classes, slaves and slave owners. Mišulin insisted that above all it was the slave rebellion organized by Spartacus that led to the fall of the Roman Republic and to the consequent birth of the Imperial regime.

From the late 1930s, Professors Mišulin, Kovalev and Maškin began to formulate and give justification to a comprehensive theory of the 'slave revolution' in ancient Rome (Kuzišin, 1980, p. 340). This theory was developed under the influence of Stalin's statement that the slave revolution eliminated the class of slave owners and abolished the slave form of exploitation of working people (Tolz, 2014, p. 80). In accordance with Stalin's remark, the professors initiated a doctrine that determined the whole development of ancient Rome in terms of a class struggle between slaves and slave owners. But since the Sicilian revolts and the rebellion of Spartacus took place many centuries before the fall of Rome, in their theory the professors introduced an idea of a permanent 'revolution of slaves', which lasted from the second century BC to the fifth century AD (see, e.g. Kovalev, 1936; Maškin, 1950; Mišulin, 1936).

This permanent revolution allegedly contained two culminating points that the authors of the theory identified, each of which occupied almost two centuries. The first took place in the second and first centuries BC and led to the fall of the Roman Republic. The second climax extended to the period from the third to the fifth century AD and resulted in the fall of the Empire and the demise of the slave system (Frolov, 1999, p. 437; Kuzišin, 1980, p. 341). In order to substantiate this theory with facts, almost any social conflict in ancient Rome had to be interpreted as a slave uprising, and that is what the authors did.

Furthermore, the slave revolution was interpreted as a mass movement that had allies among the peasantry and other disadvantaged segments of society, but, nonetheless, the slaves were depicted as an explicit class—and as the hegemon of the general revolutionary movement. The approach was evidently a projection of the official version of the Communist Revolution of 1917 in Russia to the history of classical antiquity. The Stalinist regime presented the Revolution of 1917 likewise as an uprising of a movement of workers and peasants, to which other social groups joined. And yet, in a similar vein as the theory of the 'revolution of slaves', ultimately the hegemony of the working class within this uprising was not to be challenged.

The concept of the 'slave revolution' appeared to be such an obvious vulgarization of ancient history that in the late 1940s timid attempts to revise it partially started to emerge. An example of such creeping revisionism was Alexander Dmitrev's doctoral dissertation *Social Movements in the Roman Empire in Connection with the Invasion of Barbarians*, which he defended in 1950. Historians began to focus on the diversity of social conflicts in ancient Rome. The cautious revisions emphasized that in many cases the conflicts bluntly labelled as 'slave revolts' were movements in which the main role was played not by slaves but by other social groups, namely oppressed inhabitants of provinces or religious groups, coloni (see, e.g. Dmitrev, 1940, pp. 101–114; Dmitrev, 1946, pp. 92–100; Dmitrev 1948, pp. 66–78; Dmitrev 1949, pp. 76–85; Dmitrev, 1950, pp. 66–80; Dmitrev, 1951, pp. 61–72; Dmitrev, 1956, pp. 97–126).

For this reason, the riots in Rome began to be interpreted not as slave but as popular movements, and that change of position gradually eroded the basic concept of 'slave revolution'.

The research on the problematic of social struggle in ancient Rome was developed hand in hand with studies on the essence of slave exploitation. It is thus not a coincidence that the question of the role of free peasants—who composed a relatively large social group in Roman society throughout its history—was a very difficult question for Soviet historians of antiquity. Some regarded free peasants as allies of the slave class, others as part of the slave owners class. By the same token, their economic significance fitted poorly to the model of Roman economy upheld by the historiography of the Stalinist period.

In their works, Soviet historians considered the *latifundia* as the foundation of the Roman economy. The numerous slaves who worked on the plantations of any given *latifundia* were considered as all equally marginalized, deprived of their families and property while they lived in the workhouses of the 'plantation' (*ergastula*) (Kuzišin, 1980, p. 343). Slaves were overexploited, as the owners tried to get the maximum result from them in the minimum amount of time. After the rapid death of a slave exhausted by overwork, he was replaced by a new one because in conditions of constant wars slaves were cheap. According to the predominant narrative of Stalinist historiography, the crisis of the slaveholding economy emerged immediately after the Roman Empire was no longer able to conduct further wars of conquest and had to adopt a defensive position. As a consequence, there was a transition from plantation slavery to the provision of land to slaves who were granted the right to retain part of the harvest received from the land. In a nutshell, as argued in the writings of the Soviet historians during the times of Stalinism, from that particular process the feudal relations originated (Maškin, 1950, pp. 630–631).

In the Soviet historiography of the ancient world of the Stalinist years, slave labour was considered unproductive and low-skilled and impeded technological progress. Attention was focused on the fact that slave labour in the *latifundia* ravaged small free peasants who could not stand the competition. At the same time, the low efficiency of slave labour, which generally led to the inefficiency of the ancient economy, was constantly emphasized. By concentrating on the negative aspects of the slave economy, especially on the inhumane overexploitation of slaves by their masters and the distortions of the economic structure of the society in general, but also by ignoring the historical variance and diversity of experiences in Roman society, Soviet historians depicted antiquity as a site for a constant and acute class struggle in which slave-owning relations were bound to perish.

In general, it should be noted that the manner of writing by Soviet researchers during the years of Stalinism, of works on the history of the class struggle in antiquity on the one hand and works on the historical reconstruction of the ancient economy on the other, was as if these works had not been written by the same authors. Studies on the history of uprisings and social movements in the ancient world were distinguished by a deep study of historical sources and can safely be labelled as genuine historical research. At the same time, Soviet monographs and articles on the problems of the ancient economy were more superficial. They were mainly theoretical in nature and were characterized by a weak study of the source base of the study. It is clear that the authors sought to adjust the material sources under a predetermined research scheme.

The post-Stalinist development

Stalin died in 1953. In 1956, the Twentieth Congress of the Communist Party of the Soviet Union (CPSU) was held that condemned Stalin's 'cult of personality' and political repressions that took place during his reign. At the end of the Party Congress, a resolution of the Central Committee of the Communist Party of the USSR was adopted called 'On overcoming the cult of personality and its consequences', published in the newspaper *Pravda*, N 184, July 2, 1956. Above all for Soviet historians, this seemed a direct invitation to revise the historical concepts established in the Stalin years.

As a consequence, the research on the historical development of social structures started to focus on a thorough analysis of the material sources. The methodological paradigmatic change was coupled with an aversion to using abstract theoretical constructions that had no basis in the material of historical sources. A forerunner for the post-Stalinist view on the legal history of antiquity was Maria Serģeenko, who had started her career already in the pre-revolutionary period and managed to retain her scholarly style using an in-depth elaboration of primary sources in the 1930s (Gavrilov and Kazanskij, 1993, pp. 316–328; Žmud', 2013, pp. 101–102). Inter alia, Serģeenko was a specialist of Roman agriculture (Serģeenko, 1958) and translated into Russian a lot of works of Roman agronomists. These works were originally introduced as comprehensive guides for a proper cultivation of land and the correct kind of agriculture (Serĝeenko, 1937; Serĝeenko and Protasova, 1950; Serĝeenko, 1963; Serĝeenko, 1970).

The rearrangements of organizational conditions carried out after Stalin's death supported the comprehensive revision of the dogmatic historiography of the previous decades. In addition to the pre-existing university departments of ancient history in Moscow, Leningrad, Kiev, Minsk and Sverdlovsk, departments devoted to the study of ancient history and the history of the Middle Ages were established in the universities of all major cities of the USSR (Kuziŝin, 1980, pp. 350–351).

Officially, the appeal to a new comprehensive study of the ancient economy and the various aspects of slavery was justified by the fact that alongside of the rise of 'social history' there was an increased interest in these issues in 'Western' historiography (see, e.g. White, 1970; Finley, 1968; Garnsey, 1970). In a way, the wider international turn towards 'the social' in the study of antiquity, coupled with the ideological readjustment in the political atmosphere of the Soviet Union, furbished the Russian historiography's base as a Marxist historiography. The circumstances obliged historians to turn primarily to the study of productive forces and economic relations as premises for historical processes.

Step by step, a total revision of the concept of the ancient slave-owning formation established in the Stalin years occurred. Soviet researchers of the 1960s and 1970s like Lev Elnitsky and Elena Štaerman based their studies of the social, economic and legal aspects of slavery in ancient Rome on a scrupulous and source-focused historical research (Kuziŝin, 1980, p. 352). Without denying the very concept of the slave-owning mode of production, the scholars demonstrated the diversity of the ancient economy, in which non-economic coercion to work was combined with the use of the types of economic relations of the market economy. As a result, Professor Štaerman demonstrated that the concepts of 'the estate of slaves' on the one hand, and 'the class of slaves' on the other hand were not always the same. People who were slaves from the legal point of view could be divided into groups that belonged to different social classes from the point of view of Marxist analysis (Kuziŝin, 1980, p. 353).

Furthermore, by analysing the economic historical material of the Roman provinces, it was shown in detail that alongside the slave-owning method of production, other socioeconomic structures successfully coexisted in the Roman Empire. Scholars have pointed out that the main sources of production of the Roman economy were not *latifundia* or large workshop-type manufactories but were farms and small craft workshops. In addition, the post-Stalinist historiography stressed the obvious fact that the standard of living and the level of exploitation of slaves employed in different types of enterprises varied significantly (Egorov, 1985; Elnickij, 1964; Kuziŝin, 1966; Kuziŝin, 1973; Kuziŝin, 1976; Maâk, 1971; Parfenov, 1987; Štaerman, 1957; Štaerman 1964; Štaerman, 1971; Štaerman et al., 1977; Utčenko, 1972; Utčenko, 1976).

Generalizing from these new insights, Soviet historical science in the 1970s came to the conclusion that in the society of Ancient Rome throughout its history, there were not two main social classes—slaves and slave owners—but three. The first class was the class of people who owned the means of production, though they were not engaged in productive work. The second class consisted of people who owned the means of production and at the same time they themselves took part in the production process. The third class was a class of producers deprived of the means of production (Frolov, 1999, p. 410).

In essence, the historiography of ancient history in the late USSR, and in particular the historiography of the history of Ancient Rome, differed from modern Western literature on the issue only in its hypertrophied attention to the socioeconomic aspects of ancient history and its commitment to economic determinism in explaining the phenomena of social life.

Concluding remarks

Although the development of the studies of ancient society in Soviet Russia went through different stages—each presented as revolutionary to its predecessor—the field retained all the while some traits that characterize socialist interpretations of legal history. First, the idea of the law's inevitable 'withering away' in the communist society justified and necessitated analysing the past societies as totalities, in which law did not constitute a separate domain but rather a factor among other social structures that comprised the particularity of a given historical situation within the greater narrative of world historical development. Second, the political elite showed a continuing interest in historical research. The influence of political provisions on historiography was most evident during the reign of Joseph Stalin, when scholars had no choice but to depict ancient history as a reflection of the contemporary, reductive view of social development.

Soviet historiography represented a paragon of orthodox socialist historical research to the historical sciences around socialist East Central Europe. In addition, the domestic governments in the socialist bloc tried to imitate the way in which the USSR dealt with its scientific community and sphere of higher education. Hence, a study of Soviet historiography tells a lot about the relation between the socialist regimes and the histories written within them but also about the inner dynamics of the scientific disciplines. In this sense, it is interesting—in that it reflects the nuanced phenomenon of socialist legal historiography—that within the allegedly thoroughly 'politicized' research, traits of older principles and scholarly virtues existed. In the end, the historicist viewpoint of the priority and hegemony of historical sources—a stance that in many cases derived directly from some kind of a connection to the pre-revolutionary discourse of historiography—prevailed over the sociological experimentalism of Pokrovskij school and Stalinist dogmatism.

With respect to the conception of Roman law and society, by the time of the collapse of the Soviet Union, Soviet historiography finally abandoned the concept of the slave revolution as a factor that predetermined the transition from antiquity to the feudalism of the Middle Ages. Today, there is no fundamental, ideologically constituted schism on the understanding of ancient history.

Instead, there is a wide consensus that the primary unit of the social structure of Roman society throughout its history remained the community as a self-governing association of free people. But we should not forget that this modern concept was already proclaimed in a joint report by Soviet historians of classical antiquity E. Golubcova, V. Kuziŝin and E. Štaerman on the topic 'Types of communities in the ancient world' at the XIV International Congress of Historical Sciences in San Francisco in 1975 (Kuziŝin, 1980, p. 355–356).

Notes

1 Anton Rudokvas is full professor at the Saint Petersburg State University; Ville Erkkilä is a postdoctoral researcher at the University of Helsinki.
2 See, e.g. Bucholc in this volume.
3 The title in Russian: '*Agrarnaâ istoriâ Drevnego Mira*'.
4 *Na fronte nauki: V Sovnarkome Sojuza SSR i ZK VKP (b). Partizdat ZK VKP (b)* (On the science front: In the Soviet Union's Council of People's Commissars and the Central Committee of the all-Union Communist Party) (1936), Moscow: Publishing house of the Central Committee of the all-Union Communist Party.
5 'Na fronte nauki: V Sovnarkome Sojuza SSR i ZK VKP (b) (On the science front: In the Soviet Union's Council of people's Commissars and the Central Committee of the all-Union Communist Party.)' in *Bor'ba klassov* (Class struggle), 2, (February), 1936, p. 4.

References

Alexeev-Popov, V. (1936) 'Gosudarstvennaja academia istorii material'noj kultury imeni N. J. Marra (State Academy of history of material culture named after N. J. Marr)', *Istorik-marksist (Marxist historian)*, 55:3, 193–194.

Brandenberger, D. (2006) 'Politics Projected into the Past: What Precipitated the 1936 Campaign Against M. N. Prokrovsky?', in Thatcher I. D. (ed) *Reinterpreting Revolutionary Russia: Essays in Honour of James D. White*, London: Macmillan, 202–214. DOI: 10.1057/9780230624924_12.

Cerami, P. and Petrucci, A. (2010) *Diritto Commerciale Romano. Profilo Storico*, Torino: G. Giappichelli.

Connelly, J. (2000) *Captive University: The Sovietization of East German, Czech, and Polish Higher Education, 1945–1956*, Chapel Hill and London: The University of North Carolina Press.

Dlužnevskaja, G. (2006) 'Deâtelnost Akademii istorii material'noj kultury v oblasti vostokovedenija v 1919—1940 gg. (Activities of the Academy of History of Material Culture in the Field of Oriental Studies in 1919–1940)', *Vostočnyj Arhiv (Eastern Archive)*, 14–15, 128–138.

Dmitrev, A. (1950) *Sozial'nie dviženiâ v Rimskoj Imperii v svâzi s vtorženiem varvarov (Social Movements in the Roman Empire in Connection with the Invasion of the Barbarians)*. Manuscript.

Dmitrev, A. (1940) 'Dviženie bagaudov (The Movement of Bagaudae)', *Vestnik Drevnej Istorii (Journal of Ancient History)*, 12–13:3–4, 101–114.

Dmitrev, A. (1949) 'Padenie Dakii (k voprosu o svâzi osvoboditelnih dviženij v Rimskoj imperii s vtorženiâmi varvarov) (The Fall of Dacia (on the Connection

Between the Liberation Movements in the Roman Empire and the Invasions of the Barbarians))', *Vestnik Drevnej Istorii (Journal of Ancient History)*, 27:1, 76–85.

Dmitrev, A. (1956) 'Narodnie dvigeniâ v vostočno-rimskih provinzijah v period dunajskih, vojn III v. (236–278 gg.) (Popular movements in the Eastern Roman provinces during the third-century Danubian wars (236–278 AD))', *Vizantijskij vremennik (Byzantine Chronicles)*, 8, 97–126.

Dmitrev, A. (1946) 'Bukoli (iz istorii agrarnogo dviženiâ v Rimskom Egipte) (Bucolics (from the History of the Agrarian Movement in Roman Egypt))', *Vestnik Drevnej Istorii (Journal of Ancient History)*, 18:4, 92–100.

Dmitrev, A. (1948) 'K voprosu ob agonistikah i circumcellionah (To the Question of Agonistici and Circumcellions)', *Vestnik Drevnej Istorii (Journal of Ancient History)*, 25:3, 66–78.

Dmitrev, A. (1950) 'Vosstanie vestgotov na Dunae e revoluziâ rabov (The Visigoth Uprising on the Danube and the Slave Revolution)', *Vestnik Drevnej Istorii (Journal of Ancient History)*, 31:1, 66–80.

Dmitrev, A. (1951) 'Dviženie latrones kak odna iz form klassovoj bor' by v Rimskoj imperii (The Movement of Latrones as a Form of Class Struggle in the Roman Empire)', *Vestnik Drevnej Istorii (Journal of Ancient History)*, 38:4, 61–72.

Egorov, A. (1985) *Rim na grani èpoh: problemy roždeniâ i formirovaniâ principata Avgusta (Rome on the edge of epochs: problems of the birth and formation of the Principate of Augustus)*, Leningrad: Izdatel'stvo Leningradskogo Universiteta.

Elnickij, L. (1964) *Vozniknovenie i razvitie rabstva v Rime v VIII–III v. do n. è. (The emergence and development of slavery in Rome in the VIII-III centuries BC)*, Moscow: Nauka.

Engels, F. (1970) 'Socialism: Utopian and Scientific', in Marx K. and Engels F. (eds), *Selected Works in Three Volumes. Volume 3*, Moscow: Progress.

Finley, M. I. (1968) *Slavery in Classical Antiquity*, New York: Barnes & Noble.

Fitzpatrick, S. (1979) *Education and Social Mobility in the Soviet Union, 1921–1934*, Cambridge: Cambridge University Press.

Frolov, E. (1999) *Russkaâ nauka ob antičnosti: istoriografičeskie očerki (Russian science of antiquity: Historiographical essays)*, St. Petersburg: St. Petersburg University Press.

Frolov, E. (2004) *Paradoxy istorii—paradoxy antičnosti (Paradoxes of history - paradoxes of antiquity)*, St. Petersburg: St. Petersburg University Press.

Gavrilov, A. and Kazanskij, N. (1993) 'K 100-letiû M. E. Serĝeenko (To the 100th anniversary of M. E. Serĝeenko)', *Vspomogatel'nie istoričeskie disziplìny (Auxiliary historical disciplines)*, 24, 316–328.

Garnsey, P. (1970) *Social Status and Legal Privilege in the Roman Empire*, Oxford: Clarendon Press.

Ivanova, L. (1968) *U iztokov sovietskoj istoričeskoj nauki (podgotovka kadrov istorikov—marxistov v 1917–1929 gg.) (The origins of Soviet historical science (training of Marxist historians in 1917–1929)*, Moscow: Misl'.

Kovalev, S. (1923–1925) *Kurs vseobšej istorii (Course of universal history)*. Vol. 1–2, Petrograd: Priboj.

Kovalev, S. (1936) *Istoriâ antičnogo obšestva. Čast 1. Greziâ. (The History of Ancient Society. Part 1-Greece)*, Leningrad: Socèkgiz.

Kovalev, S. (1936) *Istoriâ antičnogo obšestva. Čast 2. Hellenism. Rim (The History of Ancient Society. Part 2-Hellenism and Rome)*, Leningrad: Socèkgiz.

Kovalev, S. (1948) *Istoria Rima (The History of Rome)*, Leningrad: Izd-vo Leningradskogo universiteta.

Kozlov, D. (2011) 'Athens and Apocalypse: Writing History in Soviet Russia', in Woolf, D. (ed) *The Oxford History of Historical Writing. Volume 5: Historical Writing since 1945.* Oxford: Oxford University Press. DOI: 10.1093/oso/9780199225996.003.0019.

Kuzišin, V. (ed) (1980) *Istoriografiâ antičnoj istorii (Historiography of ancient history)*, Moscow: Vissaâ škola.

Kuzišin, V. (1966) *Očerki po istorii zemledeliâ Italii II v. do n. è—I v. n. è. (Essays on the history of agriculture in Italy II century BC - I century AD)*, Moscow: Izdatel'stvo Moskovskogo Universiteta.

Kuzišin, V. (1973) *Rimskoe rabovladel'českoe pomest'e (Roman slaveholding agricultural estate), Moscow*: Moskovskij Universitet.

Kuzišin, V. (1976) *Genezis rabovladel'českih latifundij v Italii (II v. do n. è—I v. n. è.) Genesis of slaveholding latifundia in Italy (II century BC - I century AD)*, Moscow: Izdatel'stvo Moskovskogo Universiteta.

Lenin, V. I. (1927) in Buharin, N., Molotov, V. and Skortsova-Stepanov, I. (eds) *Sochineniia (Works)*, 30 Vols. 2nd ed., Moscow: Gosizdat.

Lenin, V. I. (1929) '*O gosudarstve (On the State)*', *Pravda*, 15, 18.01.1929.

Maškin, N. (1947, 1950 and 1956) *Istoriâ Drevnego Rima (The History of Ancient Rome)*, Leningrad & Moscow: Gospolitizdat.

Maškin, N. (1949) *Prinzipat Avgusta (The Principate of August)*, Moscow: Akad. Nauk SSSR.

Maâk, I. (1971) *Vzaimootnošeniâ Rima i italijcev v III—II vv. do n. è. (do grakhanskogo dviženiâ) (Relations between Rome and the Italic peoples in the III-II centuries BC (before the movement of the Gracchi brothers)*, Moscow: Izdatel'stvo Moskovskogo Universiteta.

Mišulin, A. (1936) *Spartakovskoe vosstanie: Revoluziâ rabov v Rime v I v. do n. è. (The Spartacus Revolt: The slave revolution in Rome in the first century BC.)*, Moscow: Moskva Gosudarstvennoe Social'no-Ėkonomičeskoe Izdat.

Mišulin, A. (1936) *Revoluziâ rabov i padenie Rimskoj respubliki (The slave revolution and the fall of the Roman Republic)*, Moscow: Izdatel'stvo CK VKP(b) "Pravda".

Narodnyj Komissariat Prosveŝeniâ RSFSR. *Universitety i naučnye učreždeniâ (People's Commissariat of Education of the RSFSR. Universities and research institutions)* (1935) Second edition, revised and expanded, Moscow and Leningrad: Ob"edinennoe Naučno-Tehničeskoe Izdatel'stvo.

Parfenov, V. (1987) *Rim ot Cezarâ do Avgusta: očerki social'no—političeskoj istorii (Rome from Caesar to Augustus: essays on social and political history)*, Saratov: Izdatel'stvo Saratovskogo Universiteta.

Petruševskij, D. (1928) *Očerki èkonomičeskoj istorii srednevekovoj Evropy (Essays on the economic history of medieval Europe)*, Moscow: Gosudarstvennoe Izdat.

Pokrovskij, M. (1915–1918) *Očerki istorii russkoj kultury (Essays on the history of Russian culture)*, 1st edition, Parts 1 and 2, Moscow: Izd. T-va "Mir".

Rudokvas, A. (2017) 'IL Diritto Romano e la Privatistica Russa', in Vacca L. (ed) *Nel Mondo del Diritto Romano. Convegno ARISTEC, Roma 10-11 Ottobre 2014*, Napoli: Jovene Editore, 261–288.

Serǵeenko, M. (transl.) (1937) *O sel'skom hozâjstve. Caton, Varron, Columella, Plinij. (Cato, Varro, Columella, Plinius de agricultura) (About agriculture. Cato, Varro, Columella, Pliny)* (ed. Mečislav Burskij), Moscow and Leningrad: Sel'hozgiz.

Serǵeenko, M. (transl.) (1970) *Učenye zemledel'zy drevnej Italii (Agronomists of ancient Italy [Cato, Varro, Columella, Pliny])*, Moscow: Nauka.

Serǵeenko, M. and Protasova, S. (transl.) (1950) *Mark Porcij Katon. Zemledelie (Marcus Porcius Cato. Land cultivation)*, Moscow & Leningrad: Akad. nauk SSSR.

Serǵeenko, M. (transl.) (1963) *Varron. Sel'skoe hozâjstvo (Varron. Agriculture)*, Moscow & Leningrad: Akad. nauk SSSR.

Serǵeenko, M. (1958) *Očerki po sel'skomu hozâjstvu drevnej Italii (Essays on the agriculture of Ancient Italy)*, Moscow and Leningrad: Akad. nauk SSSR.

Serǵeev, V. (1938) *Očerki po istorii drevnego Rima 1 & 2 (Essays on the history of Ancient Rome Part 1 (Republic) & Part 2 (Empire))*, Moscow: Moskva OGIZ.

Serǵeev, V. (1926) *Feodalism i torgovyj capitalism v antičnom mire (Feudalism and commercial capitalism in the Ancient World)*, Moscow: Izdatel'stvo Kommunističeskogo universiteta im. Â. M. Sverdlova.

Serǵeev, V. (1922) *Istoriâ Drevnego Rima: Kul'turno—istoričeskij očerk v naučno—populârnom izloženii (The history of Ancient Rome: a cultural and historical essay in popular scientific presentation)*, Petrograd: Nauka i škola.

Sergeev V. (1925) *Istorija drevnego Rima (Ancient Rome history)*, 2nd ed., Moscow & Leningrad: Gosizdat.

Štaerman, E. (1957) *Krizis rabovladel'českogo stroâ v Zapadnoj Rimskoj Imperii (The crisis of the slave system in the Western Roman Empire)*, Moscow: Akad. nauk SSSR.

Štaerman, E. (1964) *Raszvet rabovladel'českih otnošenij v Rimskoj respublike (The rise of slavery in the Roman Republic)*, Moscow: Nauka.

Štaerman, E. (1971) *Rabovladel'českie otnošeniâ v rannej Rimskoj Imperii (Italiâ) (Slave-owning relations in the early Roman Empire)*, Moscow: Nauka.

Štaerman, E., Smirin, V., Belova, N., and Kolosovskaja, Û. (1977) *Rabstvo v Zapadnyh provinciâh Rimskoj Imperii v I—III vv. (Slavery in the Western provinces of the Roman Empire in the I—III centuries)*, Moscow: Nauka.

Tolz, V. (2014) *Russian Academicians and the Revolution: Combining Professionalism and Politics*, London: Palgrave Macmillan. DOI: 10.1007/978-1-349-25840-6.

Tûmenev, A. (1923) *Did capitalism exist in Ancient Greece? On the Genesis of capitalism. The experience of comparative historical research*, Petrograd: Priboj.

Utčenko, S. (1972) *Ciceron i ego vremâ (Cicero and his time)*, Moscow: Mysl'.

Utčenko, S. (1976) *Julij Cezar' (Julius Caesar)*, Moscow: Mysl'.

White, K. D. (1970) *Roman Farming*, London: Thames and Hudson.

Žebelev, S. (1932) 'Poslednij Perisad i skifskoe vosstanie na Bospore (The last Perisad and the Scythian revolt on the Bosporus)', in *Izvestiâ GAIMK (Proceedings of the State Academy of the History of Material Culture)*, 70, 9–36.

Žebelëv, S. and Kovalev, S. (1934) 'Velikie vosstaniâ rabov v II–I v. do našej èry v Rime (Great slave uprisings of the II-I centuries BC in Rome)', in *Iz istorii antičnogo obŝestva. Izvestiâ GAIMK (From the history of ancient society. Proceedings of the State Academy of the History of Material Culture)*, 10, 139–180.

Žmud', L. (2013) 'Mariya Efimovna Sergeenko (1891–1987)', *Istoriko-biologičeskie issledovaniâ (Studies in the History of Biology)*, 5:3, 101–102.

4 Strategies of covert resistance

Teaching and studying legal history at the University of Tartu in the Soviet era

Marju Luts-Sootak

Introduction

In the Soviet era (in 1940–1941 and 1944–1991), when the official name of the University of Tartu was 'Tartu State University', its Law Faculty was the only faculty of law in Estonia. The university counts its history from its establishment in 1632 during the Swedish era in Estonia. Nevertheless, it was not able to function uninterrupted. During the Great Northern War, the university was first evacuated to the harbour town Pärnu and from there on to the Swedish motherland. The Baltic provinces, which from 1710 to 1917 belonged to the Russian Empire, were thus left without a university. Since the 13th century, the local upper classes—the nobility and burghers—had been primarily German speaking, and the university, when it was finally reopened in Tartu in 1802, functioned for the following 90 years as a German university in the Russian Empire. In 1892, the university was Russified and remained Russian speaking until the end of the Tsarist state.

Although the town of Tartu is situated in the middle of ancient Estonian territory and ethnic Estonians have always been an absolute numerical majority there (about 95%), they were still at the beginning of the 19th century, almost without exception, serfs who had no contact with the university or higher education. It was only after the end of the First World War and the establishment of the Republic of Estonia that the University of Tartu was opened on December 1, 1919—now, for the first time in its history, as an Estonian-speaking university. Its status as the national university of the young Estonian state was also expressed in its official name: the University of Tartu of the Republic of Estonia. Since then, the official teaching language of the university, the Law Faculty included, has been Estonian. This is also how it remained—for the entire Soviet period, the university functioned in Estonian. In addition to the ordinary courses, there were also distance-learning courses, and for this form of studies, there was also teaching in Russian for a small group of students (approximately 20 every year). However, the main teaching language was Estonian. As a Finno-Ugric language, Estonian was somewhat hard to learn for other nationalities, and Estonians themselves were not very numerous (about one million altogether). This meant that the everyday language of teaching and university administration remained incomprehensible for Soviet 'functionaries' from elsewhere. Already the factor of this difficult-to-understand language made it hard for the Soviet central administration to control fully Estonian legal scholarship and education.

Everything that Sanita Osipova writes in this volume about Latvian legal history before and after World War II is in general terms also true about Estonia and the University of Tartu. Estonian national history and legal history writing began first in the interwar period with the Republic of Estonia, turning a formerly derided underclass—indigenous Estonians—into a subject of history and thereby opposing itself to earlier Baltic German history writing that had focused on the societal elites and the corresponding institutions. Soviet history writing sharpened this opposition even further, since now history had to be presented as a class struggle. Paradoxically, at the same time, this made it possible to continue the national history writing tradition that had been formed before the war, since Estonians had been an exploited underclass from the Middle Ages onwards and were hence a legitimate subject for a Marxist-Leninist treatment of history. It was only during the interwar era of the 20th century, in their own democratic republic, that the Estonian people had differentiated into different social classes. It was exactly this 'bourgeois republic' of the interwar period that was particularly condemned and in some ways even more 'forbidden' than earlier periods of history. But even the Soviet system included inconsistencies and windows of opportunity that allowed legal history in particular to develop into a somewhat more independent, in a certain sense even more dissident, discipline compared to the rest of the mainstream of legal studies.

In the following, I will take a look at the structural elements that allowed legal history to shake the general aims and ideology of the Soviet system. After that, I will characterise the most important academics who taught legal history at Tartu State University. More specifically, I will consider the ways and means of covert resistance employed by academics that enabled them to diverge from official party-controlled views.

The general framework of mandatory subjects in legal history

Lawyers have always been more closely associated with state power than natural scientists or, for example, historians. Compared to other colleagues in the faculty of law, it was the legal historians who consistently had the best opportunities to diverge from the Soviet political mainstream. To a degree, this was already facilitated by the general academic framework provided in Moscow, i.e. by the curriculum itself. There were rather a lot of compulsory legal historical subjects, including general or world legal history, the legal history of the USSR and the legal history of the Estonian Soviet Socialist Republic, or SSR.

The general legal history module could at different times be called *The History of the State and Law* or *General History of the State and Law* or *The History of the State and Law of Foreign Countries*, but the model was the same throughout the

Soviet era. More recent attempts to write the legal history of the whole of the world either historicise as comparative works (e.g., Glenn, 2014) or only focus on the methodological aspects of this enterprise (Duve, 2018; see also the quotations). Unlike the Soviet textbooks, they do not aspire to cover the whole of the legal history of the world since the beginning of time. But the students over the whole of the Soviet Union also learned something about ancient Babylonia or Mesopotamia—not just about the Code of Hammurabi and Hammurabi as a ruler, but also about some other things. How many persons in a normal 'Western' law faculty would have known who the *awilu*, the *mushkenu* or the *wardu* were? These were, by the way, different classes in the social hierarchy of Babylonia. Not only about Babylonia but also about ancient Egypt, India, China, Greece and Rome, medieval Europe and modern America, Soviet students acquired very specific types of knowledge in world legal history—knowledge about the upper and lower classes in the society and about the class struggle. But it should be stressed here that the General History of State and Law module also gave students the possibility of learning about the world outside of the closed borders of the Soviet Union. Newer legal history of foreign countries, not only that of the ancient or medieval world, was also a part of the curriculum.

The textbooks 'grew' together with history itself. In the 1940s, the 'most recent era' covered the time period 1917–1947 (Gurvich and Chernilovski, 1947), but in the 1980s, it also included 'the formation of the socialist world system' after World War II, the liberation of colonies in Asia and Africa and revolutions in the Latin American states (Chernilovski, 1983, pp. 570 sq.). The module, however, never covered all the states of the world. The selection from modern Europe, for instance, included the United Kingdom and the British Empire, France, Germany, Austria, Italy and in addition, from outside of Europe, the United States (Chernilovski, 1947; Chernilovski, 1983, pp. 214 sq.). In the period beginning with the Russian October Revolution, the coverage included Poland, Czechoslovakia, Yugoslavia, Bulgaria, China and Japan. The selection of smaller countries could vary between different textbooks, but the big ones were always included.

Although teachers had to follow the general curriculum, the same as that for the Soviet Union as a whole, every lecturer had some freedom to design his or her own lectures. The course in world legal history was rich enough to provide many possibilities for cherry picking. In addition to classes and class struggle, there was also teaching in the fields of legal sources, the main institutions and legal phenomena. Although the then-current Soviet law did not recognise private property or free markets, it was still possible to talk about these things in legal history (Gurvich and Chernilovski, 1947, pp. 284 sq.; Chernilovski, 1983, pp. 531 sq.). A historical introduction to classic private law was also provided by a course in Roman civil law, treated in this volume by Anton Rudokvas and Ville Erkkila. In addition to covering private law or separate parts of it (property law, family law) for different historical periods, general legal history also included an overview of criminal law, court organisation and judicial process.

I have here only referred to the Russian language, the so-called all-union textbooks. There were no substantial, original textbooks in general legal history published in Estonian. However, already at the beginning of the Soviet period, two textbooks appeared that were relevant for the earliest period covered in this module: Stepan Ketchekjan's textbook on the history of ancient Near East and Greek antiquity (Ketšekjan, 1946), and Ivan Pereterski's textbook on the ancient Roman state and law (Pereterski, 1946). These two translated textbooks subsequently remained the only published study materials in Estonian that were relevant for the course. There were no reprints after 1946, so as late as in the second half of the 1980s, the first-year students of the Law Faculty still had to compete in the library for the few extant copies that had survived after four decades of use. The textbooks covered only a small part of the course, namely, the earliest period. Concerning the period of the so-called 'general crisis of capitalism', i.e., the 20th century, some study materials in Estonian were published from the end of the 1950s until the mid-1960s by Jüri Jegorov (Jegorov, 1959; 1960/1966; 1961), whose activities will be treated in more detail below in the section on personalities. Everything else was studied from the notes made in lectures and seminars. Although there must have been some individual exceptions, the ethnically Estonian students generally did not study from Russian-language textbooks. This was not just a question of willingness or unwillingness. In spite of compulsory Russian classes from the second school year onwards, the Russian skills of Estonians were so lacking that they could not manage with textbooks in Russian.

The other big compulsory module in legal history was *The History of the State and Law of the USSR*, i.e., of the Soviet Union. This subject not only included the period beginning with the foundation of the USSR in 1922, or with the Russian socialist October Revolution of 1917, but also encompassed the whole of the legal history of the then-Soviet territory throughout the ages. Thus, the first point in the programme was 'Slave states on USSR territory'. This did not refer to the secret slave farms in Central Asia in the 1980s, exposed in the wake of Gorbachev's 'perestroika and glasnost', nor did it refer to the gulags. In the legal history syllabus, this meant the slave states of antiquity. There had been a few Greek colonies on the Black Sea, and the Persian Urartu Empire had reached the Soviet Union in the borderlands of the Armenian, Georgian and Azerbaijan Soviet Socialist Republics. Historical materialism as one part of the Marxist ideology discussed how historical societal formations would inevitably follow one another, every subsequent formation being more progressive than the previous ones, but nevertheless still presupposing the existence of the previous formations. In this way, slavery became an inevitable prerequisite of socialism. In general, studying the history of the state and law was supposed to turn students into particularly adept builders of Communism:

> Our second main task in addition to education is turning our current students into highly qualified builders of Communism. [...] In their professional education, the future lawyers must acquire the skills and abilities to use the state and law as well as possible as a means to build Communism.

> Everything changes, including the state and law. It therefore follows that their purposeful use takes various forms at different times and in different places. To inculcate a deep understanding of this fact in the students, our treatment of the state and law needs to be concrete and historical. [...] The demand for concreteness is one of the central demands of the dialectical method, and adherence to it is imperative in order to achieve objective truth. This avoids a descent into quixotic abstractionism and subjectivism. (Ibius, 1951, p. 5)

In the 1980s, there was less talk of building Communism. The last one to have predicted its arrival by the year 1984 was Nikita Khrushchev. Communism failed to arrive and George Orwell's book *1984* ended up being a more accurate prediction than Khrushchev's. However, the teaching of the history of the state and law, as of history altogether, remained in a certain way extremely 'concrete' up until the end of the Soviet period. Lecturers avoided interpretations of meanings in both their oral and written communication and limited themselves to presenting a great number of facts.

There was also one textbook of the history of the USSR that was translated into Estonian immediately after the war, again only on earlier history, although it did extend up to the reign of Peter the Great (Juškov, 1946). It was during the time of Peter the Great, amidst the Great Northern War, that Estonian territories were for the first time subjected to Russia, but earlier periods in the history of Estonia and the other Baltic countries were also taught in lectures. In the early Soviet period, Estonian legal history was covered in *The History of the State and Law of the USSR*, but later, an independent compulsory module was added.

The History of the State and Law of the Estonian SSR covered Estonian legal history, as it were, from the beginning of time. One could not locate any ancient empires in the territory of Estonia. Therefore, the starting point was later, in the Middle Ages. For me, during my studies, this course was taught in the spring term of the 1984–1985 academic year by the, at that time, very young lecturer Peeter Järvelaid (b. 1957). The first lecture was about the social order of Estonians before their land was conquered in the Crusades of the 12th–13th century. This was a proper Soviet-style topic and the fact that 'prior to the conquest the Estonians did not have any state apparatus whereby the will of the ruling class would be formulated in written form as law' was also a very 'Soviet' style of speaking. After a few lectures, Järvelaid got onto the subject of the Swedish period in Estonia (1561/1629–1710) and the lectures then turned into an amazing flood of knowledge, welded together in an adventurous way. For instance, one lecture was titled 'Hugo Grotius and Old Livonia'. Hugo Grotius (1583–1645), as one of the most important authors for the foundation of modern international law, is familiar throughout Europe. 'Old Livonia' was the collective noun used for the feudal polities established after the conquest of the territories of current Estonia and Latvia during the Crusades of the 12th–13th century. This unstable confederation of feudal principalities collapsed in the Livonian War (1558–1561), destroyed by the various great powers of the era. Northern Estonian territories became a part of the kingdom of Sweden,

Southern Estonia and Northern Latvia went to Poland as Livonia and the feudal Duchy of Courland in the south of Latvia became a vassal of the Polish-Lithuanian state. In any case, it was obvious that Grotius could not have had any real connection to the Old Livonia, which had already collapsed before Grotius was born. But thanks to Järvelaid's lecture, we learned that Grotius had existed, he had become the pensionary of Rotterdam, he had written a book *De jure belli ac pacis* (On the law of war and peace) and that this book had been borrowed six times from the library of Tartu University, founded by Swedish King Gustavus Adolphus in 1632. Moreover, *De jure naturae et gentium* by Samuel Pufendorf (1632–1694) was borrowed 11 times between 1699 and 1710, when during the times of the Great Northern War the university was moved to the coastal town of Pärnu. All these data are taken from my own lecture notes. However, I cannot find anything there about the lecturer ordering or asking us to read the textbook of the history of the state and law in Estonia (Jegorov, 1981), the same author's previous study materials on the Old Livonian Diet (Jegorov, 1966), the history of Livonian and Estonian towns and town law until the Russian imperial town law reform in 1870 (Jegorov, 1980), police institutions on Estonian territory since the beginning of the 19th century until the end of the Tsarist state (Jegorov, 1972), the court institutions of the same period (Jegorov, 1978) or the developments after the 1917 February Revolution in Estonia (Jegorov, 1969). It is possible that Järvelaid did not trust our language skills—both the textbook and the study materials, published as brochures, were all in Russian. But at the same time, our compulsory readings also did not include books in Estonian on the political system in the interwar era of the Republic of Estonia (Vihalem, 1960; 1963a; 1963b; 1971), which still in the 1970s had been a part of the mandatory literature (Vihalem, 1976). The teaching of the history of the state and law of Estonian SSR in the form of this chaotic stream of knowledge, rather than according to some structured plan or accepted programme, says something not just about the lecturer but also about that time. The era of Gorbachev had already started in the Soviet Union, and even in university lectures it was possible to freely discuss the personalities and historical events that could not have been done under the previous understanding of history, directed and constrained as it was by Marxist-Leninist ideas and 'party' policies.

What we can say about the general framework of the curriculum is that its very broad remit made it possible to bring into the lectures a very diverse set of topics, but it also made it possible to exclude many others. It should also be mentioned here that in Estonia, the presence of the state security apparatus, also in academic circles, was at least after the death of Stalin never quite as heavy and nasty as, for instance, in the German Democratic Republic.

Individual strategies of survival and resistance

The first ever Estonian with a doctorate in legal history was Leo Leesment (1902–1986). His master's dissertation, defended in 1926, concerned Old Livonian legal history (Leesment, 1926), and he continued to work in the same area in his doctoral dissertation on medieval criminal law, defended in 1930 (Leesment, 1931). Nevertheless, he could not immediately become the Professor of Legal History since this position was already taken by Jüri Uluots (1890–1945). Uluots was one of the first academics employed by the University of Tartu of the Republic of Estonia; an active politician, he was involved in the reform preparations of both Estonian civil and state law. A large part of his time was devoted to building up the Estonian state and legal order, and Leesment, a docent of civil law, had taught a fair bit of legal history already before the Soviet era. In 1939, Uluots became the Prime Minister of the Republic of Estonia, making Leesment the foremost academic teaching legal history. He was also tasked with teaching the history of Roman law. The systematic course in Roman law was taught by the Professor of Roman law Ernst Ein (1898–1956) (Siimets-Gross, 2004; pp. 116 sq.). During the first Soviet year, the courses were changed around. Uluots would have had no business at the Soviet university in any case, and he succeeded in hiding himself from the Soviet occupation in June 1940 until the German occupation in July 1941. Leesment taught the history of the state and law of the USSR, using a curriculum translated from Russian (Leesment, 1940–1949, p. 56). Ein taught (general) history of the state and law (Ein, 1940), until he was dismissed from the university in early 1941. In the 1930s, Ein had clearly expressed his sympathy for the Italian Fascist regime and Mussolini. In spite of support from university leadership, the top party officials of the Estonian SSR nevertheless considered it impossible for him to continue working for a Soviet university. When the University of Tartu was reopened after the war, now again under Soviet rule, Leesment was the only one of the three former professors still in Tartu. Both Uluots and Ein had emigrated in 1944 and Uluots had died of cancer in Stockholm on January 9, 1945.

After the war, Leo Leesment was responsible for the teaching of all courses in legal history—the general history of the state and law, as well as the history of the state and law of the USSR. As a specialist editor, Leesment also participated in the translation of legal history textbooks from Russian. Kechekjan, one of the most important legal historians in the USSR, personally thanked him for his efforts and sent him a copy of his methodological instructions meant for distance education students for independent study of the general history of the state and law (Kechekjan, 1946). Similar manuals would later regularly also be published at the University of Tartu. In addition to literature translated from Russian, there were also Leesment's own lecture notes. The manuscript collections of the library of the University of Tartu hold two typewritten copies, the second one bearing a note that this is the second edition (Leesment, 1945–46; 1947). The typescript was not only meant for the lecturer himself since according to a note of the 'Tartu State University printing office' from April 9, 1947, it had been reproduced in 150 copies (Leesment, 1947, p. 42). This must have been plenty for the students of the time: in 1945, the Faculty of Law had 11 graduates, in 1946 it had 9, in 1947 only 7 and in 1948, it had none. An increase came later: there were 27 graduates in 1949 and 1950, 49 in 1951, 71 in 1952, 65 in 1953, 56 in 1954 and 52 in 1955 (Graduates, 1989, pp. 29 sq.). Looking at the source citations in Leesment's lecture notes, it is notable that in addition to Jushkov's textbook and the classics of Marxism-Leninism, he is also referring to his own earlier writings. It is possible that during the years immediately after the war, the reference works, journals, monographs and textbooks published in the Republic of Estonia in the interwar era could still be accessed by students. Later, they were for the most part destroyed and the few surviving copies locked in the special stacks of the library, where they could be read only by special permission.

Leesment's position as an academic at the Tartu State University was uncertain from the beginning. At the University of Tartu of the Republic of Estonia, he had eventually been appointed the Professor of Civil Law. During the 1940–1941 academic year of the Soviet university, he was only allowed to teach as a docent. During the German occupation, he had been Professor Extraordinarius; in September–October of 1944 he worked at the Pärnu town museum and could thereafter return to the university as a docent. He was once again professor from October 1945 until June 1946, but was then again demoted to docent when the pre-war academic degrees were re-evaluated (Leesment, 1942–48, p. 3).

Already before the opening meeting of the new collective security organisation, the United Nations, it became clear that the USSR would not be successful in bringing in every single Soviet Socialist Republic (SSR) into the United Nations with a separate and independent right to vote (Tannberg, 2015). There was therefore no reason to tolerate their autonomy any further and, following the doctrine of party centralism, Soviet ideology had to be introduced to the fullest extent even to the most recent SSRs (Tannberg, 2010). In 1946 Russia had already started a campaign against the 'formalism' and 'services rendered to bourgeois interests' that were supposedly characteristic of the creative 'intelligentsia' (Tromly, 2014, pp. 81 sq. and passim; Roberts, 2006, pp. 329 sq.). The party leadership of the Estonian SSR tried to demonstrate its loyalty to Moscow by undertaking a grandiose project to exterminate the bourgeois remnants from the Soviet Estonian society, cultural life and educational system. In summer 1949, it was the turn of the University of Tartu. By academic and party unit, meetings were held to find out and eradicate instances of so-called bourgeois nationalism (Raid, 1995, pp. 61 sq.).

Together with some other colleagues, Leesment was accused of formalism and objectivism. The course in the history of the state and law of the USSR was also supposedly out of balance, with too much focus on earlier and too little teaching in newer, Soviet legal history. The whole faculty was blamed for the fact that not a single academic had engaged in public criticism of his or her own earlier works, published before the Soviet period. The Secretary of the Tartu City Committee of the Communist Party, who participated in the meeting, classified Leesment, together with Elmar Ilus (1898–1981), the previous civil law and current Roman law professor, as those academics who did not sincerely believe in Soviet rule and Communism and had engaged with Soviet society only mechanically, seeing it as an inevitable necessity. These accusations can be taken seriously: in his lectures, Leesment indeed taught primarily earlier legal history, less the capitalist period and no socialist legal history at all. We have already mentioned that he referred his students to his earlier writings, rather than criticising them, and his teaching style focused on conveying facts was indeed formalistic and objective—which we might just as well call an attempt to preserve at least some kind of autonomy for legal history as an academic subject against the onslaught of Soviet ideology. The party meetings continued, and in 1950, both Ilus and Leesment left the university 'by their own request'. Leesment's fate turned out to be particularly harsh. In 1951, he was arrested and deported to Siberia, sentenced to 25 years in a forced labour camp and a further 5 years of exile in the same region.

After Leesment's arrest and a few intermediary teachers, the teaching of legal history was taken over by Paul Vihalem (1910–1985), who soon also became the head of the Department of the Theory and History of the State and Law. Vihalem's background was in labour law, and he had not been previously involved in legal history research or teaching in the pre-war period. In 1941–1946, Vihalem was a member of the government of Estonian SSR as a People's Commissar of Labour. At the same time, until 1950, he worked as an academic in the Faculty of Economics, which at the beginning of the Soviet era had been split off from the University of Tartu Faculty of Law and attached to the Polytechnic Institute in the Estonian capital Tallinn. During the war, Vihalem had been active in the Soviet home front as a high Soviet functionary. Contrary to many other People's Commissars from the early Soviet period, Vihalem was spared from the above-mentioned cleansing campaign against bourgeois nationalists. However, neither was he readmitted into the top ranks of Soviet functionaries in Estonia. Perhaps the fact that his brother had emigrated to Sweden held him back. However, at the University Vihalem had in certain ways a very strong position. The sources nevertheless do not confirm the claim, found in Estonian history writing (Lust, 2010, p. 851), that Vihalem had been one of the main exposers of bourgeois nationalists at the University of Tartu's Faculty of Law. Vihalem returned to the Faculty of Law only after the bourgeois nationalists had already been driven out. His doctoral dissertation, defended as a manuscript in 1952 in Moscow and titled *Bourgeois Nationalists as Forgers of the History of the Emergence of the Bourgeois Estonian State,* was written in Russian (Vihalem, 1950). The library of the University of Tartu also preserves the Estonian manuscripts of the first and second draft of this work (Vihalem, 1945; 1946a). The second draft in particular is an exceptionally thorough piece of academic work, and even at this stage it was very accurately referenced and made effective use of sources from both earlier and more recent Estonian history. It was Jüri Uluots who had come forward with a theory of some persistence of the Estonian state or the Estonian national continuity from the 13th century Crusades until the declaration of Estonian independence during the First World War. It was this theory that Vihalem now criticised, deriving from it a justification for the Estonian nationalists' collaboration with German occupation authorities, something that Uluots' original concept certainly had not included. Notably, there was only one 'bourgeois nationalist' targeted by Vihalem's criticism, namely Uluots, though having escaped from Estonia in 1944 and having passed away in 1945, Uluots was beyond being hurt by any ideological accusations. At least in his Estonian manuscripts, Vihalem does not mention any other colleague still living, much less still living in Estonia and working at the university, whose earlier views could be classified as 'forgeries of bourgeois nationalism'.

Vihalem used partially the same materials in an article published in the journal *Estonian Bolshevik* (Vihalem, 1946b). In this article, an earlier publication by Leesment concerning the models and sources of Baltic Private Law codification is also characterised as a 'forgery of history'. Nevertheless, Vihalem quoted it to prove a point about the old-fashioned character of Baltic Private Law Act, which was also the point that Leesment was making (Leesment, 1928, p. 254). The same view of the Baltic Private Law Act is also prevalent today (Luts, 2000; Luts-Sootak, 2019).

According to the reminiscences of Vihalem's junior colleague Jüri Jegorov (born 1922), who worked at the Faculty of Law from 1947, Vihalem did not participate in the university's witch hunt for 'bourgeois nationalists'. Of all the academics in the faculty, Vihalem had the longest tenure as a member of the Communist Party—he was one of the 'June Communists' who had joined the party in 1940, immediately after the occupation of Estonia by Soviet troops on June 16. Nevertheless, many of the communists who had belonged to the leadership of the Estonian SSR and the Estonian Communist (Bolshevist) Party in 1940–41 and in the immediate post-war period were persecuted and repressed in the early 1950s, including several former People's Commissars. Among other things, they were accused of bourgeois nationalism, even though it was they who had dismantled the Estonian 'bourgeois' nation state. It is possible that it was fear of greater repressions than being dismissed as the head of the Department of Soviet Law at the Polytechnic Institute and at the Section of Academy of Sciences in Tallinn that made Vihalem leave the capital in 1951 and retreat to the university town of Tartu. Jegorov claims that Vihalem was indeed scared of the party-incited witch hunt and the party activists of the time, who in the Law Faculty were concentrated in the Department of Civil Law and Process. There was also a reason to be wary of students since some of them were extremely active in the party. Several students had played an important role in bringing about Leesment's dismissal.

Lavrentiy Beria, who became the next leader of the Communist Party of the USSR after Stalin's death, planned to put in place new 'national governments' in Soviet union republics, even if they were loyal to Soviet rule (Tannberg, 2018). Beria did not get further than the planning stage, but the 'thaw', mainly associated with the name of Khruschev, had nevertheless begun in the Soviet Empire. Even earlier, in Stalin's times, students felt that the University of Tartu had been nowhere near as 'Soviet' as, for example, the Latvian State University in Riga (Vals, 1952). In his overview of the 1950 conference of the Scientific Association of Students, the acting secretary of the association's Tartu branch, physics student Jaan Einasto, criticised the ideological passivity of the Tartu students compared to their guests from Leningrad and Riga:

> Although the theoretical and ideological quality of the treatment of topics has markedly improved, we still encounter significant deficiencies. Occasionally, the treatment of the subject at hand is ideologically defective, the discourse lacks a combative, Bolshevik attitude (humanities sections). This is especially notable if one compares the presentations of Tartu students

> in the history section to those of the guests. In the case of the latter, the ideological direction and justification of the presentation are accorded much attention. [...]
>
> Comrade I. Jonane demonstrated an exemplary treatment of her topic in the presentation 'Bourgeois Nationalists—the Fiercest Enemies of the Latvian People'. Whilst Tartu student comrade E. Kask remained superficial in the treatment of the topic in her analogous presentation, comrade Jonane presented a deep analysis also of the role and impact of bourgeois nationalists in the Latvian State University, exposing the vile means by which the remnants of reactionism attempt to conceal themselves in order to continue carrying out their dirty anti-Soviet 'work'. It was also notable that the Tartu students carefully avoided criticising the academics of their own university. In the section of legal studies, for example, comrade Mölder sharply criticised objectivist and cosmopolitan errors in the central Soviet juridical literature, but tacitly bypassed the situation in our University. (Einasto 1950)

It seems that Tartu nevertheless retained an academic spirit that was different from Leningrad and Riga. A curious example of the retention of interwar era Estonian history in scholarly research and public discourse is provided, again, by Paul Vihalem. His 735-page monograph on the establishment of the Republic of Estonia and its first couple of years of existence, published in 1960, is the most voluminous work by any Soviet Estonian legal scholar (Vihalem, 1960). Vihalem furthermore published more books than any other member of the faculty in the Soviet period. Both his 1960 magnum opus and the following shorter studies bear extremely 'Soviet' titles: *The Estonian Bourgeoisie in the Service of the Imperialists*, *White Terror in Estonia*, *Elections in Bourgeois Estonia* and *The Transition of Estonian Bourgeoisie into the Service of German Fascism*. At the same time, all these books were very 'Estonian'. The fact that Vihalem was writing about the Republic of Estonia differentiated him from many other authors. While the books were written following the key dogmas of the Soviet ideology, his method was a very positivistic one, including many facts, intensive use of primary sources and appropriate quotations. At a time when ordinary scholars or common people did not have the access to literature from the time of 'Bourgeois Estonia', such books provided much information. Still in early 2019, when the Tartu Professor of Medieval History, Anti Selart, born in 1973, encountered me in the University library carrying around Vihalem's weighty monograph, he immediately said: 'That's a good book—lots of facts!' This was exactly what made Vihalem's writings valuable: a lot of facts, together with references to primary sources. A couple of years ago, Vihalem's junior colleague Jüri Jegorov told me how Vihalem and he had discussed whether to include in the book a quotation from the Baltic Entente Treaty (12.9.1934). The Baltic Entente was not a suitably 'Soviet' topic and the direct quotation from the *Estonian State Gazette* from the interwar era was an unusual thing to have. There is furthermore a clear difference between academic writings and works addressed for a broader readership. Works especially meant for a scholarly audience (Vihalem, 1960; 1961; 1963b) contained more 'forbidden' references, while a popular scientific brochure contained almost no citations at all and its bibliography only listed works published in the Soviet period (Vihalem, 1963a, passim and pp. 173 sq.). The volume *The Transition of Estonian Bourgeoisie into the Service of German Fascism* was published in two versions. The first was published by the university publishing house and was meant primarily for use inside academia (Vihalem, 1963b). The version published by a large state publishing house does not refer to the previous version and omits its references to foreign literature, although preserving the citations of primary sources (Vihalem, 1971).

The fact that Vihalem referred quite frequently to Western literature, and even Estonian émigrés living in the West, is significant in the Soviet context. All such literary and scholarly riches were locked away in the library's special stacks and it was unthinkable for an ordinary scholar to include them in footnotes. But Paul Vihalem was not an 'ordinary' Soviet scholar; he was one of about 1,000 persons in the Estonian SSR who had been awarded the Order of Lenin. In Tartu humanities and social sciences, he was the only one to have received such a high Soviet decoration. He therefore had more freedom of speech than other people, even other professors.

It is not easy to sum up and evaluate Vihalem's activities. In an Estonian context, he was certainly a hardcore Communist. But at the same time, he was an Estonian patriot and did a lot for the research of Estonian history, also by supervising several candidate dissertations in the legal and political history of Estonia: on the emancipation of Estonian peasants from serfdom and the development of the institutions of self-government in the countryside in the 19th century (Traat, 1955), on the relations between the state and the church in the interwar period (Sillaste, 1974), on the foreign relations of the Republic of Estonia in the same period (Jaanson, 1975) and on the rise of the authoritarian regime in Estonia in the 1930s (Kiris, 1972). I am not sure the three last topics would have been 'dissertable', to use a Soviet expression, if their supervisor had not been the June Communist and Order of Lenin laureate Paul Vihalem. Dissertations about the constitution of Estonian SSR (Kärtner, 1954) and the transition of state power in the first Soviet year in Estonia (Truuväli, 1966) would, on the other hand, have been 'dissertable' even with some other supervisor.

In 1956, after Stalin's death, Leesment was freed from the prison camp and could return to Tartu. For about a year, he found it impossible to find work and made a living as a translator, translating almost anything, including reports of the state of the canteen, summaries of student dissertations and a speech by the rector of the university (Rand, 2003, p. 120). After that, he was able to find employment only in the university library, initially merely as a bibliographer, but from 1957 onward as the head of the library's manuscripts and rare books department. He held onto this job until he retired in 1965, but spent even later much time with his colleagues in the library, and has been remembered by them as a highly erudite and very helpful old gentleman. The later Professor of General History, Helmut Piirimäe (1936–2017) recalled his contacts with Leesment that had already begun in Piirimäe's student years and continued until the end of Leesment's life:

> In conversations with the revered scholar who had returned from the Siberian prison camp, I was struck by his astonishing optimism. He did talk about the horrors of the prison camp, but his main emphasis was on how wonderful the people had been who he had met there, and especially on which languages he was able to learn. As I remember, one of them was Dutch. (Piirimäe, 2007, p. 138)

Chiefly thanks to being invited by Jüri Jegorov, Leesment lectured on some topics in general and on the Soviet the history of state and law before his retirement and became a regular participant in the university's teaching activities after his retirement. The Soviet 'thaw' was not the only reason—every Soviet pensioner enjoyed the right to work for two months every year with full salary and pension. Leesment used this right to teach at the university. In addition to his activities in legal history, he helped to establish the very strong and later famous circle in Oriental studies and participated actively in the equally famous research in Scandinavian history. Leesment had always been interested in foreign languages, knew many of them and had already before the war written several articles on Swedish, Austrian and even Chinese law.

From the 1960s onwards, Leesment published a large number of articles on a great variety of topics from a wide range of different fields. His last longer piece of work was the manuscript of a textbook in the history of Baltic state and law (Leesment, 1949). The numerous articles published after his return from Siberia were generally short. However, it is impossible to agree with the claim that in these writings, Leesment was satisfied with 'merely revisiting old topics' (Järvelaid, 1992, p. 153). On the contrary, for the most part Leesment tended to take up questions that he had not given a more detailed treatment in his earlier work. Often, his writings were inspired by some curious fact, interesting source or association. They made their way to Estonian lawyers through the only law journal of the Soviet era, 'Soviet Law' (*Nõukogude Õigus*) published 1969–1989 six times a year. This journal included a separate section, 'A glance at history', that very often contained Leesment's articles. In the early 1950s they would have doubtlessly be branded as 'formalism' and 'objectivism', but in the 1970s and 1980s, scholarship was freer even in the Soviet Union and the Communist Party and state security much more indifferent towards the spoken and written word. Leesment's short articles had an even more far-reaching role in forming the field of knowledge about legal history in Estonia. Their number was remarkable. According to a list compiled by himself, he had published 215 articles between his return from Siberia in 1956 and June 1981 (Leesment, 1981); and from the following period, I found 9 more in the Estonian article database. This would of course need more thorough research, but on first sight it would seem that, given the number of his publications, Leesment was the most prolific author in the history of Estonian legal scholarship—even before the period 1956 to 1981, he managed to publish more than a hundred publications.

I have several times mentioned Jüri Jegorov, who taught at the University of Tartu a total of a hundred academic terms from 1947 to 1996. In 2019, he turned 97, and for his age, he is in an extraordinarily good shape, both mentally and physically. Thanks to what he remembers, the events that he can draw attention to and the background processes that he can explain, we have begun to understand Soviet era academic and university life so much better. Born in 1922, he graduated from high school in the summer of 1941 and was immediately conscripted into the Red Army. He was wounded at the front at Leningrad and was therefore given an opportunity to study. His first choice was the Faculty of Foreign Languages at the Leningrad State University, but he left it after a few months and continued his studies at the Higher School of Economics. After the Atlantic Charter was agreed between the United Kingdom and the United States in January 1941, the USSR began its own preparations for the new United Nations (UN). As already said, Stalin wanted to secure as many votes as possible at the UN General Assembly and therefore planned to include in the organisation either all or at least more developed republics of the Soviet Union, each with a separate vote (Russell, 1958, pp. 359, 361 sq., 433 sq., 533 sq., 596 sq.). This meant that a few diplomats from each republic needed to be trained for this purpose. Jegorov happened to be one of the two Estonians who were appointed to study at the Higher School of Diplomacy by the Ministry of Foreign Affairs of USSR. Jegorov studied there during the years 1942–1946, when the teaching staff at this academy had been recruited to be as strong as it could still possibly be after the purges that had been carried out in the Soviet Union of the 'intelligentsia' and the academic elites in the 1930s. After Stalin's plan of the broadest possible takeover of the UN had failed, the newly educated diplomats were redirected to be employed in the regular foreign service. For family reasons, Jegorov nevertheless wanted to return to Estonia. Both his father and mother were deaf and needed his help. His father, Andrei Jegorov (1878–1954), was an artist who had studied in St Petersburg under Ilya Repin and other famous Russian painters; before the war he had mingled with the political elites of the Republic of Estonia and foreign diplomats. Jüri Jegorov's sister had married a nuclear physicist and was therefore only allowed to live in a closed Russian military city. Thanks to Jegorov's good relations with Juhan Vaabel (1899–1971), a scholar of financial law and a member of the Academy of Sciences of the Estonian SSR, as well as thanks to the urgent plea by the rector of the University of Tartu stating that the university desperately needed a teacher of international law, Jegorov became an academic at Tartu State University. The rector had been somewhat disingenuous: the actual need for an international law scholar was hardly great. Roughly at the same time, another academic was appointed in the same field: Abner Uustal (1915–1985), who was later promoted to professor of the same subject (Mälksoo, 2006, pp. 483 sq.).

Jegorov with his training as a diplomat, something that was extremely rare among Estonians, was from the beginning left somewhat aside and he also himself preferred to keep away from the limelight. His views of the lectures of the colleagues who had been classified as bourgeois nationalists were rather complimentary and supportive of the denounced academics. Instead, he criticised 'socially active' students (i.e., those active in the party), who had supposedly busied themselves 'with their own' things instead of paying attention in the political education classes (Raid, 1995, pp. 162 sq.), and a colleague who had levelled accusations against others (Lust, 2010, p. 850).

During his first years of working in Tartu, Jegorov taught the 'History of International Relations' course not just to the students in the Faculty of Law but also to history students. The meticulous lecture notes of Olaf-Mihkel Klaassen (1929–2012), later the Professor of Oriental History at Tartu, give us an insight into the content of Jegorov's lectures (Jegorov, 1948–49). At the same time, Jegorov cooperated closely with the staff of the Faculty of Medicine. The doctors had been accused of lacking political education and of too little dissemination of party ideology. For that reason, Jegorov periodically gave lectures to the members of the Faculty of Medicine, but he says he did it in a quiet voice so as not to wake them: the doctors worked hard and were all permanently tired.

In 1950 Jegorov defended in Moscow his candidate dissertation in law. The topic was very 'Soviet' both in content and appearance, but the sources that he used were very 'Baltic'. The topic was *The 'Neutrality' of the Scandinavian and Baltic Countries—as one of the means of unleashing World War II and facilitating German aggression (based on materials from the pre-war and wartime)* (Jegorov, 1949). Somewhat later, the question arose whether Jegorov was qualified to work at the Faculty of Law, since 'he does not possess a specific qualification in law' (Raid, 1995, p. 192). As already said, Jegorov nevertheless continued up until the 1990s. From 1961, he was docent in the History of the State and Law. The fire that engulfed the main building of the university in December 1965 also destroyed the draft and materials of Jegorov's doctoral dissertation. He never fully recovered from this setback and his doctorate remained unfinished.

In order to survive in the Soviet system and to have as little as possible to do with the party policy and the so-called 'social assignments', Jegorov developed some of his own strategies. The Law Faculty was in the main building of the university, where the rectorate and the Communist Party also had their offices. Jegorov avoided the main building as much as possible. For this purpose, he had a workplace in the so-called permanent agitation point for the elections of Soviets, far away from the Law Faculty, in the basement of the Life Sciences building. Jegorov was the young colleague with whom Vihalem discussed the presentation of the Baltic Entente in his book. In Jegorov's own publications, one can also find long lists of so-called 'bourgeois authors' who had allegedly 'falsified' history. But it was also possible to read these lists as lists of recommended readings. Up until the second half of the 1980s, Jegorov ordered his students to use old legal history textbooks that had been translated into Estonian immediately after the war—at the time rare even in libraries, not to mention bookshops. The authors—Stepan Kechekjan (1890–1967) and Ivan Pereterski (1889–1965)—had received their education and become active as scholars already during the last years of the Tsarist state, when Russian legal scholarship was at the peak of its 'Western' orientation. Kechekjan's master's dissertation from 1914 had been on the ethical worldview of Baruch Spinoza. Pereterski was the best Soviet specialist on Roman law and international private law; he had translated some parts of Justinian's *Digest* into Russian. Their textbooks, translated into Estonian immediately after the war, had been edited by doctors and professors of law from the time of Estonian independence, namely Leesment and Ilus. We therefore see how Jegorov kept the best textbooks that were available in Estonian in the Soviet times in teaching use for a whole 50 years, approximately the entire Soviet time. And another small thing. One arbitrarily picked excerpt from the big Codification of the Baltic Private Law Act from 1864 lacked any relevant connection to the subject of town administration, but one can find it as an appendix to Jegorov's compendium on the Old Livonian Diet (Jegorov, 1966, appendix I). The private law was a matter of 'bourgeois' society and therefore had to be covered under the protective coat of medieval institutions.

It would be possible to continue the list of small tricks employed by Jegorov in his publication and teaching strategies. The older generation of Estonian lawyers still alive can tell many anecdotes about him and the things he had said, but this should suffice for the purposes of this article. Jegorov managed to survive the Soviet period without engaging in too much cooperation with the Communist Party and other Soviet institutions. In comparison to many others of his contemporary colleagues, his contribution to the 'party-oriented transformation' of the study of law was very modest indeed.

Concluding remarks

This article is the first attempt to present an overview of the practice of teaching and research in legal history in the Estonian Soviet Socialist Republic (1940–41 and 1944–91). I have particularly focused on the so-called covert resistance to Soviet regime and ideology. It appears that one of the most significant expressions of this resistance was the authors' practice of including in their publications references to primary sources as well as to publications by Western authors and Estonian emigrants. Unfortunately, this form of covert resistance had its inherent limitations: the readers were for the most part not clever enough to discover all these secret signs, and the literature that was criticised—but nevertheless quoted—was mostly not, or at least not freely, available in Soviet Estonia. It was not only students who failed to pick up such hints, but also younger academics who did not have personal memories of the interwar-era Republic of Estonia.

Vihalem published himself and also supervised several candidate dissertations by lawyers and historians on Estonian history. Leesment encouraged in particular Järvelaid, who was the Professor of Estonian Legal History at the University of Tartu in 1992–1997. After Järvelaid left Tartu, the department lacked a professor for a few years until I had the honour of being appointed the Professor of Legal History in 2003. Since then, legal historians in Tartu have developed a particularly warm and friendly relationship with Jegorov, who has shared with us his memories and observations of the Soviet era. He does not want to publish memoirs, since he is afraid of accidentally hurting someone, and says that the Soviet period had already done enough of that in Estonian history.

Finally, I wish to thank the historian of science Erki Tammiksaar (b. 1969), who kindly allowed me to read his still unpublished manuscript on the history of the University of Tartu in the last 100 years. In this way, it was possible to come across a number of sources that had not been used in previous research.

References

Duve, T. (2018) 'Global Legal History: A Methodological Approach', in *Oxford Handbooks Online*. www.oxfordhandbooks.com (accessed 9.1.2020). DOI: 10.2139/ssrn.2781104.

Ein, E. (1940) *Riigi ja õiguse ajalugu: loengud Tartu Riiklikus Ülikoolis. Üliõpilaskonspekt E. Eini loengute järgi (History of State and Law: Lectures at Tartu State University. Notes by an anonymous student following the lectures of E. Ein; in Estonian), Tartu: Tartu University Library, collection of manuscripts*, stock 55 list 2 unit 197.

Einasto, J. (1950) 'Kogemustest tuleb õppida' (One should learn from experience), *Tartu Riiklik Ülikool*, April 14, 13, 1.

Chernilovski, Z. M. (ed) (1947) *Всеобщая история государства и права. Часть III: От английской революции до Великой Октябрьской революции (General history of the state and law. Part III: From the Glorious Revolution until the Great October Revolution)*, Moscow: Juridicheskoje Izdatel'stvo Ministerstva Justitsij SSSR.

Chernilovski, Z. M. (1983) *Всеобщая история государства и права (История государства и права зарубежных стран) (The general history of the state and law (History of the state and law of foreign countries))*, 2. ed., Moscow: Vyschaja Skhola.

Glenn, H. P. (2014) *Legal Traditions of the World: Sustainable Diversity in Law*, 5. ed., Oxford: Oxford University Press. DOI: 10.1093/he/9780199669837.001.0001.

Graduates (1989) *Tartu ülikooli õigusteaduskonna lõpetanute ja õigusteadust õpetanute nimekiri 1919–1989 (The list of graduates and teachers of the Law Faculty of University of Tartu, 1919–1989)*, Tartu: Tartu Ülikool, Eesti Akadeemiline Õigusteaduse Selts.

Gurvich, G. S. and Chernilovski, Z. M. (eds) (1947) *Всеобщая история государства и права. Часть IV: Новейшее время (1917–1947) (The general history of the state and law. Part IV: The most recent times (1917–1947))*, Moscow: Juridicheskoje Izdatel'stvo Ministerstva Justitsij SSSR.

Ibius, O. (1951) *Õppetöö parteilisus nõukogude õigusteaduse õpetamisel. Van.-õp. Otu Ibiuse ettakenne TRÜ õigusteaduskonna õppejõudude koosolekul 1. juunil 1951* (The party line in the teaching of Soviet jurisprudence. A speech by senior teacher Otu Ibius at the meeting of the teaching staff of the Law Faculty of TSU on June 1, 1951), Tartu: Tartu University Library, collection of manuscripts, stock 127 unit 189.

Jaanson, K. (1975) *Kodanliku Eesti ja Skandinaaviamaade suhted aastail 1917–1925 (The Relations between Bourgeois Estonia and the Scandinavian Countries in 1917–1925)*, manuscript in the Tartu University library, Collection of Dissertations, Tartu: Tartu Riiklik Ülikool.

Jegorov, J. (1948–49) *Rahvusvaheliste suhete ajalugu: loengud Tartu ülikoolis (The history of international relations: lectures at University of Tartu)*, notes by law student Olaf-Mihkel Klaassen, Tartu: Tartu University Library, Collection of Manuscripts, stock 99 unit 26.

Jegorov, J. (1949) *«Нейтралитет» скандинавских и прибалтийских стран—как одно из средств развязывания Второй мировой войны и содействия германской агрессии (по материалам предвоенного и военного времени) (The 'Neutrality' of the Scandinavian and Baltic Countries—as one of the means of unleashing World War II and facilitating German aggression (based on materials from the pre-war and wartime))*, autoreferat of Candidate dissertation, Tartu: Ministry of Higher Education of the USSR, Tartu State University.

Jegorov, J. (1959) *Riigi ja õiguse ajalugu. 1. osa: Kapitalismi ajajärk (The history of the state and law. Part 1: The period of capitalism)*, Tartu: Tartu Riiklik Ülikool.

Jegorov, J. (1960) *Riigi ja õiguse ajalugu. 4. osa (The history of the state and law. Part 4)*, Tartu: Tartu Riiklik Ülikool.

Jegorov, J. (1961) *Riigi ja õiguse ajalugu. 2. osa: Kapitalismi ajajärk (The history of the state and law. Part 2: The period of capitalism)*, Tartu: Tartu Riiklik Ülikool.

Jegorov, J. (1966) *Вопросы истории государства и права Эстонской ССР до октябрской революции: Лифляндский ландтаг (Questions of the history of the state and law of the Estonian SSR: The Livonian Diet)*, Tartu: Tartu Riiklik Ülikool.

Jegorov, J. (1969) *Вопросы истории государства и права Эстонской ССР до октябрской революции. II (Questions of the history of the state and law of the Estonian SSR. Vol. II)*, Tartu: Tartu Riiklik Ülikool.

Jegorov, J. (1972) *Вопросы истории государства и права Эстонской ССР до октябрской революции. III: Полицейские органы в Эстонии в XIX столети - октябрь 1917 (Questions of the history of the state and law of the Estonian SSR. III: Institutions of police in Estonia in the 19th century—October 1917)*, Tartu: Tartu Riiklik Ülikool.

Jegorov, J. (1978) *Вопросы истории государства и права Эстонской ССР до октябрской революции. IV: Судебные органы в Эстонии в XIX столети - октябрь 1917 (Questions of the history of the state and law of the Estonian SSR. IV: Institutions of justice in Estonia in 19th Century—October 1917)*, Tartu: Tartu Riiklik Ülikool.

Jegorov, J. (1980) *Вопросы истории государства и права Эстонской ССР до октябрской революции. V*: Городское управление в Лифляндии и Эстляндии до применения буржуазной городской реформы 1870 г. (*Questions of the history of the state and law of the Estonian SSR. V:* , Tartu: Tartu Riiklik Ülikool.

Jegorov, J. (1981) *История государства и права Эстонской ССР. Дооктябрский период (XIII век—окт. 1917 г.) (The history of the state and law of the Estonian SSR. The pre-October period (13th century—October 1917)*, Tallinn: Valgus.

Juškov, S. V. (1946) *NSVL riigi ja õiguse ajalugu. 1. osa 1. vihik: Vanimast ajast kuni Peeter Suureni (The history of the state and law of the Union of SSR. Part 1, issue 1: From the oldest time until Peter the Great)*, Tartu: Teaduslik Kirjastus.

Järvelaid, P. (1992) 'Leo Leesment (1902–1986)—90', *Eesti Jurist*, *2*, 152–153.

Kechekjan, S. F. (1946) Letter to Leo Leesment, Moscow, 24.6.1946 (in Russian), Tartu: Tartu University Library, Collection of Manuscripts, stock 93 unit 141.

Ketšekjan, S. F. (1946) *Üldine riigi ja õiguse ajalugu I: Vanaaeg, I vihik: Vana-Ida ja Vana-Kreeka (General history of state and law I: The ancient times, I issue: Ancient Orient and Ancient Greece)*, Tartu: Teaduslik Kirjastus.

Kiris, A. (1972) *'Põhiseaduse kriis' ja täidesaatva võimu tugevdamine kodanliku Eesti 1933. aasta konstitutsioonis (The 'Constitutional Crisis' and the Strengthening of the Executive Branch in the 1933 Constitution of Bourgeois Estonia)*, manuscript in the Tartu University library, Collection of Dissertations, Tartu: Tartu Riiklik Ülikool.

Kärtner, H. (1954) *Eesti NSV konstitutsiooni areng (The development of the Constitution of the Estonian SSR)*, manuscript in the Tartu University library, Collection of Dissertations, Tartu: Tartu Riiklik Ülikool.

Leesment, L. (1926) *Der Livländische Rechtsspiegel und seine Abweichungen vom Sachsenspiegel*, Tartu: Tartu Ülikool, manuscript in the Tartu University Library, Collection of Dissertations,.

Leesment, L. (1928) 'Märkmeid Balti Eraõiguse allikaist (Notes on the sources of Baltic Private Law Act)', *Õigus*, 8, 254–258.

Leesment, L. (1931) *Die Verbrechen des Diebstahls und des Raubes nach den Rechten Livlands im Mittelalter*, Tartu: K. Mattiesens Buchdruckerei.

Leesment, L. (1940–49) *NSVL rahvaste riigi ja õiguse ajalugu. Loengud Tartu ülikoolis koos peetud loengute tunnikavade ja osavõtjate nimekirjadega (The history of the state and law of the peoples of the USSR. Lectures with time schedules and lists of participants; in Estonian)*, October 1, 1940–1949, Tartu: Tartu University Library, Collection of Manuscripts, stock 93 unit 99.

Leesment, L. (1942–48) *Lisa 1937 Curriculum Vitae'le (Appendix to the Curriculum Vitae from 1937)*, Tartu: Tartu University Library, Collection of Manuscripts, stock 93 unit 1.

Leesment, L. (1945–46) *NSVL riigi ja õiguse ajalugu. Loengute konspekt (The history of the state and law of the USSR. Lectures)*, Tartu: Tartu University Library, Collection of Manuscripts, stock 93 unit 100.

Leesment, L. (1947) *NSVL riigi ja õiguse ajalugu. Loengute konspekt. II väljaanne (The history of the state and law of the USSR. Lectures. 2nd edition)*, Tartu: Tartu University Library, Collection of Manuscripts, stock 93 unit 101.

Leesment, L. (1949) *Materjale Baltimaade riigi ja õiguse ajaloole (Lühike Eesti riigi ja õiguse ajalugu) (Materials to the history of the state and law of the Baltic countries (A short history of the Estonian state and law))*, Tartu: Tartu University Library, Collection of Manuscripts, stock 93 unit 58.

Leesment, L. (1981) *Leo Leesmenti tööde nimestik (The list of works of Leo Leesment)*, 19. June 1981, Tartu: Tartu University Library, Collection of Manuscripts, stock 93 unit 46.

Lust, K. (2010) '"Terava kriitika ja enesekriitika korras...". Allumisest ja vastupanust Tartu ülikooli sovietiseerimisele õigusteaduskonna näitel (1944–1953) ('As rigorous criticism and self-criticism...'. On the subjugation and resistance to the Sovietisation of Tartu University using the example of the Faculty of Law (1944–1953))', *Akadeemia*, 10, 841–875.

Luts, M. (2000) 'Private Law of the Baltic Provinces as a Patriotic Act', *Juridica International: Law Review of Tartu University*, vol. *V*, 157–167.

Luts-Sootak, M. (2019) 'Zur Verortung des Baltischen Privatrechts (1864/65) unter den europäischen Privatrechtskodifikationen', in Hamza, G., Hlavačka, M. and Takii, K. (eds) *Rechtstransfer in der Geschichte. Internationale Festschrift für Wilhelm Brauneder zum 75. Geburtstag*, Berlin: Peter Lang 2019, 219–243.

Mälksoo, L. (2006) 'The Science of International Law and the Concept of Politics: the Arguments and Lives of the International Law Professors at the University of Dorpat/Iurþev/Tartu 1855–1985', *The British Year Book of International Law 2005*, Oxford: Clarendon Press 2006, 383–501. DOI: 10.1093/bybil/76.1.383.

Pereterski, I. S. (1946) *Üldine riigi ja õiguse ajalugu I: Vanaaeg, II vihik: Vana-Rooma (The general history of state and law I: Ancient times, II issue: Ancient Rome)*, Tartu: Teaduslik Kirjastus.

Piirimäe, H. (2007) 'Leo Leesment—Tartu Ülikooli õigusteaduse professor ja orientalist (Leo Leesment—Professor of Jurisprudence and the orientalist at Tartu University)', *Tuna*, no. 2, 137–138.

Raid, L. (1995) *Vaevatee. Tartu Ülikool kommunistlikus parteipoliitikas aastail 1940–1952* (The way of pain. University of Tartu in the policy of the Communist Party in the years 1940–1952), Tartu: Tartu Ülikooli Kirjastus.

Rand, M. (2003) 'Leo Leesment 100', *Tartu Ülikooli Raamatukogu aastaraamat 2002*, Tartu: Tartu Ülikooli Raamatukogu, 120–121.

Roberts, G. (2006) *Stalin's Wars: From World War to Cold War, 1939–1953*, New Haven, London: Yale University Press.

Russell, R.B. (1958) *A History of the United Nations Charter: The Role of the United States 1940–1945*, Washington: The Brookings Institution.

Siimets-Gross, H. (2004) 'Leo Leesment ja Rooma õigus (Leo Leesment and Roman law; with German summary 'Leo Leesment und römische Recht', 124–125)', *Annales Litterarum Societatis Estonicae 2002*, Tartu: Õpetatud Eesti Selts, 114–125.

Sillaste, H. (1974) *Luteri usu kiriku ja riigi vahekorra õiguslik reguleerimine kodanlikus Eestis (The Legal Regulation of the Relationship between the Lutheran Church and the State in Bourgeois Estonia)*, manuscript in the Tartu University library, Collection of Dissertations, co-supervisor Lembit Raid, Tartu: Tartu Riiklik Ülikool.

Tannberg, T. (2010) *Политика Москвы в республиках Балтии в послевоенные годы (1944–1956): Иследования и документы (The politics of Moscow in the Baltic Republic in the years after the war (1944–1956): Studies and documents)*, Moscow: Rosspen.

Tannberg, T. (2015) 'The First Diplomats of Soviet Estonia on the Eve of the Cold War: The Creation of the Estonian SSR People's Commissariat for Foreign Affairs in 1944', in Tannberg, T. (ed) *Behind the Iron Curtain: Soviet Estonia in the Era of the Cold War*, Frankfurt am Main: Peter Lang, 15–34. DOI: 10.3726/978-3-653-06082-9/4.

Tannberg, T. (2018) 'After Stalin: The Kremlin's "New Nationalities Policy" and Estonia in 1953', in Fleischman, L. and Weiner, A. (eds.) *War, Revolution and Governance. The Baltic Countries in the Twentieth Century*, Boston: Academic Studies Press, 207–238. DOI: 10.1515/9781618116215-012.

Traat, A. (1955) *Talurahva õiguslik olukord Liivimaal feodalismi lagunemise perioodil (The Legal Situation of the Peasantry in Livonia during the Period of the Disintegration of Feudalism)*, Tartu: Tartu Riiklik Ülikool, manuscript in the Tartu University library, Collection of Dissertations.

Tromly, B. (2014) *Making the Soviet Intelligentsia: Universities and Intellectual Life Under Stalin and Khrushchev*, Cambridge: Cambridge University Press. DOI: 10. 1017/CBO9781139381239.

Truuväli, E.-J. (1966) *Kodanliku riigiaparaadi purustamine ning sotsialistliku riigiaparaadi loomine Eestis 1940/1941.a. (The Demolition of the Bourgeois State Apparatus and the Creation of the Socialist State Apparatus in Estonia in 1940/1941)*, Tartu: Tartu Riiklik Ülikoo, manuscript in the Tartu University library, Collection of Dissertations.

Vals, H. (1952) 'Vennasülikooli külastamas (Visiting the sister university)', *Tartu Riiklik Ülikool*, May 31st, 18, 1.

Vihalem, P. (1945) *Eesti kodanliku õigusteaduse reaktsioonilisest ja natsionalistlikust ilmest. Teine mustand (On the reactionary and nationalistic face of Estonian bourgeois legal scholarship)*, December 1945, Tallinn: manuscript in Tartu University Library, Collection of Manuscripts, signature Mscr. 1466.

Vihalem, P. (1946a) *Eesti kodanliku õigusteaduse reaktsioonilisest ja natsionalistlikust ilmest. Teine mustand (On the reactionary and nationalistic face of Estonian bourgeois legal scholarship)*, June 1946, Tallinn: manuscript in Tartu University Library, Collection of Manuscripts, signature Mscr. 1467.

Vihalem, P. (1946b) 'Kuidas Jüri Uluots ja teised kodanlikud natsionalistid võltsisid eesti rahva ajalugu (How Jüri Uluots and the other bourgeois nationalists falsified the history of Estonian people)', *Eesti Bolševik*, 1, 6–16.

Vihalem, P. (1950) *Буржуазные националисты как фальсификаторы истории возникновения буржуазного эстонского государства (Bourgeois Nationalists as Falsifiers of the History of the Emergence of the Bourgeois Estonian State)*, Moscow: Institute of Law by USSR Academy of Sciences.

Vihalem, P. (1960) *Eesti kodanlus imperialistide teenistuses (1917–1920) (The Estonian Bourgeoisie in the Service of the Imperialists (1917–1920))*, Tallinn: Eesti Riiklik Kirjastus.

Vihalem, P. (1961) *Valge terror Eestis 1918–19 (White Terror in Estonia 1918–19)*, Tartu: Tartu Riiklik Ülikool.

Vihalem, P. (1963a) *Valimised kodanlikus Eestis (Elections in Bourgeois Estonia)*, 1963, Tallinn: Eesti Riiklik Kirjastus.

Vihalem, P. (1963b) *Eesti kodanluse üleminek saksa fašismi teenistusse (The Transition of Estonian Bourgeoisie into the Service of German Fascism)*, Tartu: Tartu Riiklik Ülikool.

Vihalem, P. (1971) *Eesti kodanluse üleminek saksa fašismi teenistusse (The Transition of Estonian Bourgeoisie into the Service of German Fascism)*, Tallinn: Eesti Raamat.

Vihalem, P. (1976) *Tööjuhend õigusteaduskonna III kursuse kaugõppijatele Eesti NSV riigi ja õiguse ajaloo õppimiseks 1976/77 ja 1977/78. õppeaastateks (Guidelines for distance learning of the History of the State and Law of Estonian SSR for year three students at the Law Faculty in the academic years 1976/77 and 1977/78)*, Tartu: Tartu Riiklik Ülikool.

5 The Western legal tradition and Soviet Russia

The genesis of H. J. Berman's *Law and Revolution*

Adolfo Giuliani

Introduction

The Western legal tradition (henceforth WLT), a central presence in legal historiography following the immensely popular two volumes published by the Harvard legal historian Harold J. Berman *Law and Revolution I: The Formation of the Western Legal Tradition* (1983) and *Law and Revolution II: The Impact of the Protestant Reformations on the Western Legal Tradition* (2003), is in search of a precise definition.

This chapter traces the origin of this idea to the Cold War era. It shows that it was conceived by Berman in his 1950 book on *Justice in Russia*, a work in which he wanted to explain to a Western audience what lay beyond the Iron Curtain. To this purpose, he constructed an account in which he placed the West and Soviet Russia in opposition and concluded that they were made of the features that were missing in each other. A chapter in that book is the blueprint for his two well-known volumes on *Law and Revolution* published in 1983 and 2003 (and for a third volume left unfinished).

The WLT grew from another legacy received from the Cold War era: human rights history. Recent scholarship tells us that this theme attracted scholarly attention beginning from the 1970s following contemporary concerns with human rights in Eastern European countries. This chapter shows how this theme was absorbed by WLT by hijacking a core component of continental legal science (*subjectives Recht*), then re-engineered by political theorists into the major identitary element of the WLT in an eternity history rooted in medieval canon law.

Harold J. Berman and the construction of the Western legal tradition

When legal scholars speak of the WLT, we swiftly understand what they mean. This expression belongs to common parlance and is a useful and quick shorthand to summarise a host of ideas immediately labelled with a precise identity. It only works, however, at a general level. As soon as we begin to see it more closely and wonder for instance about its content and geographic boundaries, we realise we are facing difficult questions, and we soon understand that this successful phrase is relying more on an instinctive or even emotional appeal than on a rational basis.

The only way to dispel the uncertainty over the WLT is to analyse it historically and tackle the questions which a historian would typically ask: where does this expression come from, who introduced it, for what purposes, who were her audience, and what did she want to do by using this expression? These are the questions this chapter aims to answer. This is not difficult, as the author who introduced this expression and, by placing it at the heart of one of the most successful legal-historical accounts published in the 20th century, gave it the broadest dissemination, is well known: the American legal historian Harold J. Berman (1918–2007). Berman offered a grandiose account of the growth of a WLT in his two monumental volumes, *Law and Revolution I: The Formation of the Western Legal Tradition* (1983) and *Law and Revolution II: The Impact of the Protestant Reformations on the Western Legal Tradition* (2003). Less known is the overall project, left unfinished, and even less its original purpose. In spite of the attention it attracted, it has been left unnoticed that this overwhelming project was first conceived as part of his book *Justice in Russia: An Interpretation of Soviet Law*, published in 1950.

This chapter goes back to this project's formative stage, offering an essay in the history of legal history. At its heart is a question about the historical consciousness of legal history because one of the features of this discipline is that of having forgotten how deeply the categories with which legal historians think and write about the legal past are embedded in ideas rooted in the 20th century.

My purpose in what follows will be to explain the rise of the WLT focusing on three points: (1) to show how Berman's idea of a WLT arises from his 1950 book *Justice in Russia* and that the idea is a mirror-image of another projection: the legal tradition of Soviet Russia; (2) to show the philosophical premise upon which his historical project is based, to be found in his university mentor Eugen Rosenstock-Huessy; and (3) to demonstrate the question of human rights history is the main building block of the WLT and, further, that in building that account, the idea of the 'Eastern tradition' without human rights served as a convenient context.

Harold J. Berman's *Justice in Russia* (1950)

The American legal historian Harold J. Berman is unquestionably one of the major contributors to 20th century legal history. His two massive volumes, *Law and Revolution I* (1983) and *Law and Revolution II* (2003), redirected this discipline with his compelling thesis about legal evolution. He suggested that "the Western legal tradition was born out of a 'revolution' and thereafter, during the course of many centuries, has been periodically interrupted and transformed by revolutions" (Berman, 1983, p. 1).

This thesis is fleshed out in a rich account branched out in many fields and developed in significant detail through a long temporal arch. Its influence has been considerable; it has received appraisals and fostered countless debates (Duve, 2013). It is true that matters of detail have attracted the attention of his critics, but its chief contribution is not in particular aspects of the many fields touched upon, mostly drawn from secondary sources, but in the broad evolutionary hypothesis that as a vestment clothes his narrative. The powerful message brought forward by his evolutionary account is an auto-representation of the Western identity.

We would not understand his project, however, without knowing its origin. It was in fact conceived in his book *Justice in Russia* (1950) and presented in a chapter (Ch. 6: 'The Western Legal Tradition') in which we find the major thesis of a legal evolution through successive revolutions. This is the blueprint of his lifelong project, which he then developed in *Law and Revolution I* (Berman, 1983) focused on the Papal Revolution; then carried forward in his *Law and Revolution II* (Berman, 2003) on the German and English Revolution; and was meant to be continued, as we learn from John Witte, in a further volume on the American, French and Russian revolutions, which, however, remained unfinished as a result of his untimely death (Witte, 2014, p. 146). The overall project is summarised in the following table that ends the chapter (Berman, 1950", p. 121).

Berman's *Justice in Russia: An Interpretation of Soviet Law* (1st ed. 1950; 2nd ed. 1963: *Justice in USSR: An Interpretation of Soviet Law*) was written to offer a key to make sense of Soviet Russia. During the Iron Curtain era, Soviet Russia was beyond the reach of Westerners: mysterious, distant as an ancient civilisation, and felt to be in dramatic opposition to the West. More than a doctrinal analysis of the laws and institutions of the Soviet system, Berman's purpose was to illustrate Russian life as

Year	*Revolution*	*Law movement*	*Constitutional principles*	*Private-law contributions*
1075	Papal revolution	Renovation of Roman and Canon law	Visible, hierarchical, legal church; separation of church and state.	Principles of Reason, Conscience, and Precedents.
1517	German reformation	Reception of Roman law	Absolute monarchy: secular civil service (Bureaucratic, Rational State).	Freedom of contract, freedom of wills; conceptualist law
1640	English Revolution	Restoration of Common law	Parliamentary system; landed aristocracy; judiciary independent of politics.	Family settlements; feudal property without feudalism; traditionalist law.
1789	French Revolution	Napoleonic codes	Individualist democracy; separation of powers; government by public opinion.	Absolute private property conceived in contractual terms; contractualist law.

Figure 5.1 The Western legal tradition.

reflected in legal materials. The work was about 'justice' in Russia, purposefully addressed to explaining the sense of right and wrong and the broad principles that structured Soviet society.

If the purpose is to understand Soviet life, Berman tells us, we need legal history. It would be misleading, he continues, to focus on socialist theory only: we should turn to the intellectual forces that, more powerfully than theories, shape human societies, their laws and institutions. The key to explain that legal world is in a historical account of the legal past. He also adds that Soviet legal scholars have been conscious of their Russian heritage: they were aware not only of Marx and Engels, Lenin and Stalin, but for the purposes of continuity and stability they also turned to pre-Revolutionary Russia (Berman, 1950, Ch. 4, *Marxism and the Russian Heritage*). Soviet leaders therefore broadened legal education to include Russian legal history and Latin to understand Roman law, in which Russia imagined her roots. Westerners, however, have no hope of understanding Russian legal history in its own terms; they must first turn to their own Western legal tradition because of 'the polarity that has existed between Russian history and Western legal history for almost a thousand years' (Berman, 1950, p. 110). The Russian tradition was autonomous, unrelated to the common tradition that united the various systems of the West.

The major interest for us in his *Justice in Russia* is Chapter 6 on the WLT. Those who are familiar with his later big volumes will be surprised by the dazzling speed with which Berman deals with his topic. They may also notice some rather unexpected statements, such as the notion that the German Reformation (the second revolution according to Berman's plan) occurs at the same time as the reception of Roman law (bringing it forward a century), though this suggestion is then corrected in the later volumes. Another feature is the inclination for macro-structures. We learn that the Western legal tradition is set in motion by

> [...] three leading principles: the principle of Reason, the principle of Conscience, and the principle of Precedents [...] and the ideas associated with them of the supremacy and completeness of law, the equality of law, and the growth of law [...] [which] remain the foundation of the legal system of every Western people.

To this, Berman quickly adds:

> It is more than mere coincidence that only now, with the collapse of the European system of national states and the rise to power of Russia [...] we are able to rediscover the unity and continuity of the Western legal tradition which modern nationalisms have for so long observed. (Berman, 1950, p. 121)

The main purpose was not to define a legal tradition perceptible as Western but to make sense of the political world that lay on the other side of the Iron Curtain. In Berman's account, the West and Soviet Russia are in diametrical opposition and hence define each other. Thus, those features that produced Western legal evolution are those Russia lacked, and their absence explained the special features of Soviet law.

It would be misleading to look at Berman's book without keeping in mind how powerfully the divide between the West and the East lurked in the background. Berman's thesis about the WLT arose from a storage of memories whose dominant note was fear—fear about the polarity between Soviet Russia and the West, about nuclear destruction, about further military expansion towards the West and the expansion of Communism in the West. Berman tells us of Lenin's theory of a 'contest of two systems': 'in which West and East could survive alongside, but without ceasing to determine the class struggle' (Charter 77, 1977, p. 119). Such fears materialised in the image of an Iron Curtain, an image that gave free rein to imagined threats and to an opposition in which Eastern Europe was invented as an intellectually and culturally separate land (Judt, 1990).

Berman's book tells us that East and West were also separated juristically in that they belonged to different legal traditions. In this sense, the Iron Curtain influenced the formation of the WLT. It gave rise to a narrative written in reaction to a very different post-war world in which Westerners saw Easterners as their opposite and designed a Western legal identity in contrast to the Eastern. This Western identity arose from the acceptance of some fundamental principles that were supposedly lacking in Soviet Russia—among which were the rule of law, human rights and private property. These principles acquired an unquestionable authority by being carried over from generation to generation by tradition, which leads us to a natural question, what do we mean by 'tradition'?

Rosenstock-Huessy: An outsider ahead of his time

The essence of Berman's project is in the two words 'tradition' and 'revolution' in his title *Law and Revolution I. The Formation of the Western legal tradition* (1983) and *Law and Revolution II: The Impact of the Protestant Reformations on the Western Legal Tradition* (2003). They mean first that legal rules must be understood as a tradition and, second, that they change in time according to a pattern punctuated by successive revolutions.

This simple idea risks being misunderstood if one is not aware of its philosophical basis, which is to be found in an important and original book, *Out of Revolution: Autobiography of Western Man*, first published in 1938 by Berman's former university mentor Eugen Rosenstock-Huessy (1888–1973). This book dismissed the conventional academic historiography practised in Germany and generally followed in European universities (Iggers, 2012). This book indicated another and captivating approach towards the past consciously based on an original philosophical foundation. The aim was to revitalise the vital link of history and memory.

Eugen Rosenstock-Huessy was a learned and highly original German scholar who emigrated to the United States in 1933. He first taught at Harvard and then at Dartmouth, where Berman was among his students. He is remembered as a compelling teacher and pioneering mind who paid the price for his originality by being ignored by academia, as he notes in a sombre conclusive note to his *Out of Revolution* (1938). Today we know Rosenstock through Berman, who refers admiringly to him in the introduction to his own *Law and Revolution I* (1983) and in a substantial introduction to Rosenstock's *Out of Revolution. Out of Revolution* was ahead of its time: first, because its interdisciplinary approach aimed at bringing to light the collective memory of the legal past explained through law, theology, natural sciences, linguistics and even cartography and numismatics. Second, its historical narrative goes backwards: because it is meant to explain the intellectual identity of his generation, it begins from the present time moving towards the past through successive revolutions, beginning from the Russian Revolution down to the French, English, German and Papal revolutions. Third, the connective theme of his book, tradition, at that time was unconventional. Those who read *Out of Revolution: Autobiography of Western Man* as a sharp turn away from conventional academic history were unquestionably correct.

In *Out of Revolution,* Rosenstock-Huessy wanted to offer not only an account of European history but also a theory of history: he had a compelling view about how history should be understood and made (Rosenstock-Huessy, 1938, p. 692). There are two approaches to the past, he argued: one is history, understood as the academic discipline taught and practised in German universities, and the other is memory. This distinction is at the heart of his own attempt to capture a viable identity for his generation. It required two bold steps: first, to reject the philosophical basis (Cartesian rationalism) upon which the history he criticised rested and, second, to seek another approach to understand the past based on memory and tradition.

In this context should be placed the rise of interest for legal tradition as an explanatory concept. While today this is one of the standard concepts of legal-historical research (Glenn, 2014), the idea of a legal tradition in its progress toward acceptance has meant another explanation of law creation that replaced the legislative-based idea of sources of law. They are two competing explanations of how legal rules come into being, and references to legal traditions surged when the sources of law started to be examined critically as an insufficient and doubtful explanation of law creation (Calasso, 1954; Jestaz, 2015).

Rosenstock-Huessy's major appeal is in a philosophy of history aimed at understanding and explaining the Western identity. What is the leading force in its evolution? How does one explain legal change? Rosenstock replies that the game changers are critical moments that impact the human world at its various levels (social, economic, legal), and a feature of European history is the number and intensity of those turning points. They are waves of changes that invested different countries at different times: Bolsheviks in Russia, Jacobins in France, Cromwell in England, Luther in Germany, popes in Italy. They are the generative forces that recurrently occur, forwarding evolution to the next step.

Rosenstock-Huessy's revolutions cannot be separated from his account of memory and tradition. In his going backwards from the present to the past, he sees the linearity of time interrupted by crises that are harbingers of new forms of consciousness and new ways of thinking and living, then made perceptible in new institutions, language modifications, new conceptualisations of time and representation of space or of reasoning. Revolutions produce semantic shifts and new vocabularies. Humans modify and reformulate their language: they are name-giving animals who construct their world making use of language: 'Our passions give life to the world, our collective passions constitute the history of mankind' (Rosenstock-Huessy, 1938, p. 3). They arise from a storage of collective memories, as it were. They re-semaniticise their environment, redirecting the impulses that govern the flow of information. At the same time, they create a web of interactions between present and past in a chain of responses and dialogues from which the European tradition is made.

Along with tradition, the other interface between Rosenstock-Huessy and Berman is the reference to revolutions. In Berman, however, the sequence is turned upside down. While Rosenstock-Huessy moves backwards from the Soviet Revolution to the medieval Papal Revolution, Berman goes forward: his account of the WLT begins from the Papal Revolution of the period 1050–1200. This phase is the one that has attracted the greatest attention by far. His thesis focuses on the 'revolutionary' impact of the period 1050–1200, which he presents as the time that produced the deepest transformations in the legal world. The bishops of Rome claimed control over the Church, and their newly acquired autonomy from secular powers transformed the legal world. It reformulated legal thinking, giving rise to coherent bodies of laws and legal studies whose major fruit was the learned legal science of canon and civil law. Berman's thesis was original. Departing from the Romanists' orthodoxy, and particularly from Koschaker, the focus shifted from Roman to canon law. It is therefore from religion and canon law that the WLT found its beginning. This argument then expanded by including the dissemination of canon law on a European scale that included English law (Helmholz, 1996). By turning to canon law, Berman broadened legal-historical studies to the interplay between the religious and secular component of the law, giving life to the most fruitful stream of research (Prodi, 2000; Decock, 2013; Gordley, 2006). Yet in the context of this volume, it is notable that Berman's approach to legal history was initiated by a comparison with the East and the West. As Berman himself wrote in *Justice in the USSR*:

> Russian law, therefore, challenges us to rediscover the unity and continuity of the Western legal tradition [...] to find the link between the political-legal and the moral-spiritual aspects of our own heritage. (Berman, 1963, pp. 268–269)

The Western legal tradition and natural rights history

The period between Berman's early formulation of the Western legal tradition in his 1950 book *Justice in Russia* and the immensely successful 1983 volume

Law and Revolution saw the formula of WLT acquiring currency in a bipolar world locked in the strident rivalry between the Soviet bloc and Western countries. The WLT represented the West in its essential traits in a way that summarised both its identity and emblematically its success in the ideological battleground. Of the many themes that made up the WLT, the most compelling was that of human rights history, according to a formula that condensed the essence of Western identity in a way that transcended earlier references to rights *tout court*, natural rights and the rights of man.

Samuel Moyn made a case to show how this was a powerful inspirational concept that entered political language with a universal ring and was soon absorbed into political consciousness as a centrepiece of political language (Moyn, 2011). It spoke of a natural freedom possessed by individuals who were members of a moral community of universal nature irrespective of state boundaries. Whereas the Truman Doctrine (1947) addressed people with a choice 'between alternative ways of life'—freedom or oppression, control, and terror—human rights presented a cosmopolitan vision of a universal humanity, the fruit of an immemorial inheritance grown into maturity at a time of stark political confrontation. In the latter stages of the Cold War, human rights became a veritable cult object. 'America did not invent human rights,' asserted President Jimmy Carter in 1981, '[i]n a very real sense, it is the other way round. Human rights invented America' (Moyn, 2014, p. XIV). During the bipolar stalemate of the Cold War, human rights functioned to identify the moral community that Soviet Russia threatened. If in the West they were vital, their absence in the East signalled the perceived failure of the Soviet bloc (Moyn, 2014, p. XIX). This was one of the chief features that supposedly distinguished the West from Soviet Russia. If human rights made America, their absence made Soviet Russia.

The heated political atmosphere coincided with Berman's elaboration of his thesis about the WLT. As the bipolar mentality of the 1950s had led Berman to formulate this notion as a mirror image of the legal tradition of the Soviet Russia, his pioneering work inspired a multitude of studies that further derived from that fundamental distinction between the East and the West in their attempt to depict the past of the contemporary (and politically loaded) dilemmas. From the 1980s, the idea of WLT rose to become a prominent field in its own right. Like a magnet, it attracted diverse themes that were only briefly outlined in Berman's book. Filling these slots, other scholars supplemented the original narrative with additional argumentative blocks, making the concept broader, more persuasive and electrifying. One of these expansions was natural rights history.

What was almost entirely missing from the legal-historical scholarship of 1980s was some clarity about the origin of rights: in academic research, it was terra incognita.[1] Yet this was about to change, and in the consequent debate on the natural rights history, the idea of WLT played a significant role by providing the strongest possible basis. Few arguments have more impact than a creation in immemorial time and an eternal history that has been with us forever.

In 1988 a *Festschrift* was published to celebrate Harold J. Berman (*The Weightier Matters of the Law: A Tribute to Harold Berman*). It opened with an essay 'Villey, Ockham and the Origin of Individual Rights' by the British-American legal historian Brian Tierney (1922–2019), which soon became the most cited article in the new field of rights history (Tierney, 1988). The real question, according to Tierney, was about 'the origin of Western rights theories.' By saying this, he manifested his preoccupation not with their essence, but with their genesis, which had to be reformulated. Rights were qualified by various adjectives (individual, subjective, natural, and modern), but the one that counted most was to be 'Western' (Tierney, 1988, p. 13).

Although indicated with a vague denomination, the concept which Tierney's article borrowed from Continental law was extremely precise—*droit subjectif, diritto soggettivo, Subjectives Recht*. In moving from the continent to the new Anglo-American home, it acquired some additional features. The first was to be presented as the winning argument that defeated the French Romanist and philosopher Michel Villey. No effort was spared by Tierney in his piece to annihilate his adversary. As a result, covered by a veil of oblivion, Villey was then accurately cited in the ensuing deluge of studies only to remember his defeat in that memorable dialectical duel. But to be fair, Tierney and Villey were talking about different things: Tierney's focus was the 'origin of Western right theories' (Tierney, 1988, p. 13), while Villey's was the 'origin of *droit subjectif*' (*genèse du droit subjectif*), an expression untranslatable in English for the lack of a corresponding concept. They were talking from different disciplines (political theory and law); for different purposes (Villey explaining a technical component of continental legal systems, Tierney building the core of the WLT); and in different languages (English and French).

Michel Villey (1914–1988) belongs to the group of jurists who wanted to reformulate the 19th century intellectual legacy received from the theory-centred and hugely influential strand of German legal science, Pandectism. He sought to enlarge what he perceived to be a field impoverished by the demise of justice, which he believed to be intrinsic to legal science, but at the same time he shared the preoccupation of his generation to separate the legal from the interference of politics, religion and morality. At the heart of Pandectist systems bequeathed to 20th century legal science, he saw a foundational idea: *droit subjectif*.

The Roman law-based legal systems of continental Europe are designed to begin from a basic unit indicated as *droit subjectif*. This notion serves the following purposes. The first function is explanatory: it explains how individuals can create effects in law. Broadly speaking, why is a contract binding (and by analogy, a law, a sentence, an administrative act), and why does it create obligations? The *droit subjectif* doctrine answers by imagining an individual who exerts will. The main idea is that individuals possess an inner power that produces effects of juristic relevance. The second purpose is constructive: the creative power in the individual is the starting point for designing the legal system conceptually. This idea is deemed to belong to the essentials of continental legal science, and it has been minutely analysed by an immense mass of scholarship and brought to a considerable degree of sophistication by 19th century Pandectism.[2]

Villey wanted to deactivate the bewitching power of *droit subjectif* by analysing it historically. He looked at the Pandectist constructions of Savigny, Puchta and Windscheid searching for their philosophical foundations. He noted that behind those constructions, whose source was usually attributed to Grotius, was a specific philosophy arising from medieval nominalism and suggested that the primary contributor was the logician William of Ockham.

The fundamental objection posed by Villey was to denounce that these 19th century constructions were the fruit of philosophical theories based on the view of an abstract individual. They produced systems of *droits subjectifs* (with its corollaries of absolute property, real rights and will theories) and created legal institutions whose starting point was an abstract individual, not the many communities in which humans effectively lead their lives, from the family to the natural environment. Secondly, such theories, operating at such a level of abstraction, produced a sort of legal thinking that expelled justice from the scope of jurisprudence. Its ultimate fruits were lists of human rights, comforting declarations of good intentions but no more effective than noble and illusionary dreams.[3]

In his article, Tierney wanted to take the first and important step in the direction of natural rights history. However, instead of beginning with a clean slate, he thought to begin by launching an attack on Villey's thesis about the origin of the *droit subjectif.* He was disturbed by the suggestion that *droits subjectifs* could be the fruit of the voluntarism and individualism brought about by the resurgence of nominalism between the 16th and 17th centuries.[4] His article endeavoured to antedate the origin to the Papal Revolution of the 12th century, and here he leaned on Berman's account of WLT. As Berman put it:

> Maitland called the twelfth century 'a legal century.' It was more than that: it was *the* legal century, the century in which the Western legal tradition was formed. (Berman, 1983, p. 120)

One of the features of the 12th-century Renaissance, according to Berman, was that canon law writings 'permeated the doctrines based on individual intentions and individual will in areas like the law of torts, the law of contract, the law of marriage' (Tierney, 1988, p. 135). Prudence would have advised clarifying what the phrase 'doctrines based on individual intentions and individual will' meant, but to Tierney that phase seemed the ideal seedbed to nurture the rise of rights doctrines:

> The doctrine of individual rights was not a late medieval aberration from an earlier tradition of objective right or of natural moral law. Still less was it a seventeenth-century invention of Suarez or Hobbes or Locke. Rather, it was a characteristic product of the great age of creative jurisprudence that, in the twelfth and thirteenth centuries, established the foundations of the Western legal tradition. (Tierney, 1988, p. 31)

Tierney's attack on Villey's theory (and on the idea that the origin of natural rights was Ockham's philosophy) was fierce—and questionable.[5] The major doubt about the method followed by Tierney is his confidence in relying on a limited set of texts to demonstrate such a far-reaching theory as individual rights. Those texts are in fact a necessary but not sufficient condition. Texts are one element in a broader institutional architecture in which questions of philology, interpretation and hierarchical structure determine their effective application. Tierney was in fact correct in spotting the difference that divided him from Villey:

> [H]is [Villey's] prior conviction [was] that major shifts in legal and political ideas could occur only after an appropriate pattern of thought had been created in the sphere of pure philosophy. (Tierney, 1988, p. 20).

Legal science operates indeed by proceeding conceptually according to changeable philosophical models embedded in a plurality of philosophical dimensions. It would therefore be misleading to separate law from the dominant philosophies, for example to separate the pre-1650 period from Scholasticism, the following period from Rationalism, the 19th century from Kant, the 20th century from linguistic philosophies, and the 21st century perhaps from the philosophy of information.

Another observation is that the shift from *droit subjectif* to natural rights history in the 1980s signalled the regression of legal science's boundaries. *Droit subjectif*, a topic originally at the heart of continental legal science, was captured by political theorists, translated into a cluster of denominations (individual, subjective, natural, modern, Western) and its origins reengineered into an eternity history that ironed out the recurrent shifts in philosophical, and hence legal, thinking. It is perhaps the case that another shift has occurred, by which the self-congratulatory account of a rise of the WLT in a direct line of development that indicates both the mythical origin and the way ahead, has lost its original appeal. As we learn from recent scholarship, human rights history entered political debates in the 1970s, and it arrived, as Moyn suggests, with 'a recognizably utopian program: for the political standards it champions and the emotional passion it inspires' (Moyn, 2011, p. 1).

Conclusion: the WLT and the Cold War

The Western legal tradition arises from the Cold War. Conceived by the Harvard legal historian Harold J. Berman in a chapter of his 1950 book on *Justice in Russia*, and then developed in his well-known 1983 and 2003 volumes (and in a third left unfinished), since then this idea has been a staple concept to make sense of the legal past.

In his *Justice in Russia*, Berman wanted to explain to a Western audience what lay beyond the Iron Curtain. He constructed his idea of WLT in an account set out in opposition in which the West and Soviet Russia define each other in a mirror image. The WLT's almost ubiquitous currency grew from another legacy from the Cold War era: human rights history. This chapter shows how the WLT absorbed this theme, hijacking a core component of continental legal science (*droit subjectif*) reengineered by political theorists into the major identitary element of the WLT in an eternity history rooted in medieval canon law. Paradoxically, natural rights history was further used in depicting a future in which the world would be something that the East was not.

The chapter addresses the question of the historical consciousness of legal history. One of the features of this discipline is that of having forgotten how deeply the language with which legal historians think and write about the legal past is embedded in ideas rooted in the 20th century. This chapter has attempted to look back at those times and to bring to light those ideals and hopes that legal scholars invested in the project of the WLT. It also recognises how much of that project was the fruit of the fear that marked the bipolar standoff of the Cold War, which today we can still glean from Harold J. Berman's works written at that time.

My purpose was not to offer an argument about the historical relativism of WLT's identitary narrative. I rather believe that making explicit its formation and attempting to understand the role it served then is a necessary step to figuring out how it can be transcended.

Notes

1 In the 1970s, human rights history was a minor field without adherents or audience. To have an idea of the state of the art in this field we must turn to a bibliography 'On the Nature and Foundations of Rights, 1947–77,' published by the journal *Political Theory* in 1978. It was limited in size (comparable to the bibliography on Hobbes studies in the German language published during 1968–1981) and was only partially focused on human rights specifically (the requirement for a research field is agreement on the subject matter). It is also worth mentioning that in British universities in the 1970s, human rights were taught as one among other rights traditions: one was Utilitarianism, centred on Bentham, who described rights as 'nonsense upon stilts,' while other rights traditions at that time included J. S. Mill, Isaiah Berlin and Michael Oakeshott (Gray, 2011). Universalism was not necessarily connected with rights. As Moyn wrote, '[a] universalism based on international rights could count as only one among others in world history' (Moyn, 2011, p. 13).

2 Briefly, a definition: the Pandectist Georg Friedrich Puchta (1798–1846) in his *Lehrbuch der Pandekten* defined 'Recht in subjectiven Sinne' as follows: 'A right (according to a subjective meaning) is present if an object is given in the Power of a Person by the right (according to an objective meaning)' (*ein Recht (im subjectiven Sinne) ist vorhanden, wenn ein Gegenstand durch das Recht (in objectiven Sinne) in die Macht eitner Persongegeben ist.*) (Puchta, 1838, p. 30). The adjective 'subjective' is a legacy of 18th century Scholastic Latin: 'subjective' is the attribute to the subject and belongs to its essence, as explained in a standard logic textbook published by Isaac Watts in 1725 (Logick, II, ii, §. 8): 'Objective certainty, is when the proposition is certainly true in itself; and subjective, when we are certain of the truth of it. The one is in things, the other is in our minds.'

3 As we have learned from recent scholarship, the recognition of humanity is not guaranteed by being inserted into lists of human rights (Moyn, 2011; Douzinas, 2000, p. 372).

4 'Seventeenth century thinkers [...] were influenced not only by the circumstances of their own age but also by an earlier tradition of thought they had inherited' (Tierney, 1989, p. 623).

5 The stringent voluntarism upon which Ockham framed his natural law was one of the intellectual forms used by 16th–17th century jurists in their thinking, and their source was Ockham (Vazquez, Suarez). Moreover, the linguistic philosophy that complemented that voluntarism to justify the binding power of human will was nominalism, and again their source was Ockham. It is also true that in some medieval texts we can read 'ius' and 'habere ius,' but they do not demonstrate a theory of right. 'Ius' is a slippery term. Still in late 16th century university teaching, students were taught the 36 meanings of the word 'ius' (Bolognetti, 1551). On the other hand, 'habere ius' means several things, one of which is to share a greater good, and even today in neo-Latin languages we have the notion of 'avere ragione,' 'tener razon,' 'avoir raison' (to 'hold' or 'have' reason). In Rome, the 'habere ius' of one who has committed parricide was the right to be thrown into the River Tiber in a bag filled with vipers. Other texts presented by Tierney are equally questionable. He observes that the divine commandment 'Honour thy father and mother' can be rephrased by saying that 'parents have a right to the respect of their children' (Tierney, 1988, p. 33), which is simply a conjecture that has been pushed too far.

References

Assmann, J. (1992) *Das Kulturelle Gedächtnis: Schrift, Erinnerung und Politische Identität in frühen Hochkulturen*, Munich: Verlag C. H. Beck.

Berman, H. J. (1963) *Justice in the USSR: An Interpretation of Soviet Law (rev. ed.)*, Cambridge (Mass.): Harvard University Press.

Berman, H. J. (1950) *Justice in Russia: An Interpretation of Soviet Law*, Cambridge, (Mass.): Harvard University Press.

Berman, H. J. (1983) *Law and Revolution I: The Formation of the Western Legal Tradition*, Cambridge and London: Harvard University Press.

Berman, H. J. (2003) *Law and Revolution II: The Impact of the Protestant Reformations on the Western Legal Tradition*, Cambridge: Harvard University Press.

Bolognetti, G. (1551) *Tractatus de differentia iuris et facti*, Napoli.

Calasso, F. (1954) *Medioevo del diritto*, Vol I, Le Fonti. T. 1, Milano: Giuffrè.

Charter 77 (1977) *White paper on Czechoslovakia*, International Committee for the Support of Charter 77 in Czechoslovakia, Paris.

Decock, W. (2013) *Theologians and Contract Law: The Moral Transformation of the Ius Commune (ca. 1500–1650)*, Leiden and Boston: Martinus Nijhoff. DOI: 10.1163/9789004232853.

Douzinas, C. (2000) *The End of Human Rights: Critical Thought at the Turn of the Century*, Oxford and Portland: Hart Publishing.

Dummett, M. (1994) 'Testimony and Memory', in Matilal B. K. and Chakrabarti (eds) *Knowing from Words. Western and Indian Philosophical Analysis of Understanding and Testimony*, Dordrecht: Springer, 251–272. DOI: 10.1007/978-94-017-2018-2.

Duve, T. (ed.) (2013) 'Law and Revolution—Revisited', *Rechtsgeschichte - Legal History* 2013, no. 21: 156–159. DOI: 10.12946/rg21/156-159.

Giaro, T. (2013) 'The East of the West. Harold J. Berman and Eastern Europe', *Rechtsgeschichte*, 21, 193–197. DOI: 10.12946/rg21/193-197.

Glenn, H. P. (2014) *Legal Traditions of the World: Sustainable Diversity in Law*, Oxford: Oxford University Press. DOI: 10.1093/he/9780199669837.001.0001.

Gordley, J. (2006) *Foundations of Private Law: Property, Tort, Contract, Unjust Enrichment*, New York: Oxford University Press.

Halbwachs, M. (1992) *On Collective Memory*, in Coser L. A. (ed), Chicago and London: University of Chicago Press.

Helmholz, R. H. (1996) 'The character of the western legal tradition. Assessing Harold Berman's contributions to legal history', in Hunter H. O. (ed), *The Integrative Jurisprudence of Harold J. Berman*, Boulder and Oxford: Westview Press, 29–50.

Iggers, G. G. (2012) *The German Conception of History: The National Tradition of Historical Thought from Herder to the Present*, Middletown: Wesleyan University Press.

Jestaz, P. (2015) *Les Sources Du Droit*, Paris: Dalloz.

Judt, T. (1990) 'The Rediscovery of Central Europe', *Daedalus*, 119:1, 23–54.

Koselleck R. (1985) *Futures Past*, Cambridge (Mass.): Massachusetts Institute of Technology Press.

Maritain, J. (1922) *Antimoderne*, Paris: Édition de la Revue des jeunes.

Moyn, S. (2011) *The Last Utopia: Human Rights in History*, Cambridge (Mass.): Harvard University Press. DOI: 10.2307/j.ctvjk2vkf.

Moyn, S. (2014) *Human Rights and the Uses of History*, London and New York: Verso.

Prodi, P. (2000) *Una storia della giustizia. Dal pluralismo dei fori al moderno dualismo tra coscienza e diritto*, Bologna: Il Mulino.

Puchta, G. F. (1838) *Lehrbuch der Pandekten*, Leipzig: Barth.

Rosenstock-Huessy E. (1938) *Out of Revolution: Autobiography of Western Man*, New York: Morrow and Co.

Rosenstock-Huessy E. (1970) *Speech and Reality*, Norwich: VT Argo Books.

Tierney, B. (1988) 'Villey, Ockham and the Origin of Individual Rights', in Witte, J. and Alexander, F. S. (eds) *The Weightier Matters of the Law: Essays on Law and Religion; a Tribute to Harold J. Berman*, Atlanta: Scholars Press, 1–31.

Tierney, B. (1989) 'Origins of Natural Rights Language: Texts and Contexts, 1150–1250', *History of Political Thought*, 10:4, 615–646.

Villey, M. (1983) *Le droit et les droits de l'homme*, Paris: PUF.

Witte, J. and Alexander, F. S. (eds) (1988) *The Weightier Matters of the Law: Essays on Law and Religion; a Tribute to Harold J. Berman*, Atlanta: Scholars Press.

Witte, J. and Manzer, C. J. (2014) 'A Prequel to Law and Revolution: A Long Lost Manuscript of Harold J. Berman Comes to Light', *Journal of Law and Religion*, 29, no. 1, 142–169. DOI: 10.1017/jlr.2013.3.

Part II

Legal historians of socialist regimes

6 Juliusz Bardach and the agenda of socialist history of law in Poland

Marta Bucholc

Introduction

The history of law is situated somewhat ambiguously among other historical disciplines. On the one hand, the history of law is a 'history of something' (see Popper, 1994, pp. 470–471), confined to a particular object and to a discipline-specific point of view from which history can be written. On the other hand, law is a special 'something' for at least two reasons.

One is the temporality of law, which makes it different from other subjects of historical inquiries. Current mathematical knowledge results from a long and winding path of historical development, but no awareness of this path is required to learn and apply state-of-the-art mathematics. Historical consciousness may sometimes be an enhancement, but it is always a luxury. However, historicity is inherent to law, at least in its form dominant in the modern West, because this form of law states the conditions of its own validity in temporal terms. Legal order is a succession of norms, which are either in force, no longer in force, replacing each other, or repealing and amending each other. Finding one's way round in this normative nexus requires some form of historical consciousness. This brings us to the second reason why law is a specific object of a 'history of something', namely, its direct connection to political power. History of law implies the situatedness of lawmakers. It has a side effect of relativizing and historicizing legal orders. While some legal orders, especially democratic ones, may be relatively immune to this operation, some others find it too much of a risk for their legitimacy to admit that there was a law before them, as that may imply that there will be a law after them.

That the latter point should apply to socialist regimes in Central and Eastern Europe after 1917 and 1945 is far from obvious. The Marxist philosophy that inspired the official ideology comprised an expressly historicist approach to social norms. Even though it insisted on the finality of history, it also posited a long succession of changing forms of production, each of them with its own particular normative setup. An examination of this historical process was the crux of historical materialism. The history of law should actually thrive under socialism. In most cases, however, it demonstrably did not, and one of the reasons was the fact that the philosophical and ideological tenet about history ending in communism could not withstand the pressure of detailed analysis of the variety of the laws of the past and their political and cultural embeddedness. This objection against the history of law would in fact be common to all monocratic systems for which pluralism is a threat, even if it is only extending into the past. Incidentally, the argument should also work against comparative law: there would be little point in comparing socialist countries to one another, as they were all supposedly steering towards legal standardization, and the results of any comparison between a socialist and a capitalist legal order were taken for granted.

Furthermore, the role that the history of law played in the late 19th and early 20th centuries should be considered. At the time, in Europe, the history of law, especially if we include Roman law, was traditionally a necessary element of legal training and an important playfield for debates weighing on the legal reforms at the time, both in public and in private law. The political relevance of the history of law was indisputable, and so was the role of law as a carrier of national identities. In the early modern and modern period, law was ultimately tied to the national project and to the model of a nation-state, a connection reinforced by the high wave of modern constitutionalism (see Thornhill, 2011). The history of law was thus embedded in national history (for Germany, see Haferkamp, 2018). It became a natural point of resistance against any form of post-nationalist or internationalist modes of thinking. By the same token, the history of law could also form a foundation of the identity of the legal profession as a carrier of a disciplinary and professional ethos.

This brief overview of some among the many reasons why legal history could not thrive under socialism makes any proof to the contrary valuable. In this chapter, I undertake an analysis of the biographical and scientific trajectory of a Polish legal historian Juliusz Bardach (1914–2010). He was a scholar of exceptional standing in a socialist country, a remarkable feat in many ways. Poland was not only 'the merriest barrack in the Soviet camp', but it was also an exception from the point of view of academic history (for the socialist period, see Connelly, 2000). The old argument, according to which Poland can be treated as a mirror of all the problems of Central and Eastern Europe (Garrison Walters, 1988, p. 170), does not work for the history of law. However, an exception makes it possible to triangulate an image of what might otherwise be mistaken for a universal course of a social process. The same reasoning applies to Bardach. He was not typical or representative—indeed, he was quite the opposite—but his biography 'allows us to follow almost a hundred years of uneasy history of Eastern Europe' (Sokalska, 2017, p. 18). His influence makes Bardach's case an excellent starting point for a study of the vicissitudes of legal history in Poland under socialism. The opinion of Henryk Olszewski that 'almost all historians of law in Poland can think of themselves as his students' (Olszewski, 2010, p. 163) is certainly shared by many: '[I]n retrospect, Bardach deserves to be called the most important figure in the historiography of law in Poland in the second half of the 20th century' (S. Salmonowicz quoted in Zakrzewski, 2016, p. 62).

Although Bardach's autobiographical notes remain unpublished (Szlachta, 2014, p. 80), it is only a matter of time before he becomes the subject of a full-fledged biography. As Tadeusz Rutkowski observed in his seminal book on political aspects of the organization of historical science in Poland in the first 25 years of the People's Republic, biographical studies of Polish historical sciences are still 'in a bad state' (Rutkowski, 2008, p. 19). However, a number of biographical sketches have been published, many of which I cite here. A detailed synopsis of Bardach's work on Lithuanian law by Tomasz Siewierski (2010) is particularly precious for a non-specialist. As Rutkowski has pointed out (Rutkowski, 2008, p. 15), there are still too few critical monographic works on the history of historical science under socialism, and the same applies to historical-legal science. Nonetheless, a number of valuable contributions, first and foremost in *Czasopismo Prawno-Historyczne,* covered some aspects of the development of legal history under socialism and after 1989.

In this chapter, I do not attempt a prosopography of the history of law under socialism in Poland. Apart from a few concluding remarks, I do not read Bardach's life's work as a model for his (or any other) generation or cohort. Instead, I suggest reconstructing his contribution to what could be called 'the agenda of the history of law' in Poland after 1945: its general direction of research, including the selection of topics and the methodological strategies, as well as its relation to other disciplines and to its own disciplinary past before 1945.

Bardach's life at a historical intersection

Juliusz Bardach was born into an assimilated Jewish family in Odessa in Russia in 1914, the oldest son of Mejer Bardach and Ottylia Neuding.[1] His father was a dentist. In 1922, the family was repatriated to Poland, to Volodymyr-Volynskyi (then Włodzimierz Wołyński). At this point, Bardach—according to his handwritten curriculum vitae attached to his university enrolment file—started to learn Polish. At home, he was prepared for the second grade of gymnasium, and for six years he attended a public gymnasium in Włodzimierz. In his final grade, he changed to a private gymnasium, passed his maturity exam, and in 1933 enrolled as a law student at the Faculty of Law and Social Sciences of Stefan Batory University in Vilnius (then Wilno in Poland). On his registration form, Bardach entered his nationality and his mother tongue as Jewish.

The beginnings of an academic career and the Second World War

Poland before 1939 had five state universities and more than 20 state and non-state academic higher schools (not to mention institutions of religious formation, one of them, *Chachmei Lublin Yeshiva*, among the most renowned in the world) (see Bajerski, 2016). In this academic scene, legal science enjoyed an important place. The curricula in law were dominated by the Austro-Hungarian model, since only in the Austrian partition had Polish been the language of university teaching before 1918, which gave the former Austro-Hungarian academics an advantage. In 1920, a ministerial ruling introduced a unified university curriculum in legal sciences that lasted until the first decade after the war (Wołodkiewicz, 2015). The balance between scientific formation and the needs of practical professional training was achieved by the domination of theoretical and historical subjects in the first two years, including Roman law as a propaedeutic of civil law, legal theory, the history of Polish law and state regimes, and the history of law and state regimes in Western Europe. From the very beginning, this concept of legal education was heavily contested (see Marszał and Srokosz, 2010).

The high prestige of the history of law as well as its crucial role in academic teaching were an incentive for outstanding students. From the beginning of his studies, Bardach was a member of the seminar of Polish and Lithuanian law of Professor Stefan Ehrenkreutz (1880–1945). Ehrenkreutz would later become the last Rector of Batory University; he was a senator of the Polish Republic until 1938 and, in 1939, he supervised Bardach's master's thesis. Bardach also participated in seminars of Henryk Łowmiański (1898–1984) and of Wiktor Sukiennicki (1901–1983), who had once belonged to the Kelsen Circle in Vienna. During his studies, Bardach made a number of intellectual connections, which survived the war and proved vital for his later personal ties and his academic profile. He also became a political activist, a member of the socialist youth movement and, after 1935, a member of the Polish Socialist Party (for details on Bardach's student years, see Filaszkiewicz, 2016).

In 1939, Bardach had to leave Vilnius to escape the Soviets. In 1942, the Nazis killed his first wife, his parents, his sister and his uncle's family, who had all remained in Włodzimierz. The only surviving member of the family was Juliusz's brother, Janusz Bardach (1919–2002), who was sent to the Gulag. After the war, Janusz emigrated to the United States and made a name for himself as a surgeon as well as an author.[2]

Having survived in various parts of the Soviet Union until 1944, Juliusz decided to join the First Polish Army, organized by the Soviets. He would remain in the army for some time, reaching the rank of colonel in the political division. Soldiers with the rare benefit of higher education were often placed there and given the task of politically educating soldiers, many of whom had very little sympathy with Marxist-Leninist ideology. In 1946, Bardach was nominated military attaché at the Polish Embassy in Moscow, where he remained until 1948. He was approached by the authorities of the Faculty of Law of the newly established University of Łódź in 1945 as a potential docent. However, the army refused to let him go, even though Łódź in post-war times was a political project of pivotal importance, including a new people's university meant to take up the space left by the devastated bourgeois Warsaw academia (see Zysiak, 2018).

Second beginnings

While still in active service, Bardach obtained a doctorate at the prestigious Faculty of Law of the Jagiellonian University in Cracow, based on a dissertation on *Adoption in Lithuanian Law of the 15th and 16th centuries*, which he had published in 1938. His supervisor was Professor Adam Vetulani (1901–1976), an excellent specialist in church and canon law (a subject that disappeared from university teaching after the war) and the history of Polish law. Olga Filaszkiewicz explains that the reason to approach Vetulani was that the original supervisor, Ehrenkreutz, died in 1945 (Filaszkiewicz, 2016, p. 94). Vetulani was most definitely not a politically correct figure after 1945. Nevertheless, upon his return from abroad in 1947 he became the Chair for the History of Polish State and Law and later a dean of the Faculty of Law, although he was never a party member and for many years was under surveillance by the Secret Service. Bogdan Szlachta quotes Bardach remembering his concern that because of his declared Marxist views and his pre-war socialist card, he could have been an undesirable supervisee for Vetulani, an unwanted addition to 'his school' (Szlachta, 2014, p. 80). Bardach remained close to Vetulani throughout his academic career, and he was one of the eight doctoral students supervised by him who would all become law professors. In this way, the influence of Bardach is also a part of a larger historical trend. Vetulani was a direct continuator of the 19th century 'Cracow school of historians' (see Mączak, 1993, p. 236; Wandycz, 1992). Bardach's influence would thus be instrumental in extending this school's impact into the 20th and then the 21st century. Vetulani was also known in the West: among other things, he received honorary doctorates from Strasbourg and Nancy, which he could not receive in person because the authorities would not let him travel abroad. Through liaison with Vetulani, Bardach, still a high-ranking officer of the People's Army, would thus become a friend with a person of high-bourgeois origin, close to the Church, including the future pope John Paul II, Karol Wojtyła, who also studied at Jagiellonian University and was later Bishop of Cracow (see *Dobra starość...*, 2007). Bardach even protected Vetulani from a politically and ideologically motivated relocation to Wrocław (cited in Szlachta, 2014, pp. 81–82).

In 1950, Bardach was released from the army with very unfavourable notifications in his personal file: 'heard to express views hostile to the Soviet Union', and 'a pre-war socialist'. An official remark of this kind was a career killer in the army. However, as a Marxist researcher, Bardach was good enough for a university job (Zakrzewski, 2016, p. 58) and the Faculty of Law of the University of Warsaw employed him.

In my brief history of Polish sociology (Bucholc, 2016), I argued that there were two distinct roles that academics with a pre-war education played immediately after the war: survivors and supervisors. The war brought about catastrophic destruction of Polish universities, and two of them, Lwów and Wilno, were lost (while Germany lost the university in Breslau to Poland). However, those professors and docents who lived through the war, the Holocaust, the Nazi and Soviet occupations and the Warsaw Uprising of 1944, or who returned from emigration after 1945 were still a significant component of the human resources on which the new academia could be based. They brought with them their pre-war research agendas, knowledge and international networking capital but also intellectual habits and academic ethos. They were survivors themselves, but through them and with them the traditions of pre-war university also survived, though sometimes in disguise. Many of the survivors never joined the party, and indeed the phenomenon of highest-ranking academics who were not party members was one of the particularities of Poland among the Eastern bloc countries. However, the survivors were few and moreover, from the point of view of the Communist Party, they were too unreliable, even though some of them, like the prominent sociologist Józef Chałasiński, seemed genuinely to link their fate to that of the new regime early on (see Bucholc, 2016, pp. 20–21). Hence the political necessity of politically reliable supervisors.

Most of the supervisors were recruited from the cohort born in 1920. They ensured ideological cohesion, attacked pre-war academics and were quickly included in the academic teaching, transmitting the new ideology to their students. Many of them would later emigrate and become well-known European scholars, like some of the members of the so-called Warsaw school of the history of ideas, including Leszek Kołakowski or Bronisław Baczko (see Bucholc, 2017a). However, they were naturally themselves educated either before the war or by survivors after the war, thus—through a kind of intellectual osmosis—becoming carriers of pre-war, bourgeois academic culture and scientific knowledge. The 'survivor effect' translated into very practical things that were far from obvious in the academy in the late 1940s and early 1950s: the command of foreign languages, the experience of travelling abroad for research, the direct or indirect link with colleagues in the West and the personal experience of pluralism and free debate in science.

Bardach's role was initially one of a supervisor, and 'was often perceived as a political imposition on science' (Salmonowicz cited in Zakrzewski, 2016, p. 58). Rutkowski summarized the period of Stalinism at the University of Warsaw thus:[3]

> The years 1949–1955 were a time of strong ideological pressure at the University of Warsaw [...]. It was followed by personal changes in the academic staff, first and foremost at the faculties which were important for ideological reasons: Philosophy, History, Law, Political Economy and the Faculty of Journalism, which was founded at the end of this period. Academics came to them by way of a speedy 'party' promotion (including Juliusz Bardach, Rafał Gerber, Stanisław Ehrlich, Julian Hochfeld). (Rutkowski, 2016, p. 442)

In the 1950s, Bardach spoke at a number of congresses and symposia, following the party line, sometimes using a very sharp tone (Rutkowski, 2008, p. 153). He also performed a 'party lustration' at the *Instytut Zachodni*[4] in 1952 (Rutkowski, 2008, p. 226). In the late 1940s, some form of methodological pluralism was still in place by sheer force of facts. As Rutkowski points out, commenting on the first post-war (and seventh ever) General Congress of Polish Historians in 1948 in Wrocław, which was dedicated to the so-called 'Recovered Territories' (*Ziemie Odzyskane*)—'there was next to no Marxist historical scholarship on the Recovered Territories' at the time (Rutkowski, 2008, p. 124). Polish historical science had to learn Marxism as it went along, and the political reinforcement of history departments was a necessity. Hence, the interplay of ideology and science, a development that was much more complicated than any retrospective projection could possibly imagine. To name just one example: Bardach emphatically opposed the presence of 'political Catholics' in the Instytut Zachodni (Rutkowski, 2008, p. 226), but Stanisław Alexandrowicz remembers that it was his intervention in 1952–1953 that saved the university job of Brygida Kürbis, who was fired because she regularly attended Catholic masses (Alexandrowicz, 2010, p. 155). Bardach's argument was the high quality of Kürbis' scientific work, and she did indeed become a history professor herself.

In 1950, Bardach was, according to Rutkowski, 'the rising star of party historical science' (Rutkowski, 2008, p. 153). He was, of course, a party member, and even though he underlined his pre-war socialist commitment on many occasions, he did not resign his Communist Party membership until 1990, which many others did, especially in 1968 and 1981. In 1950, Bardach became an Acting Professor and an Acting Dean of the Faculty of Law as a result of the Marxist reorganization of the academia in historical science. In the same year, any ties with the Western community of historians were cut and a period of intensive party work on the new design of Polish historical science followed (Rutkowski, 2008, p. 160). In this process of ideological restructuring, the history of law and state was perceived as part of the agenda of the Marxist science of history more than the Marxist science of law. It was no longer the history of state regime, and in 1950 Bardach himself requested the terminological shift from 'state regime' (*ustrój*) to 'state' (*państwo*) as better expressing the new Marxist orientation (*Z prac...*., 1950, p. 99). However, already in 1951, he insisted on the relative autonomy of the history of law, arguing as follows:

> Just as we cannot separate the legal and state developments from their socio-economic basis as it was usually done by bourgeois scholars, we cannot reduce the interest in state and legal developments to the study of their base or, which also did happen, to the study of the development of the forces of production. To replace law with economics, and the history of the state and the law with social or economic history would be a vulgarisation of Marxism. (Bardach, 1951, pp. 2–3)

The Thaw and 1968

The universal *cesura* of post-war academic and political history alike is, as in the Eastern bloc as a whole, the year 1956, which in Poland goes by the name of the 'October Thaw of 1956'. The second half of the 1950s was a period of revival in Polish intellectual life, of renewing or establishing new contacts in the West and of a certain relaxation in ideological rigor. In 1955, Bardach became a university professor, and in 1960 an 'ordinary professor', employed in the Institute of History of Law established in 1952. He also held a post at the Polish Academy of

Sciences, where he directed the historical part of the Institute of Legal Sciences. As a direct consequence of the Thaw, the contacts between Polish and French historians were renewed, and in June 1957, Bardach, as one of three Polish delegates, participated in a conference entitled 'The Days of History of Law' in Paris (Rutkowski, 2008, p. 314). In the 1950s, Bardach joined a number of committees responsible for preparing a new framework of historical studies in Poland.

The Thaw did not last long, an ideological offensive was soon relaunched and Bardach's star, one of the brightest immediately after 1956, started to fade. Halfway through the 1960s the opinion that he was 'too liberal' for the taste of the party was established (Rutkowski, 2008, p. 350). By 1967, Bardach lost his influence on the political line in science (Rutkowski, 2008, p. 435). In July 1963, still a member of the History Section of the Department of Education of the Central Committee, he became an object of interest to the Security Service and remained so until 1974 (Rutkowski, 2008, p. 435). In 1962, he had to move with all his team from the University of Warsaw to the Institute of History of Polish Academy of Sciences, directed by the leading medieval historian, Tadeusz Manteuffel. There he stayed on until his team was dissolved in 1968.

The year 1968 is a turning point whose ripple effect in Polish intellectual history is far from adequately reconstructed. As a result of the anti-Semitic campaign sponsored by the Soviet authorities, a purge was orchestrated by the party with little or no social resistance. Student protests at the University of Warsaw in March 1968, apparently analogous to those in the West, led to the expulsion of student leaders. A few professors who supported them were also fired, including Bronisław Baczko, Zygmunt Bauman, Włodzimierz Brus, Maria Hirszowicz, Leszek Kołakowski, and Stefan Morawski. Most of them would soon emigrate.

Bardach was one of the supporters of the students' protests. He was among the signatories of a letter to the Minister of Education defending students victimized by the security forces after a rally in Warsaw (Rutkowski, 2008, p. 470). His precarious situation at the time is reflected in the following words of the rector of the University of Warsaw at a meeting in which the crisis at the university was discussed:

> It has been stressed that there is a strong pressure exercised on the part of professors on younger academic staff, for example in the Faculty of History by Prof. Gerber, Herbst, Manteuffel, in the Faculty of Law by Prof. Ehrlich, Katz-Suchy, Maneli, Bardach, and in the Faculty of Philosophy by Prof. Szacki, Baczko, Hirszowicz, Morawski. (Cited by Rutkowski, 2008, p. 522)

In this collection of names Bardach is accompanied by Baczko, Hirszowicz and Morawski, who would lose their jobs, but also, among the others, by Jerzy Szacki, a historian of ideas and the main representative of the Warsaw School of the history of ideas, and by Stanisław Ehrlich, who would soon supervise the doctorate of Jarosław Kaczyński, the future leader of the national-conservative party *Prawo i Sprawiedliwość*.

The year 1968 was a hard blow for the intelligentsia and for the academy. By the end of the 1960s, as many as 20,000 persons (the counts vary substantially),

Figure 6.1 In 08.03.1968 thousands of students gathered in the courtyard of the University of Warsaw in protest against the violations of the extraterritoriality of the university. The militia attacked the youth and dispersed the demonstration.

persecuted or discriminated against due to their real or alleged Jewish origins or Zionist sympathies, left Poland with one-way travel documents stating that their holders were not Polish citizens. Those who did not emigrate were harassed and intimidated, and a deep re-organization of academic life followed. Bardach's team at the Polish Academy of Sciences was dispersed and the director himself was fired from the Academy. In his farewell speech, he stated his outrage at the scale of personnel changes in scientific institutions and journals, and he declared that the circumstances of 1968 reminded him of the 'worst methods of Stalinism' (Rutkowski, 2008, p. 499). The Security Service recorded the speech. However, Bardach remained a professor at the University of Warsaw, and he was neither removed from the party nor isolated from the international historical community, even though in 1970 during the XIII International Congress of Historical Sciences in Leningrad, Polish authorities recommended him especially to the attention of the Komitet Gosudarstvennoy Bezopasnosti, the Soviet Committee for State Security (KGB) (Rutkowski, 2008, p. 532).

Public appreciation after 1989

Bardach lived through the Russian Revolution, two World Wars, the communist takeover in Poland and the many ups and downs of the Polish socialist state ending in the transformation of 1989. His life passed at a historical intersection between the East and the West, between the old imperial Europe of the 19th century, the totalitarianisms of the 20th and the new turn towards the West after the fall of the Eastern bloc. After 1989, Bardach as a senior scholar enjoyed public acknowledgment of his work and person. He obtained three honorary doctorates, two from Polish universities, Łódź (1995) and Warsaw (1996),[5] followed by the University of Vilnius (1997). Jagiellonian University celebrated a renewal of his doctorate in 1999. Bardach, who had been decorated many times in his army days, received a number of civilian honours and awards after 1989, including the Grand Cross of the Order of *Polonia Restituta* (2002) and the Order for Merits to Lithuania (2006). He was also honoured by many *festschrifts* (the last one on his 90th birthday).

Bardach lived in Warsaw until his death in 2010. In 2013, an award named after him was funded by the Institute of the Grand Duchy of Lithuania in Kaunas (Szlachta, 2014, p. 84). In many eulogies, he was remembered by his colleagues, as well as by his students and supervisees, many of whom belonged to the elite of Polish historians.

Bardach's oeuvre and how to understand it

Bardach insisted that narrow specialization is not advisable in science. It would be neither possible nor necessary to characterize his large oeuvre in full (for a discussion in Polish, see Olszewski, 2010; Siewierski, 2012; Zakrzewski, 2016), but an overview of the most relevant features is crucial for an understanding of Bardach's role in the formation of the agenda of legal history in Poland.

The Lithuanian connection

The most remarkable aspect of Bardach's work is his lifelong study of Lithuanian law, in which he became the best-known specialist in Europe next to Łowmiański (Olszewski, 2010, p. 162). When still a student, he gave a talk on Lithuanian law at the General Congress of Polish Historians in Vilnius in 1935, and in 1938 he published a dissertation on adoption in the Lithuanian law. His warm feelings for Lithuania were born in his student days in Vilnius and never ceased throughout his lifetime. These sentiments were as useful as they were genuine: they were in line with Ehrenkreutz's seminar and it was an established area of research at the Stefan Batory University. The importance of Lithuanian law and in particular of the Lithuanian statutes for legal developments in Eastern Europe was an additional argument: in the early 1930s, it was neither an exotic interest nor a marginal one. Moreover, studies on the legal traditions of Poland-Lithuania were of great political relevance in the 1930s, and to pick Lithuania as a subject of research might have been at the time a good career move.

This was less the case after 1945. Poland-Lithuania, a sworn enemy of the Grand Duchy of Moscow was, after all, a feudal state that ruthlessly suppressed its peasantry, so its laws would hardly deserve much attention unless as an illustration of the tenets of Marxist philosophy. However, Bardach's initial pre-war research was, in fact, far from it. In his work on adoption, he set out to document the existence of adoption as an institution of customary law, pointing out that even though it was not regulated in the statutes it was a part of everyday legal practice. It was not only a study in customary law (see Siewierski, 2012, p. 109): Bardach's analysis went in the direction of the historical study of 'living law' (*lebendes Recht*) à la Eugen Ehrlich and it proved a far-reaching independence of socially generated normative order from the statutory 'law in books'.

In all Bardach's work on Lithuania, he stressed the independence and originality of Lithuanian law and the fact that it was never 'colonized' (my term) by Polish tradition. This was, again, a double-edged argument: on the one hand, it went against pre-war and pre-partition Polish nationalism; on the other hand, it documented the longstanding independent legal tradition of Lithuania (then a Soviet republic). Conscious of this ambiguity, Bardach opposed nationalistic interpretations of Lithuanian legal history. Siewierski (2012) remarks that a paper that deserves attention in this context is Bardach's review of a book by a Lithuanian historian Jonas Žmuidzinas published in Paris in 1978 under the title *Commonwealth polono-lithuanien ou l'Union de Lublin (1569)*. In the review, Bardach insisted on the multifaceted, historically informed use of the notion of nationhood (see also Bardach, 2009). Bardach's interest in Lithuania was not popular with the communist authorities: in 1969, during the 10th General Congress of Polish Historians in Lublin, Bardach's presentation on the Polish-Lithuanian Union of Lublin was downgraded from a plenary lecture to an ordinary session (Zakrzewski, 2016, p. 60).

Bardach never prepared a comprehensive history of Lithuanian law, but among his 637 publications the Lithuanistic part (more than 120 according to Andrzej Zakrzewski, 2016, p. 59) is the largest coherent corpus, pertaining not only to the law but also to culture and the political history of the land, not only as a part of the union with Poland.[6] Some of these works were written before the war and the vast majority after 1956. Many of them were translated into foreign languages, mostly French and Russian, but also Lithuanian, Belarusian, Italian, Ukrainian, English and Flemish.

History of the Polish state and law

Bardach's *magnum opus* reflected an encyclopaedic inclination shared by some of his contemporaries (see Sułek, 2012). It was a five-volume synthesis of the history of the Polish state and law, the first volume of which was dedicated to the period before the 15th century and which Bardach authored himself while at the same time acting as an editor for the whole work. Five volumes published in Warsaw between 1957 and 1982[7] cover the history of Polish state regimes and law, including public law, private law and procedure, until 1939. It is still a standard reference work, with an outreach far exceeding the field of legal history.

That the ambition to carry out such a far-reaching project became realizable at this very point bespeaks a need to synthesize the science of legal history based on new Marxist premises. On the other hand, it also indicates that there was a continuity between the pre-war efforts and the developments in the socialist historiography of law. In particular, Bardach contributed significantly to the study of Polish parliamentarism in the early modern and modern period, whose development he depicted with great attention to the internal logic of a form of polity, which developed parallel to the Western representative monarchies but under very different political and cultural conditions. The grand synthesis partly resulted from Bardach's teaching duties, and one additional product of this effort was a handbook *Historia państwa i prawa polskiego,* co-authored by Bardach, Bogusław Leśnodorski and Michał Pietrzak, which was first published in 1976. The book was reprinted, revised and republished several times until 2009. As a result, for more than 30 years Bardach's work remained a standard handbook for law students in courses on Polish history, whose share in legal education gradually sunk after 1989, in line with the turn to 'dogmatic' aspects of law.

Disciplinary ethos, methodology and the problem of periodisation

In socialist Poland, the history of law was not separated from history in general, and legal historians played crucial roles in institutional historical science (Rutkowski, 2008, p. 14). Their impact seems, indeed, to have been stronger in history than in legal science. This is probably because in Poland—as opposed to certain other academic traditions—legal historians would usually specialize in the history of law only, doing little scholarly work in dogmatically oriented branches of law and not engaging in teaching beyond the historical subjects.

Bardach perceived historical-legal sciences as an interdisciplinary field, 'whose particular vocation it is to use its research techniques and its own approach to enrich both legal and historical science' (Bardach, 2001, p. 33). Even though this quote comes from a late paper, it does summarize Bardach's disciplinary attitude throughout his life rather well: he felt comfortable between epochs, languages and discourses (see Zakrzewski, 2016, pp. 60ff).

One particular feature of Bardach's general philosophy of legal historical research was his appreciation of the role of culture (Olszewski, 2015, p. 16). This was particularly evident in his attention to legal language and its link to vernacular languages. He was a student of 'travelling concepts' *avant la lettre*, and he endorsed the main tenet of this approach in today's cultural studies (see Bal, 2002), according to which the use of concepts and their transformations are part of cultural practices and cannot be separated from them. Particularly his work on the reception of law and on the comparative method belong to this field, in which he consciously traced the pathways of legal institutions, concepts and terminologies. The attention to customs, uses and habits—including linguistic habits—continued from pre-war times, and in his later work Bardach insisted that the history of law forms the core of socio-legal studies, which cannot put culture aside (Olszewski, 2015, p. 17). This, in turn, made his stance problematic from the point of view of orthodox Marxist historiography: already in the 1950s, Bardach opposed the view that law was 'detached from general culture' and stressed continuities between the law and culture of Poland in various historical epochs (Olszewski, 2015, p. 17). In this manner, he did incorporate the dangers of the history of law to Marxism as a political ideology. Despite his self-declared commitment to Marxist methodology, his research was concerned with the historical and cultural contingencies of law and not with its determination by the forces of production and class struggles.

Against this culturalist interpretation of Bardach's work, an argument could be raised that he remained very much focused on the problem of periodization, particularly in the history of the Polish state and Polish representative government. The focus on periods of development as relatively closed units of historical progress was typical for Marxist historiography seeking finality and determination in the succession of phases. Rutkowski cites a significant clash between Polish and Soviet legal historians at a conference held in Poland in 1952, where Bardach himself reported a vivid discussion with Soviet guests, who very sharply criticized the 'negativist' vision of periodization presented by one of the speakers pleading for different periodizations for different socioeconomic formations. The Soviet guest, Arkady Sidorov, opted for a 'monist', linear and universalist model of periodization as the only one compatible with historical materialism (Rutkowski, 2008, p.196). Bardach adhered to the party line in this respect, but already in 1949, quoting Lenin, he argued that 'each division, each periodization is an attempt to impose a certain scheme, to divide the existing unity of history for our cognitive purposes' (Bardach, 1949, p. 23) and that it was in full accordance with historical materialism. Bardach's influence on the periodization of history of the Polish state, combined with his role as editor-in-chief of an encyclopaedic synthesis, was decisive and has only relatively recently been challenged (Zakrzewski, 2016, p. 59). Olszewski thus characterized Bardach methodological stance:

> Juliusz Bardach created his workshop over decades. He construed it on the go, in the course of researching specific subjects. He did not think of himself as a methodologist of scientific research. His methodological texts were not conceived of as ambitious preaching on how historians of law should do their research, but they emerged as a result of years-long, persistent, in-depth studies of sources. (Olszewski, 2015, p. 24)

There is an analogy here between Bardach and the historians of ideas from the Warsaw school. They remembered the role of methodology in their discussions, and to an extent also in their work, as marginal and ancillary (see Bucholc, 2017a): their method was dictated by the subject and was, in the sense of Paul K. Feyerabend, 'opportunistic'. From this point of view, Bardach's statement of

1955, according to which 'the history of the state and law has no method of its own' (*Historia*... 1955, p. 3), is probably more than just lip service to the Marxism of the age.

Numerous miscellanea, including the problem of Roman law

Bardach's work included a large variety of miscellanea. One important section of this work were his biographical essays, most of which were dedicated to important figures in Polish 19th century historiography (Olszewski, 2015, p. 23). He also honoured many of his friends and colleagues with eulogies and memories. Olszewski interprets this as resulting from his conviction that science needs great personalities. However, it could also be seen as a commitment to the disciplinary tradition of history, which was also a national scientific and intellectual tradition, predating both the independent modern Polish state and socialism. Bardach's biographical essays may be indicative of a sense of belonging to a historically continuous community of scholars, and it may also be seen as a self-legitimizing effort: remembering is an instrument of inclusion. This focus on national tradition was common to many scholars of the time, including in particular Szacki (see Bucholc, 2017b). The feeling that tradition was not summarized in a satisfactory manner, that it was, in a way, left free-floating by the ideological turn after 1945, seems to have been pervasive in socialist Poland. It is somehow telling of the general climate in academia that this feeling evolved into reconstructive and commemorative projects initiated by scholars once affiliated with the Marxist party vanguard in their respective disciplines.

One other section of Bardach's miscellanea was Roman law. He dedicated little attention to this branch of historical legal studies, but in 1999, he published *Statuty litewskie a prawo rzymskie*.[8] This book was a critical commentary to the new edition of the Lithuanian statutes, and it is, as far as can be confirmed based on the available bibliographies, the only major reference to Roman law in Bardach's oeuvre. It was a continuation of work started before 1939: Bardach remembered that Ehrenkreutz held a talk on the influence of Roman law on the Lithuanian statutes at a conference in 1935 in Vilnius, and he appointed Bardach as a discussant of his paper (Bardach, 2016, p. 521).

The position of Roman law in Polish socialist universities was marked by an interesting ambivalence. Some authors insist that the communist takeover with its subsequent law-making did in fact destroy the pre-war legal tradition in Poland as it did in other socialist countries of Central and Eastern Europe (see Kühn, 2011). However, the continued presence of Roman law as an important element in this tradition would be an argument to the contrary. Church law and canon law vanished from universities immediately after the war, sharing the fate of theology. Witold Wołodkiewicz cites a discussion during the First All-Polish Conference of Legal Historians in 1950, when Rafał Taubenschlag overtly stated that he 'did not see any chance for Roman law to develop in Poland' apart from legal papyrology and the studies of influence of Roman law on Polish law (Wołodkiewicz, 2012, p. 209).

But Roman law—though criticized heavily by the new authorities—held on. Moreover, in the 1950s, Latin was still perceived as a must for law students, even those taking advantage of a speedy educational track created after the war to make up for the decimation of legal professions in the years 1939–1945 (Olszewski, 2017, p. 39). During the many reforms of university curricula, Roman law was reduced alongside other historical subjects and was perceived as a course of less and less propaedeutic value. Nevertheless, in the years 1944–1975, Roman law was taught throughout the land (see Czech-Jezierska, 2015). In the reform of 1975, however, based on the project of Bardach's student Jan Baszkiewicz, Roman law was combined with other historical subjects and separate lectures on Roman law were abandoned, which antagonised many legal historians (Wołodkiewicz, 2012, p. 210). In the 1980s, Roman law was reinstated as a subject in its own right, only to become subject to quite new adverse pressures after 1989. Throughout the socialist period, there was both human and intellectual capital in the field of Roman law in Poland, but Bardach's connection to this field was weak. For example, among the many personages he wrote about as a biographer or a friend there was not one Romanist. A passionate reviewer, he wrote only one review of a book on Roman law (more precisely, about its influence in Poland) (Bardach, 1991).

While the division of labour in the history of law after 1945 continued the prewar categorizations, the stress on Roman law and ancient law in the research agenda gradually weakened. A quantitative study of the contributions to the most important historical-legal journal published in Polish, *Czasopismo Prawno-Historyczne*, since the 1990s, shows that Romanist papers were a thematic minority, with more than six times fewer contributions than Polish legal history, but also twice fewer than universal legal history and the history of legal and political doctrines and also almost twice fewer than various miscellanea (Materniak-Pawłowska and Krzymkowski, 2018, pp. 349–350). Roman law seems to have fallen victim to ideological considerations much more than any other branch of history of law.

Vicissitudes and serendipities

In the very tentative and incomplete balance of Bardach's biography and oeuvre, there are a few elements that have been given relatively little attention in the existing scholarship. The first of them is Bardach's Jewish origins. As Olena Sokalska remarked (Sokalska, 2017, p. 14): 'It is ironic to note that in Poland, it is often only after the death of an eminent Pole that two things about him are noticed: that he was eminent and that he was Jewish.'[9] While in some biographical notes he is described as coming from a Jewish or Polish Jewish family, in many others it is not mentioned at all. Bardach was included in a publication edited by Wiesław Kozub-Ciembroniewicz on scholars of Jewish origins at the Jagiellonian University with a very informative biographical essay by Bogdan Szlachta (2014). However, in this essay, apart from the first sentence of the biography, there is no mention of Jewishness as a factor in Bardach's life or career, even though the very nature of the publication seems to suggest that gathering a number of scholars under the same heading was dictated by the perceived salience of the criterion. Bardach's Jewish origins almost certainly played a role in his life after 1945 at least once, in 1968, but even in the narratives of this year, it is not mentioned at all. As far as publications are concerned, Bardach wrote one article in which the legal situation of Jews was discussed (Bardach, 1990, translated into French and English), and in 1989 he reviewed one book on the history of Jews in Poland in the 17th–18th centuries. Too little information is available precisely to assess the impact of Bardach's Jewish origins on his work or career, but the same factor played a key role in the biographies of many of his contemporaries in various scientific disciplines. Any prosopography of Polish legal historians should take this into account to ensure correspondence and synergy with studies in intellectual and academic history in Poland and in Central and Eastern Europe in general.

Another factor, which is definitely understated, is that Bardach was a native speaker of Russian. This aspect is not discussed in any of his biographies or eulogies cited here apart from one, by Stanisław Alexandrowicz:

> I was particularly impressed by Juliusz Bardach during the joint meetings of Polish and Soviet historians. (…) During the sessions, the interventions by Prof. Bardach as a speaker, and even more as a discussant, were always very much to the point, and they were also bold. (…) Professor was able to conduct a polemic with the Soviet colleagues, very intelligently, but also in a very civil and diplomatic manner. In this, he spoke excellent literary Russian, more pre-revolutionary than Soviet. In view of his unusual tactfulness, his criticisms were never directly repudiated. (Alexandrowicz, 2010, p. 155)

An excellent command of Russian was not, by and large, a unique feature in academia, but it was not a universal feature either, and it was certainly a significant cultural asset. Among the historians educated in Poland before 1939, the orientation to the West was self-explanatory, which entailed a command of Western languages, in particular French and German.[10] Russian was not a language of Polish historical science, apart from specialists in thematic fields where it was relevant. It does not take much to realize that a person capable of using an 'excellent' Russian would find it much easier to display tact and diplomatic skills in difficult talks with Soviet partners.

The part of Bardach's work published in Russian has been underplayed in recent accounts, and the focus is mostly on his many ties to Western academia and on his recognition in the West to which his numerous memberships and affiliations attest.[11] However, he was also a regular member of various committees of socialist historians, in which Soviet academics played varying but important roles. Even though Polish historiography has liberated itself from full dependence from the Soviets since 1955 (Rutkowski, 2008, p. 265), it did not mean a break of bilateral and multilateral contacts and coordination within the Eastern bloc.

Bardach's bibliography shows 11 books, articles and chapters published in Russian (including translations from Polish), at least 5 of them published after 1989, and 11 reviews of books published in Russian, some of them after 1989 and representing a wide range of topics. A few papers on the state of historical science in the USSR, on the debates with Soviet historians and on Soviet historiography, as well as eulogies for Soviet historians,[12] also form a part of this category, only outnumbered by works in French (over 50, including, however, only one aforementioned review of a book published in French). It is important to realize that the connection to Soviet academia was the only viable Eastern connection for a socialist historian before 1989 and that it was critical in the 1950s, which was also the formative period of Bardach's career. For example, in 1955 he was a representative of Polish historical sciences delegated to discuss the publication in Russian of a comprehensive history of Poland prepared by Soviet historians (*Istorija Polszi*), a debate in which Polish historical science took a critical stance concerning the Soviet view of Polish history, albeit phrased with the usual lip service to Soviet colleagues (see Rutkowski, 2008, p. 263ff).[13] That Bardach was not unilaterally westward looking was an important asset for the new institutionalization of the history of law.[14]

Conclusion

Bardach's impact on the agenda of the history of law in socialism was complex and multidimensional, though not easy to measure in an exact manner. In the 1950s, he held a key position as a party scholar in determining the new organizational forms and research directions for Marxist historical science in Poland. In the 1960s, he lost much of his political influence, but he remained an established author, able to travel abroad much easier than many of his colleagues, well connected both in the East and in the West, keeping in touch with Soviet historical science while making a name for himself in Western international organizations and institutions. His work was largely a continuation of pre-war research agendas via direct personal links. He combined his commitment to the pre-socialist science of history, including its relative methodological openness and interdisciplinarity, with a focus on certain typically Marxist research topics, in particular on periodization. He was a very well-connected historian, an editor and an author of much-used reference books. In Bardach, the history of law gained a valuable asset in its constant interplay with historical science, but much less so in legal science, which contributed to its distancing from other branches of legal science.

Bardach's biographical trajectory shares certain transdisciplinary patterns observed in socialist academia. His status as a supervisor combined with the possibility that he was indeed a 'survivor in disguise'. It was not unusual in scholars born between 1910 and 1919 who seem to have been affected by a kind of a post-factum 'generational underdeterminacy'. Those born before 1910, like many of those with whom Bardach kept crossing paths constantly, including, for example, the influential sociologist and historian of ideas Nina Assorodobraj-

Kula (1908–1999), managed to finish their education well before the war and to take the first steps in their academic careers according to the European pre-war model, the memories of which they then carried on as survivors of bourgeois academic culture. Those born in the 1920s had no pre-war academic formation themselves; they were open to academic Marxism, predestined to play the role of supervisors of ideological takeover. They would include future revisionists like Leszek Kołakowski (1927–2009) or Zygmunt Bauman (1925–2017).

This generational mechanism was somehow reflected by the consequences of March 1968. Rutkowski wrote:

> The effect of the March events was a takeover of the main role in historical science by historians of the younger generation, born at the turn of the 1920s and 1930s. Some of the scholars whose scientific activity culminated in the 1940s and 1950s, whose position was an established one, were pushed aside from the mainstream of state politics. They were tolerated because of their work and their position abroad, their functions at the universities and in foreign institutions, but they were treated with suspicion, so they were removed from influencing decisions in matters of science. This referred, among the others, to Juliusz Bardach (…). (Rutkowski, 2008, p. 589)

Younger historians who did not fall for the charms of revisionism and were loyal to the system made a speedy advance after 1968. Survivors—some of them—managed to survive, but their impact was meagre to the extreme apart from direct personal influence on their immediate students and colleagues. Bardach, who by his birthdate would qualify as a survivor, started his academic path with an almost five-year delay due to his army service, and it put him in an in-between position. He was established enough by 1968, but he was not considered trustworthy as a party scholar after that. This might have been a blessing for his work: he was no longer working on the ideological frontline. His scientific biography demonstrates the involvement of legal history in political, academic, cultural and intellectual agendas over the timespan of more than six decades. It also demonstrates the pivotal importance of an understanding of these agendas for a fuller grasp of what the history of law was and could be under socialism.

Notes

1 The biographical information in this section is based on the following: Filaszkiewicz (2016); Rutkowski (2008), p. 153; Olszewski (2010); Siewierski (2010) (2012); Szlachta (2014); and Zakrzewski (2016) as well as two scans of Bardach's admission documents from Stefan Batory University (a handwritten curriculum vitae and an enrolment form), kindly made available to me by Olga Filaszkiewicz, to whom I am very grateful.

2 His memories were published by the University of California Press in two volumes: *Man Is Wolf to Man: Surviving the Gulag* (1999) and *Surviving Freedom: After the Gulag* (2003) (both volumes together with Kathleen Gleeson).

3 My translation.

4 A research institution established in 1944 to study the history of Polish-German relations, especially in the Recovered Territories.

5 Bardach received his PhD from Jagiellonian University; therefore, despite being a professor at the University of Warsaw, he was eligible for an honorary doctorate from the same.

6 Bardach's bibliography is available on the website of the Institute of History of Law of the Faculty of Law, University of Warsaw: http://bibliografia.ihp.wpia.uw.edu.pl/biblio2.php (retrieved December 17, 2019).

7 J. Bardach, *Historia państwa i prawa Polski do połowy XV wieku*, Warsaw 1957; Z. Kaczmarczyk, B. Leśnodorski, *Historia państwa i prawa Polski od połowy XV wieku do 1795 roku*, Warsaw 1957; *Od rozbiorów do uwłaszczenia*, J. Bardach, M. Senkowska – Gluck (eds.), Warsaw 1981; K. Grzybowski, *Od uwłaszczenia do odrodzenia państwa*, Warsaw 1982; *Historia państwa i prawa Polski 1918–1939*, F. Ryszka (ed.), cz. 1–2, Warsaw 1962, 1968.

8 In 1997, Bardach published a paper on the same subject, 'Wpływ prawa rzymskiego na Statuty litewskie oraz ich oddziaływanie na kraje sąsiednie' in the journal *Lituania* (1–2/1997, pp. 12–36).

9 'У Польщі іронічно зауважують: часто лише після смерті видатного поляка стає відомо про нього дві речі, що він був видатний і що він був єврей.'

10 In 1936 and 1937, Bardach reviewed of two volumes of a book by G. Wirschubski, *Das Strafrecht des Litauischen Statuts*, for the journal *Ateneum Wileńskie* (1936, vol. 11, pp. 516–518, and 1937, vol. 12, pp. 604–606).

11 He was a member of Société Jean Bodin and Société d'Histoire du Droit, as well as of Accademia Nazionale dei Lincei (since 1974) and Accademia Mediterranea delle Scienze (since 1982). He was also a Vice President of the Commission des Anciens Pays et Assemblées d'Etats et du Parlamentarisme and was President of the Commission for Slavonic Studies of the International Committee of Historical Sciences (1980–1985).

12 Including Boris Grekov, Lev Tcherepnin, Vladimir Pashuto, S. Youshkov.

13 A review, co-authored by Bardach, S. Arnold and S. Kieniewicz, of the first volume of this book was published in Polish in 1954 (*Kwartalnik Historyczny* 1954, No. 4, pp. 222–233) and in Russian (authored by Bardach alone) in 1955 ('Wiestnik Akademii Nauk SSSR' 1955).

14 Another trajectory of disciplinary development is shown by sociology, which did not have a comparable asset to legitimise a turn to the East—and avoided this turn almost entirely (see Bucholc, 2016).

References

Alexandrowicz, S. (2010) *Wspomnienie o Profesorze Juliuszu Bardachu* (3 XI 1914, Odessa–26 I 2010, Warszawa), *Zapiski Historyczne*, 4 (LXXV), 153–156.

Bajerski, A. (2016) *Szkolnictwo wyższe międzywojennej Polski. Ujęcie geograficzne*, Poznań: Wydawnictwo UAM.

Bal, M. (2002) *Travelling Concepts in the Humanities: A Rough Guide*, Toronto: University of Toronto Press.

Bardach, J. (1949) 'O periodyzacji dziejów w historiografii radzieckiej, *Przegląd Historyczny* 40, 22–52.

Bardach, J. (1951) 'Perspektywy rozwoju nauki historii państwa i prawa', *Czasopismo Prawno-Historyczne* 3, 1–10.

Bardach, J. (1990) Żydzi w Birżach radziwiłłowskich w XVII–XVIII wieku, *Przegląd Historyczny*, 81:1–2, 199–220.

Bardach, J. (1991) Rec. J. Kodrębski, Prawo rzymskie w Polsce XIX wieku (Łódź 1990), *Przegląd Historyczny*, 82:2, 335–337.

Bardach, J. (2001) *Themis a Clio, czyli o potrzebie podejścia historycznego w prawoznawstwie*, Warsaw: Liber.

Bardach, J. (2009) 'About Natives, Nativeness and Native Patriotism—Past and Present', in *A Book of the Grand Duchy of Lithuania: Towards the Tradition of European Community. A Joint Publication of Scientists and Writers from Belarus, Lithuania and Poland*, Sejny: Pogranicze.

Bardach, J. (2016) 'Ze wspomnień o Karolu Koranyim', in Baraniewski W., Tygielski W. and Wróblewski A. K., (eds) *Portrety Uczonych. Profesorowie Uniwersytetu Warszawskiego po 1945 (A–K)*, Monumenta Universitatis Varsoviensis, Warsaw: Wydawnictwa UW, 521–525.

Bucholc, M. (2016) *Sociology in Poland: To Be Continued?*, London: Palgrave. DOI: 10.1057/978-1-137-58187-7.

Bucholc, M. (2017a) 'The Warsaw School of the Historians of Ideas as a Thought Collective: Together, Separately', *The Interlocutor* 1:1, 141–161.

Bucholc, M. (2017b) '*Nachruf für Jerzy Szacki. Historie*', *Jahrbuch des Zentrums für Historische Forschung Berlin der Polnischen Akademie der Wissenschaften*, 11, 251–253.

Connelly, J. (2000) *Captive University*, Chapel Hill and London: University of North Carolina Press.

Czech-Jezierska, B. A. (2015) 'Powojenne losy nauczania prawa rzymskiego w Polsce Ludowej (1944–1989)', *Krakowskie Studia z Historii Państwa i Prawa*, 8:1, 77–92.

Dobra starość… (2007) 'Dobra starość to umiejętność wykorzystania doświadczenia', in *A. Kobos, Po drogach uczonych. T. 2.* Kraków: Polska Akademia Umiejętności, 491–524.

Filaszkiewicz, O. (2016) 'Juliusz Bardach—wileńskie lata', in Dąbrowski P. and Szpoper D. (eds) *Stefan Ehrenkreutz i historycy prawa okresu dwudziestolecia międzywojennego*, Olsztyn: GWS, 87–98.

Garrison Walters, E. (1988) *The Other Europe: Eastern Europe to 1945*, Syracuse: Syracuse University Press.

Haferkamp, H.-P. (2018) *Die historische Rechtsschule*. Frankfurt am Main: Vittorio Klostermann.

Historia… (1955) *Historia państwa I prawa polskiego, Cz. I, według wykładów prof. J. Bardacha przygotowali M. Pietrzak, W. Rostocki i St. Russocki*, Warszawa: PWN.

Kühn, Z. (2011) *The Judiciary in Central and Eastern Europe: Mechanical Jurisprudence in Transformation*, Leiden and Boston: Brill and Martinus Nijhoff. DOI: 10.1163/9789047429005.

Marszał, M. and Srokosz, J. (2010) 'Rzymianie czy barbarzyńcy? Z dyskusji nad reformą programu studiów prawniczych w Polsce w Latach 1931–1937', in *Acta Universitatis Wratislaviensis 3264*, Przegląd Prawa i Administracji Lxxxiii, Wrocław: Wydawnictwo UWr, 263–286.

Materniak-Pawłowska, M. and Krzymkowski, M. (2018) "Siedemdziesiąt lat 'Czasopisma Prawno-Historycznego"', *Czasopismo Prawno-Historyczne*, 70:1, 345–352.

Mączak, A. (1993) '*National Traditions in the Historiography of the State: the Case of Poland*', *Actes du colloque de Rome (18–31 mars 1990)*, Publications de l'École Française de Rome, Année 1993, 171, 235–248.

Olszewski, H. (2010) 'Wspomnienie o Juliuszu Bardachu (1914–2010)', *Nauka* 1, 159–163.

Olszewski, H. (2015) *Ludzie Uniwersytetu w mojej pamięci*, Poznań: Wydawnictwo UAM.

Olszewski, H. (2017) *Kilka uwag o prawniczych studiach II stopnia w latach 1952–1954, Acta Universitatis Wratislaviensis 3780 Studia nad Autorytaryzmem i Totalitaryzmem*, 39:2, 89–113.

Popper, K. R. (1994) *The Open Society and Its Enemies*, New Jersey: Princeton University Press.

Rosner, A. and Wąsowicz, M. (eds) (2004) *Z dziejów kultury prawnej: studia ofiarowane Profesorowi Juliuszowi Bardachowi w dziewięćdziesięciolecie urodzin*, Warsaw: Liber.

Rutkowski, T. (2008) *Nauki historyczne w Polsce 1944–1970. Zagadnienia polityczne i organizacyjne*, Warsaw: Wydawnictwa UW.

Rutkowski, T. (2016) 'Na styku nauki i polityki. Uniwersytet warszawski w PRL 1944–1989', in Baraniewski W., Tygielski W. and Wróblewski A. K. (eds) *Dzieje Uniwersytetu Warszawskiego po 1945*, Monumenta Universitatis Varsoviensis, Warsaw: Wydawnictwa UW, 375–692. DOI: 10.31338/uw.9788323522041.pp.375-692.

Siewierski, T. (2010) 'Juliusz Bardach (1914–2010): o lituanistycznej pasji uczonego' (http://mlodszaeuropa.pl/index.php?option=com_content&view=article&id=71:juliusz-bardach-1914-2010-o-lituanistycznej-pasji-uczonego&catid=18:dziedzictwo-artykuy&Itemid=6; retrieved 17.12.2019).

Siewierski, T. (2012) 'Juliusz Bardach (1914–2010): o lituanistycznej pasji uczonego', in Czyżewska U., Siewierski T., Tabaszewski R. and Żołnierz J. (eds) *Multum, non multa. Młodzi badacze w poszukiwaniu prawdy*, Lublin: Wydawnictwo KUL, 107–120.

Sokalska, O. (2017) 'Юліуш Бардах—Історик Права На Перехресті Епох І Держав (До Витоків Родоводу Вченого)', *Вісник Пенітенціарної Асоціації України*, 2, 13–19.

Sułek, A. (2012), 'Jerzy Szacki, encyklopedysta', *Przegląd Filozoficzno-Literacki*, 35:4, 43–45.

Szlachta, B. (2014) 'Juliusz Bardach (1914–2010)', in Kozub-Ciembroniewicz W. (ed) *Uczeni żydowskiego pochodzenia we współczesnych dziejach Uniwersytetu Jagiellońskiego*, Kraków: Wydawnictwo UJ, 77–85.

Thornhill, C. (2011) *A Sociology of Constitutions*, Cambridge: Cambridge University Press. DOI: 10.1017/CBO9780511895067.

Wandycz, P. S. (1992) 'Historiography of the Countries of Central and Eastern Europe: Poland', *The American Historical Review*, 97:4, 1011–1025.

Wołodkiewicz, W. (2015) 'Nauczanie prawa czy przepisów prawnych', *Czasopismo Historyczno-Prawne*, 67:1, 233–247. DOI: 10.14746/cph.2015.68.1.12.

Wołodkiewicz, W. (2012) 'Czy prawo rzymskie będzie istnieć?', *Palestra* 9–10, 203–212.

Zakrzewski, A. (2016) 'Juliusz Bardach. 1914–2010', in Baraniewski W., Tygielski W. and Wróblewski A. K. (eds) *Portrety Uczonych. Profesorowie Uniwersytetu Warszawskiego po 1945 (A–K)*. Monumenta Universitatis Varsoviensis, Warsaw: Wydawnictwa UW, 57–62. DOI: 10.31338/uw.9788323523314.pp.56-63.

Z prac… (1950) 'Z prac Podsekcji Prawa I Kongresu Nauki Polskiej', *Państwo i Prawo* 11:5, 97–114.

Zysiak, A. (2018) 'Postwar Modernization and the University for the Working Classes in Poland', in Karady V. and Hincu A. (eds) *Social Sciences in the Other Europe Since 1945*, Budapest: Pasts, Inc., Central European University, 29–51.

7 Valdemārs Kalniņš (1907–1981)

The founder of Soviet legal history in Latvia

Sanita Osipova

Introduction

In natural sciences, existing knowledge is fundamentally revised only in the light of new scientific findings. This is certainly the case in biology, physics, chemistry, and astronomy. However, history, including the history of law, belongs to the humanities, and the message it communicates can be exploited, among other things, for political purposes. Raymond Aron viewed history as an ever-evolving time-linked myth (Aron, 2000, p. 480). Like myths, the stories that are part of history can be told in different ways, with certain facts brought to the fore and others concealed, with past events construed or falsified. Events of the past have an impact on an individual's worldview as, in the process of socialisation, they lay the foundations for the individual's national identity as well as his or her understanding of the state, justness, or historical injustices that need to be repaired. In telling history to a nation, the teller shapes its identity, national identity being a historical-cultural phenomenon (Smits, 1997, pp. 6–7). By altering the narrative of past events, we can influence the minds of society. By means of history, the existing order, power, state, and law can be rendered illegitimate or, conversely, legitimised in the public consciousness and the values prevailing in society can be changed. That is the reason why history, unlike the natural sciences, has undergone 'rewritings' not only on account of new scientific developments but also for political reasons, with the change of the ruling ideology and power.

The development of Latvian legal history from the 19th to the mid-20th century

Latvian legal history as it has been recorded in the works of legal historians since the 19th century is itself worth a serious study. Depending on the ethnicity (nationality) of the historian, on the state to which the territory of Latvia belonged in a particular period, and on the ruling ideology of that period, the same historical facts and sources of law are either emphasised or concealed, as well as interpreted in directly opposite ways. This explains why legal history books housed in Latvian libraries give drastically different ideas of the nature and social implication of law that used to be in force in the Latvian territory. The following schools of legal historians can be identified as having studied the legal history of Latvia from different perspectives and using different methodologies.

1 In the 19th and early 20th century, interest towards the history of law was maintained by the historical school of jurisprudence (Lazdiņš, 2006, pp. 21–23). During this period, studies were mainly carried out by Baltic German historians of law, who viewed the history of Baltic law as part of German legal history (Meļķisis, 1998, p. 1).[1] This was because Livonia was a vassal state of the German Empire and also because it was the Baltic Germans who constituted the elite of the Russian Empire's Baltic 'Governorate' (*Guberniya*), and the German language was a state language there until the last quarter of the 19th century. One of the more widely known Baltic German historians of law was Friedrich Georg von Bunge (1802–1897) (Lazdiņš, 2000, p. 12).

However, during this period, alongside the Baltic Germans' efforts in studying the local law as part of the German legal culture, scholarly activity was also carried out by Russian legal historians. In their studies, especially at the end of the 19th century, after the Empire had been centralised and the policy of Russification had begun, they emphasised the historical presence and influence in the Baltics of Russian, or, at least, Slavic legal culture and Eastern Orthodox Christianity.[2] Thus, matters of Latvian legal history were mainly discussed between German and Russian scholars (Lazdiņš, 2000, pp. 10–19). Moreover, Latvia itself did not yet exist at that time, as the territories populated by Latvians, which would be united into a state in 1918, were divided into various governorates of Russia.

2 Latvian legal culture and its history were studied at a qualitatively new level and in the 20th century time with support from the national state in the Republic of Latvia, during the period between the two World Wars. It was in this period, after the Latvian people had established their state, that the foundations of Latvian legal history were laid. A substantial contribution to the studies of Latvian legal history was made in the inter-war years of the 20th century by Arveds Švābe (1888–1959)[3] and Vasīlijs Sinaiskis (1876–1949) (Kovaļčuka and Eļtazarova, 2009, pp. 12–13). The notion of Latvian legal history, as formed by the Baltic German lawyers, was revised. Jānis Straubergs writes the following with respect to the revaluation of history:

> Every major work in the field of Latvian history has to come up against certain traditions shaped by the German historians, and to face the skepticism with which the departure from those traditions is received. (Straubergs, 1936, p. 5).

The development of legal history as a scholarly discipline was still influenced by the historical school of jurisprudence (Lazdiņš, 2006, pp. 41–42). However, in contrast to the studies by Baltic Germans, who had been emphasising the dominance of German legal culture in the former territory of Livonia, during this time an expressly Latvian perspective was developed (Birziņa, 1999, p. 157). Scholars during the inter-war period pointed out that the true essence of Latvian legal consciousness lay in folklore, particularly in short quatrain songs called *dainas* (Sinaiskis, 1938).

3 The whole legal system and jurisprudence of Latvia were substantially changed as a result of the Soviet occupation (1940/1941 and 1944–1990/1991). The changes affected not only substantive and procedural law and the judiciary but also academic legal disciplines such as legal theory, philosophy, and history, which were fundamentally revised to comply with Marxist-Leninist dogmas (Osipova, 2007). The previously existing state was declared a state of reactionary bourgeois exploiters hostile to the people, and the legal history maintained by it was discredited as being 'falsified' and a 'pseudo-discipline' that had to be consigned 'to the dustbin of history' (Kļava, 1953). The methods used by legal historians during the inter-war period were declared antiscientific, and their works ended up in closed library archives.

Rapid changes or how the school of legal history was destroyed in Latvia

Metamorphosis of the legal system and doctrine was only possible because, within half a year of the occupation, the laws of the Russian Soviet Federative Socialist Republic came into force in the territory of Latvia (*Latvijas PSRS Augstākās Padomes Ziņotājs*, 1940), just as they did in Estonia and Lithuania. Simultaneously the Soviet programme of legal studies was introduced, which had to be taught using textbooks approved at the all-Union level.

As early as 1940, Soviet legal history in the University of Latvia was taught to students by Valdemārs Kalniņš (1907–1981) (Birziņa, 1999, p. 265). Within a very short time (a couple of months between the proclamation of Soviet power in the summer of 1940 and the beginning of a new academic year in autumn), he replaced the inter-war period idea of legal history, formed under the influence of the historical school, with a diametrically opposite concept of legal history. In other words, the teaching of a political discipline complying with Soviet ideology started immediately following the occupation, and Latvian legal history within this discipline was viewed in the context of that of the USSR, based on the periodization of history adopted by the Communist Party of the Soviet Union (CPSU) (Kalnin, 1954, p. 4).

The University of Latvia Library still keeps Soviet textbooks in legal history from the time immediately after World War II—books in Russian on the history of state and law of the USSR (Denisov, 1947; Jushkov, 1950). The history of state and law of the USSR was also the name of the first course in legal history, which complied with the Soviet doctrine and was taught to students in 1940. Even during my own studies, matters were not substantially different. Although between 1986 and 1991, I was part of a Latvian-speaking group, we studied the history of state and law of the USSR using Russian textbooks approved as 'good' at the all-Union level. At the heart of the history of state and law of the USSR, there was the teaching of the state and law history of Russia, in which the state and legal histories of other Soviet republics were touched upon as a subordinate subject (Zhidkov, 1988–1991).

However, to legal students in 1940–1941 and 1944–1945, these books on the USSR state and law history were not yet available in sufficient quantities. It is also not entirely believable that at the time immediately following the occupation students had a sufficient knowledge of the Russian language allowing them to learn from those books.[4] Therefore, they mainly studied by listening to lectures and making notes. Thus, the lecturers played the most important part in introducing the Soviet teaching of legal history.

To keep the lectures in line with the Soviet legal dogma, that is, politically correct, the lecturers' work was under constant supervision. Professor Līna Birziņa (1910–2007) writes in her memoirs that during the post-war years, lectures were attended, without prior notice to the lecturer, by a 'visitor' and a shorthand writer who took down notes on the lecture. From the 1950s, lectures were recorded using a technical innovation such as a magnetic tape recorder. If 'departures' from the ideological course set by the Communist Party of the Soviet Union were found by reviewers in the recorded lectures, meetings were called and held at the 'Great Hall' (*Magna Aula*) of the University of Latvia to publicly criticise the politically incorrect utterances made during the lectures and to shame the guilty teacher in front of colleagues and co-workers. This was how the Soviet system controlled the 'lecturers' political stance' (Birziņa, 1999, p. 269). Furthermore, one should not forget another system functioning alongside this open surveillance, namely, KGB informants. In the Soviet system, there were KGB agents among students as well as among university teachers who collected information about misconduct during lectures. The consequences of such information being reported were not public, but they were considerably more serious than mere public correction.

The work of the historical legal school previously formed in Latvia (mainly constituted by Professor Švābe and the students) ended, as none of the Latvian legal historians of the inter-war period went on to work in Soviet legal studies after World War II. The 1940–1941 experience motivated many scholars to flee at the end of the war. For a second time now, Vasīlijs Sinaiskis, a historian of Roman law, fled from the Bolsheviks to the West (Feigmane, 2010).[5] Arveds Švābe and his student Benno Ābers, too, left Latvia at the end of the war (Strods, 1988). Another student of Švābe, Tālivaldis Jānis Zemzaris, remained in Latvia and even continued working in science after the establishment of Soviet power, albeit in meteorology, not law. However, Zemzaris lost his job in 1949, having been 'accused of participating in "organisations of bourgeois Latvia" and included among the individuals unwanted by Soviet power' (Auns, 2002, p. 149). Thus, for various reasons, none of the specialist legal historians of the inter-war period were engaged in the development of Soviet legal history.

Soviet legal history in Latvian SSR was taught by Valdemārs Kalniņš; later on, he turned this field of study into a discipline, becoming the founder of the Soviet

Latvia school of legal historians. Among the members of this school were Professor Līna Birziņa and assistant to Kalniņš, future Professor Romāns Apsītis (1939) (Birziņa, 1999, p. 272).

Valdemārs Kalniņš's controversial scientific work: Before and after the Soviet occupation of Latvia

How did Valdemārs Kalniņš find his way into legal history studies? He was a polyglot: apart from his native Latvian, he was fluent in Latin, German, and Russian. He was a lawyer: after graduating, in 1931, from the University of Latvia, Department of Law, Professor Sinaiskis prepared him for research and teaching work in civil law and Roman civil law. Thus, during his studies and at the beginning of his scholarly career, Kalniņš did not specialise in Latvian legal history. Before the Soviet occupation, he taught civil law (Kalniņš, 1939), Roman law, and Roman law history at the university. In 1938, he defended his doctoral thesis entitled *Universal Succession in Roman Inheritance Law* (Birziņa, 1999, p. 265).

It would have been easier to analyse the changes introduced into legal history studies by the Soviet ideology if there had been works by the same author published both before and after the establishment of Soviet power. However, as already mentioned, none of the Latvian legal historians of the inter-war period went on to work in Soviet legal studies. Kalniņš, for his part, worked in the field of civil law and Roman private law. Still, the substantial differences between inter-war period jurisprudence and the Soviet doctrine in their understanding of the essence of law, the sources of law, and legal methodology, in other words, in their treatment of historical legal norms, can be clarified by comparing Kalniņš's publications before and after 1940.

First of all, it should be stressed that before 1940, Kalniņš only used works by lawyers in analysing and evaluating the history of Roman legal institutions. His publications contain references to works by jurists from the Roman Empire (Gaius, Ulpianus, Paulus, etc.); the Russian Empire (Pokrovsky I. A.); Germany (Bachofen J., Fehr M., Dernburg H., etc.); and, of course, by his teacher Vasīlijs Sinaiskis (Kalniņš, 1939, p. 7). Unlike many other scholars, who in their works praised Latvia's authoritarian ruler at the time, Kalniņš was apolitical. Working in the field of civil law, he was using the term 'the Civil Law of Latvia' (Kalniņš, 1939, p. 2), not 'President Ulmanis' Civil Law' (Vīnzarājs, 1938, p. 803). In fact, there is no evidence of an ideological impact on his pre-1940 works that analysed legal institutions, nor is there servility to authoritarian state rule—simply objective legal analysis.

Developed in a similar manner, his 1939 civil law studies programme contains, in section II, a brief overview of the historical development of civil law, including the reception of Roman law, as well as of legal philosophy, where he mentions the school of natural law and the historical school, Hegel's teaching, and the influence of sociology—a popular research area at that time—on civil law. The programme, however, does not mention either Marxism-Leninism (Kalniņš, 1939, p. 2) or National Socialism—the ideology some Latvian scholars of that time sympathised with (Gailīte, 2014, pp. 97–98). My guess is that the objective academic style of lectures and publications, alongside his reticence to express enthusiasm about an authoritarian Latvia or critical opinions on Soviet ideology and law, were precisely the reasons (Kovaļčuka, 2011, pp. 81–95)[6] why the Soviet powers found Kalniņš eligible to continue working at the university and to teach Soviet legal history, an ideologically important course. In fact, prior to 1940, Kalniņš had never publicly expressed his political views. He had not 'stained' himself by demonstrating loyalty to the authoritarian state. In addition, Kalniņš's good knowledge of Russian might have played its part, for he could use it not only in everyday situations but also in the academic context. As Professor Birziņa wrote: 'sadly, on official occasions [in the Soviet state], especially in academia, only Russian would do' (Birziņa, 1999, p. 268).

Kalniņš's publications from the Soviet period, however, invariably start with citations from Lenin (Kalniņš, 1963, p. 3), Stalin (Kalnin, 1954, pp. 2–4), and materials from the programme and regular congresses of the Communist Party (Kalnin, 1962, p. 3). A similar tendency can be observed in the studies course programmes: in the pre-occupation period, they only included sources of law and the legal doctrine (Kalniņš, 1939, pp. 1–3), while in the Soviet times, the recommended reading list began with numerous works by Karl Marx, Lenin, and Pēteris Stučka (1865–1932), followed by materials from CPSU congresses and decisions of the plenum. Only after tribute was paid to the ruling regime were legal sources and sources of Soviet legal doctrine that were necessary for studying given (Kalnin, Apsitis, 1970, pp. 20–30). One can only imagine the degree of intimidation required to make an individual as Kalniņš drastically change his scholarly style to please the ruling regime.

During the Soviet period, not every person could pursue a career in academia and freely choose to become a scholar in the field of Soviet legal history, as the politically unreliable individuals were denied the possibility of working in a number of professions, including scientific and academic work (Auns, 2002, p. 149).[7] Furthermore, the academic freedom of those allowed to work as scholars was also restricted; for example, scholars could not freely choose research objectives, all of which were clearly defined in the party policy documents. Legal historians in the Soviet state were entrusted with a politically important task, namely, to substantiate the claim that 'the Soviet state is the new, superior and historically ultimate type of state' (Kalnin, 1954, p. 2). For this purpose, the whole course of history of the future Soviet peoples up to the Great October Socialist Revolution had to be rearranged as a class struggle on the way to communism.

The research objective mentioned in Kalniņš's doctoral thesis written and defended in 1954 (in Russian) was:

> to show how the Latvian people, led by the communist party, in a fierce struggle with class enemies broke free of the bourgeois power and established a dictatorship of working people, joined the family of friendly nations of the USSR, developed and consolidated its national Soviet statehood and socialist law. (Kalnin, 1954, p. 1)

To achieve this purpose, history as a discipline was fundamentally revised to introduce periodization complying with, as Kalniņš wrote in his thesis, 'historical materialism—the scientific approach developed by Marx and Engels, and advanced by Lenin and Stalin, based on regularities in the evolvement of society and on the laws of the course of history' (Kalnin, 1954, p. 3). This is also clearly reflected in Kalniņš's later works; for example, in the 1964 publication devoted to Pēteris Stučka's contribution to the study of Roman law:

> P.I. Stučka endeavoured to evaluate Roman law from scientific, that is, Marxist-Leninist perspectives. [...] As P.I. Stučka wrote, 'ours is a revolutionary viewpoint which presupposes paying special attention to epochs.' (Kalnin, 1964, p. 37)

The history of Latvia, too, was re-divided into 'epochs' (Kalniņš, 1972, pp. 49–50). It should also be noted that a new state and law history discipline was created from the legal history (German *Rechtsgeschichte*) influenced by the historical legal school because, according to Marxist dogma, law only emerges and changes along with the state and therefore must not be viewed in isolation from it.

The second task that Soviet legal historians were entrusted with was to mark the rights of exploiters in different periods as an instrument of oppression and an impediment to the development of working people, as 'also the earlier history serves to ideologically boost the driving forces of people in their struggle for building communism' (Kalniņš, 1963, p. 3). Soviet legal history described the ancestors of Latvians—the tribes of the Balts and Livs—as a class oppressed by their conquerors, that is, working people subjected to exploitation. They appear in history books as peasant serfs and poor rightless townspeople (Kalniņš, 1972, pp. 49–50). Another concept that Soviet historians had to incorporate in their publications was that of the Russian people being friendly to the peoples of the other Soviet republics. In the case of Latvia, it was emphasised that at a certain point in history Russians had stepped in to support Latvians in their fight against the German occupants, the Crusaders (Sudrabkalns, Drīzulis, 1951, p. 21).

It was thus only logical from the Marxist-Leninist standpoint that a previously oppressed people—the Latvians—should be included in the Soviet Union, a family of liberated working peoples. This way of presenting history, with the development of history viewed as a result of the insatiable struggle between antagonistic classes, directly determined the structure of history-telling. For example, *The State System and Law of the Duchy of Courland (1561–1795)*, a book published in 1963, is structured as follows. First comes the history of the state, which describes the respective historic period and the political situation in the state (Kalniņš, 1963, pp. 5–9), including its division into classes. The ruling class in the work in question constituted landowners; priests; burghers; or wealthy townsmen; and free farmers (Kalniņš, 1963, pp. 10–12). Then came the exploited class: peasants, broken down into seven groups depending on their material status (Kalniņš, 1963, p. 14).

The description of each class contains information on the legal status of the individuals belonging to it, with references to the legal sources where that status was regulated. Next comes a description of the state system, with a special emphasis on the judiciary (Kalniņš, 1963, pp. 25–27). Part two of the book is legal history, mainly referring to, describing, and citing various sources of law (Kalniņš, 1963, pp. 28–47). The book contains no analysis of the branch of law dealing with public law. Other legal history textbooks (Kalnin, 1962) from which the state and law history of Latvian SSR was taught (Kalnin, Apsitis, 1970), as well as the respective studies programmes, were structured in a similar way.

What especially strikes the eye in the contents of the studies' programme is the third task entrusted to the Soviet legal historians—to use scholarly ways to condemn as false or wrong all other versions of legal history and to prove the reactionary nature of the previous state, that is, to criticise the Republic of Latvia and its laws (Kalnin, Apsitis, 1970, pp. 12–13). There was only one 'right' version of legal history, and that was Soviet legal history. There was only one state enjoying justness and equality—the USSR. There was no such thing, not could there be such a thing, as bourgeois justice, the Soviet dogma maintained. I will not analyse the vocabulary developed for criticising liberal national or bourgeois states, as it should be studied as a separate research subject. Moreover, I doubt whether this vocabulary is at all translatable into languages that have never been used to put Soviet ideology into effect. For example, Kalniņš, referring to Stučka, criticised the dogmatic representation of Roman law in bourgeois literature and emphasised the advantages of the Soviet approach to research (Kalnin, 1964, p. 37).

Kalniņš, however, did not take part in the politically ordered disparagement of works by expatriate Latvian legal historians, even though it was a widespread practice, especially during Stalin's lifetime (Kļava, 1953). Quite the opposite: despite the censorship and the strict boundaries set by the Soviet ideology for research in the field of legal history, Professor Kalniņš managed to ensure continuity in Latvian legal history studies. While being politically correct in his publications, he still included references to sources that contained alternative information and opinions of 'reactionary' scholars.[8] For example, when writing about urban law, Kalniņš preserved the previously developed terminology (created by Baltic German rather than Latvian legal historians: e.g., Švābe wrote about 'townsmen' (***namnieki***) (Švābe, 1940, p. 257), thus Latvianising the German term 'burghers,' whereas Kalniņš returns to 'burghers' in his books. Kalniņš remained loyal to historical facts discovered by his predecessors: for example, he stepped back from the idea of constant antagonism between Latvians and Germans. He wrote that 'at the onset of [the city of] Riga, it was rather easy to become a burgher. Not only Germans, but also the local non-Germans (Livs, Latvians, Russians, etc.) were included as burghers at the time' (Kalniņš, 1972, p. 44). In his publications, Kalniņš provided references to works by Baltic German legal historians as well as to publications by the legal historians working in the period of the Republic, albeit not during Stalin's lifetime but only from the 'Khrushchev Thaw' onwards.

Rounding up the topic, I asked myself only one question. Is the Soviet state and law history at all an academic discipline? Can we recognise as a discipline a mass of information purposefully generated at the request of, and under the management and supervision of, a totalitarian state? Can there be such a thing as science or the humanities without the academic freedom to create; can a discipline exist where it is closely supervised, censored, and customised to reach certain political goals? Soviet legal history was created without observing the key prerequisites of academia—scholarly objectivity and neutrality. I have come to the conclusion that Soviet legal history was created not as an academic discipline but as a vehicle for propaganda, aiming to consolidate the Soviet ideology in the mind of *homo sovieticus*, as well as to spread it outside the state borders.

Conclusion

Latvia was founded in 1918. The Latvian legal history originated in the inter-war period re-evaluating and revising the legal history understandings of the German and Russian scholars of the 19th century. The entire legal system and jurisprudence of Latvia were substantially changed as a result of the Soviet occupation (1940/1941 and 1944–1990/1991). The changes affected not only substantive and procedural law and the judiciary but also academic legal disciplines such as legal theory, philosophy, and history, which were fundamentally revised to comply with Marxist-Leninist dogma. The work of the historical legal school previously formed in Latvia (mainly inaugurated by Professor Švābe and his students) was ended, and the Latvian legal history was discredited.

Scholars' freedom to choose to work in the Soviet legal history field was restricted, and the key prerequisites of academia—scholarly objectivity and neutrality—were not respected. The loyalty of scholars and content of their lectures were under permanent CPSU and KGB surveillance, performed by different methods. Legal historians in the Soviet state were entrusted with several politically important tasks, namely, to substantiate the claim that 'the Soviet state is the new, superior and historically speaking the ultimate type of state,' to mark the rights of exploiters in different periods as an instrument of oppression of working people, to use scholarly ways to condemn as false or wrong all other versions of legal history, and to prove the reactionary nature of the previous state.

In the light of the above, I conclude that Soviet legal history was created not as an academic discipline but as a vehicle for state ideology. Therefore, the contribution of Soviet legal historians is contradictory.

Notes

1 A number of outstanding Baltic German legal historians were active in the 19th century Baltics: Friedrich Georg von Bunge, August von Bulmerinq, Astaf Transehe-Roseneck, Leonid Arbuzov, and others.

2 For example, Russian civil law historian S. V. Pakhman (Семен Викентьевич Пахман 1825–1910) in his monograph *История кодификации гражданского права* (Москва: Зерцало, 2004) analyses the history of Baltic law as part of Russian

legal history. This was consistent with the political reality, as the whole territory of Latvia had been part of the Russian Empire starting from the 18th century.

3 For example, Švābe A. *Latvijas vēsture. 1800–1913.* Trešais izdevums, Rīga: Avots, 1991, Švābe A. *Latvijas vēsture 1800–1914.* Trešais izdevums. Rīga: Avots, 1991, Švābe A. *Latvijas cilšu tiesības.* Rīga: [b.i.], 1939, Švābe A. *Latvju kultūras vēsture. II. daļa.* Rīga: A. Gulbja apgādībā, 1922, *Latvju kultūra.* Zin red. Arveds Švābe. [b.v.] A. Klāvsona apgāds, 1948.

4 Even though, from the Soviet occupation on, a Russian language exam was part of the university entrance exams.

5 Vassily Sinaisky spent the last years of his life in Belgium, where he died in 1949.

6 The situation in Soviet Russia, its treatment of the church and religion, private property, kolkhozes, etc., was widely discussed in the Latvian press. In turn, Russian émigré lawyers used Latvia as a centre for publishing their periodical *Statute and Law* (Закон и Право) (1929–1938).

7 Here, we can once again recall *Tālivaldis Zemzaris.* 9.

8 E.g., Baltic Germans such as Ch. G. von Ziegenhorn, C. von Rummel, F.G.von Bunge; see: Kalniņš V. *Kurzemes hercogistes valsts iekārta un tiesības (1561.–1795.),* Rīga: Pētera Stučkas Latvijas Valsts universitāte, 1963, pages 8, 10, 15. Also, works by legal historians of the inter-war period, such as Arveds Švābe, Benno Ābers, Tālivaldis Zemzaris.

References

1940. Gada 6. novembra PSRS Augstākās Padomes Prezidija dekrēts 'Par KPFSR kriminal-, civil-, un darba likumu pagaidu piemērošanu Lietuvas, Latvijas un Igaunijas Padomju Sociālistisko Republiku teritorijās' (Decree of the Presidium of the Supreme Soviet of the USSR of November 6, 1940 'On the temporary application of the criminal, civil and labour legislation of the USSR in the territories of the Soviet Socialist Republics of Lithuania, Latvia and Estonia.') (1940), Latvijas PSRS Augstākās Padomes Ziņotājs, 74, 1.

Aron, R. (2000) *Vvedenije v filosofiju istoriji (Introduction to the philosophy of history),* Moscow: Universitetskaja kniga.

Auns, M. (2002) 'Jānim Tālivaldim Zemzarim—100 (100th Anniversary of the birth of Janis Talivaldis Zemzaris)', *Latvijas Arhīvi,* 1, 149–154.

Birziņa, L. (1999) *Latvijas Universitātes tiesībzinātnieki. Tiesiskās doma Latvijā XX gadsimtā (Lawyers at the University of Latvia. Legal thought in Latvia in the 20th century),* Rīga: Zvaigzne ABC.

Denisov, A. I. (ed) (1947) *Istorija gosudarstva i prava SSSR: chast 2 (History of State and Law of the USSR: 2 part),* Moscow: Institut juridicheskih nauk Ministerstva justiciji SSSR.

Feigmane, T. (2010) 'Vasīlijs Sinaiskis', *Latvijas krievi,* http://www.russkije.lv/lv/lib/read/vasily-sinaysky.html (accessed 30.09.2019).

Gailīte, D. (2014) 'Valstiskuma jautājums vācu juridiskajā presē Latvijā. Rigasche Zeitschrift für Rechtswissenschaft (1926–1939) (The question of statehood in the German legal press in Latvia. Riga's Journal of Law (1926–1939))', in Rozenfelds, J., Čepāne, I. and Osipova, S., (eds) *Tiesību efektīvas piemērošanas problemātika. Latvijas Universitātes 72. zinātniskās konferences rakstu krājums,* Rīga: LU akadēmiskais apgāds, 96–106.

Jushkov, S. V. (1950) *Istorija gosudarstva i prava SSSR: chast 1 (History of State and Law of the USSR: 1 part),* Moscow: Gosjurizdat.

Kalniņš, V. (1939) *Civiltiesību programma. Pēc Latvijas un Vakareiropas civillikumiem (Programme for Civil Law. After German and Western European civil law)*, Rīga: Latvijas Universitāte.

Kalniņš, V. (1939) *Romiešu ķīlu tiesību attīstība (Development of the Roman Lien Law)*, Rīga: Jurists.

Kalniņš, V. (1963) *Kurzemes hercogistes valsts iekārta un tiesības (1561–1795) (State Order and Law of the Duchy of Courland (1561–1795))*, Rīga: Pētera Stučkas Latvijas Valsts universitāte.

Kalniņš, V. (1972) *Latvijas PSR valsts un tiesību vēsture. I daļa. Feodālisma un topošā kapitālisma laikmets XI–XIX gs (State and legal history of the Latvian SSR. Part I. The Era of Feudalism and developing Capitalism in the 11th–19th century)*, Rīga: Zvaigzne.

Kalnin, V. E. (1964) 'P. I. Stuchka o rimskom prave i jego recepciji v burzhuaznih stranah (P. I. Stučka on Roman law and its reception in bourgeois countries)' in *Nauchnaja konferencija o teoreticheskom naslediji P.I. Stuchki v sovetskoj pravovoj nauke*, Riga: LGU.

Kalnin, V. E. (1954) *Istorija gosudarstva i prava Sovetskoj Latviji (State and Legal History of Soviet Latvia)*, Riga: Latvijskij Gosudarstvennij Universtitet im. P. Stuchki.

Kalnin, V. E. (1962) *Obshchestvenno-politicheskij stroj i pravo foedalnoj Latviji v XI–XVI vekah (Sociopolitical System and Feudal Law in Latvia in the XI–XVI Centuries)*, Riga: Latvijskij Gosudarstvennij Universtitet im. P. Stuchki.

Kalnin, V. E. and Apsitis R. V. (1970) *Programma po Istorii gosudarstva i prava Latvijskoj SSP (Study Programme on the Political and Legal History of the Latvian SSR)*, Riga: Latvijskij Gosudarstvennij Universtitet im. P. Stuchki.

Kļava, G. (1953) 'Grāmata par buržuaziskajiem Latvijas vēstures viltotājiem (*A book on bourgeois counterfeiters of Latvian history*)', *Cīņa*, 2:7, 5.

Kovaļčuka, S. (2011) 'Oskars Gruzenbergs: žurnāla «Likums un Tiesa» (1929–1938) galvenais redaktors (Oskar Gruzenberg: Chief Editor of the journal *Law and Justice* (1929–1938))', in Krūmiņa-Koņkova, S. (ed) *Kultūras identitātes dimensijas,*Rīga: Latvijas Universitāte, 81–95.

Kovaļčuka, S., Eļtazarova, K. (2009) 'Bez kultūras nav tiesību, bez tiesībām nav īstas dzīves (There is no right without culture, no real life without rights)' in *Jurista Vārds*, 39:582, 12, 1.

Lazdiņš, J. (2000) *Baltijas zemnieku privāttiesības (XIX.gs.) (Private Law of the Baltic Peasants (19th century))*, Rīga: Biznesa augstskola Turība.

Lazdiņš, J. (2006) 'Vēsturiskā tiesību skola un Latvija (Historical school of jurisprudence and Latvia)' in *Latvijas Universitātes Raksti. Juridiskā zinātne*, 703, 41–45

Meļķisis, E. (1998) 'Ievadam (The Introduction)', in Meļķisis, E. (ed) *Latvijas tiesību avoti. Teksti un komentāri. I sējums, Seno paražu un Livonijas tiesību avoti 10.gs.- 16. gs.* Rīga: LU žurnāla "Latvijas Vēsture" fonds, 1–2.

Osipova, S. (2007) 'Lettische Rechtswissenschaft nach der Gründung des lettischen Staates 1918', *Zeitschrift für neuere Rechtsgeschichte*, 29:1–2, 60–65.

Osipova, S. (2009) 'Vēsture, tiesību vēsture un nacionālā identitāte Latvijā XX gs. (History, history of law and national identity in Latvia in the 20th century)', *Jurista Vārds*, 589:46, 5–9.

Pakhman, S. V. (2004) *Istorija kodifikaciji grazhdanskogo prava (The History of the Codification of Civil Law)*, Moskva: Zercalo.

Savčeno, V. (1952) 'Grāmata, kas atmasko Latvijas vēstures viltotājus (A book revealing the forgers of Latvian history)', *Padomju Jaunatne*, 12:19, 3.

Sinaiskis, V. (1938) *Latviešu senā sabiedriskā iekārta tautas dziesmu spogulī (The Ancient Latvian Social Order in the Mirror of Folk Songs)*, Rīga: A. Gulbis.

Sinaiskis, V. (the year of publication not identified) *Sērdieņu dainas (The Orphan Folk Songs)*, Rīga: Literatūra.

Smits, E. (1997) *Nacionālā identitāte (The National Identity)*, Rīga, AGB.

Straubergs, J. (1936) *Rīgas vēsture (The History of Riga)*, Rīga: Grāmatu draugs.

Strods, H. (1988) 'Un gars ritēs mājup… (And the spirit will go home…)', *Dzimtenes Balss*, 18, 4, p. 7.

Sudrabkalns, J. and Drīzulis, A. (1951) *Mūsu Rīga (Our Riga)*, Rīga: Latvijas Valsts izdevniecība.

Švābe, A. (1922) *Latvju kultūras vēsture. II. daļa. (History of Latvian Culture. Part II)*, Rīga: A. Gulbja apgādībā.

Švābe, A. (1939) *Latvijas cilšu tiesības (The Tribal Rights of Latvia)*, Rīga: A. Gulbja apgādībā.

Švābe, A. (1940) *Latvijas vēstures avoti. II sējums. Senās Latvijas vēstures avoti. 2. burtnīca (1238–1256) (Sources of Latvian History. Volume II. Sources of Ancient Latvian History, Book 2 (1238–1256))*, Rīga: Latvijas Vēstures institūta apgādiens.

Švābe, A. (1991) *Latvijas vēsture 1800–1914. Trešais izdevums (History of Latvia 1800–1914. third edition)*, Rīga: Avots.

Vīnzarājs, N. (1939) 'Bulletin de la Société de Législation Comparée', 1938. g., *Tieslietu Ministrijas Vēstnesis, 3*, 803.

Zhidkov, O. A. and Krasheninnikova, N. A. (eds) (2004) *Istorija gosudarstva i prava zarubezhnih stran (History of State and Law of Foreign Countries)*, Moskva: Norma.

8 Getaway into the Middle Ages? On topics, methods and results of 'socialist' legal historiography at the University of Jena

Adrian Schmidt-Recla and Zara Luisa Gries

Introduction

This paper chooses a personal and local approach to interpreting legal history in East Germany. It examines the topics and results of Gerhard Buchda's (1901–1977) own works and of the works of his graduate students at the University of Jena, where Buchda held the chair of German civil law, commercial law and German legal history from 1949 to 1967. 'Buchda and his students at Jena' may sound surprising, as Jena produced one of the most famous forerunners of socialist theory on the state, government and the law, namely Gerhard Haney (1926–2012). So why did we not focus on him and his work? The answer is: Haney's doctoral and postdoctoral theses (Haney, 1961; Haney, 1964a) did not focus on legal historiography, nor did they use legal history as a scheme or model of socialist law. His major project (Haney, 1967) is addressed to theory and philosophy of law. Moreover, Haney's publications on Theodor Maunz (1901–1993) (Haney, 1964b) were politically driven and not legal historiography (even though today they are most certainly a topic of legal historiography). In fact, Haney did not start publishing articles on legal history earlier than 1989 (Haney, 1989).

For the above reasons, this paper does refer to a person who ran legal history at Jena throughout the first decades of the German Democratic Republic (GDR)—Gerhard Buchda. Buchda is nowadays only little known as an expert of medieval Saxon law who studied the *Sachsenspiegel* as well as medieval municipal law. Born in Stadtroda near Jena, he studied law, finished his doctoral thesis in 1929 and was awarded the *venia legendi* in 1936 at Jena. After a short engagement in Berlin he was offered a professorship of German civil law and German legal history at the University Halle in 1937. In 1943 he joined the German army (*Wehrmacht*) as a private. After having returned to civilian life in 1945 he was dismissed by the University of Halle (cf. Lieberwirth, 1997, pp. 11–16), probably due to his membership in Nazi organizations. Buchda joined the National Socialist Association of German Legal Professionals (*Nationalsozialistischer Rechtswahrerbund*, NSRB) in 1933, the National Air Raid Protection League (*Reichsluftschutzbund*, RLB) in 1934, the National Socialist Teacher's League (*Nationalsozialistische Lehrerbund*, NSLB) in 1935, the paramilitary unit of NSDAP (*Sturmabteilung*, SA) in 1937, and the National

Socialist German Workers' Party (*Nationalsozialistische Deutsche Arbeiterpartei*, NSDAP) in 1939. There is to date no evidence that Buchda held leadership positions in any of them.

After his dismissal from Halle, he decided not to leave the Soviet occupation zone, joined the Liberal Democratic Party of Germany (*Liberal-Demokratische Partei Deutschlands*, LDPD) in 1946, and gained a second chance at (his beloved) Jena. It is reported that Buchda would have had a chance to take offers from universities in West Germany, but he 'stood his ground.' In 1963 he was Dean of the Jena Faculty of Law. He was Chairman of the 'Institute for State and Legal History' (*Institut für Staats- und Rechtsgeschichte*) by the time of his retirement. Moreover he was granted several visas to travel to congresses held in Austria, France and West Germany and was able to publish in Western publishing houses from 1950 up to 1974. At least once (in 1956) he spoke at the German Legal History Conference (*Rechtshistorikertag*) (cf. Buchda, 1958, pp. 274–348, 274).

As far as this study can assess, Buchda's articles in foreign journals and his contributions to congresses abroad did not bring any immediate benefit for GDR authorities or East German Universities—at least on the basis of the topics of Buchda's contributions and the methods he utilized, it is hard to see him furthering the socialist cause. Possibly his mere participation in international legal scientific events in the role of an 'elder statesman' or a 'notable colleague' was estimated to be beneficial from the point of view of the SED. Such an interpretation remains nevertheless speculative since one will hardly find any solid biographical proof of the fact that authorities tried to utilize 'old' or 'traditional' scholarship to their own ends. Anyway, Buchda took his leave in 1967 shortly before the 'Third Higher Education Reform' (to which cf. Kaiser, 2010) overruled traditional structures, values and contents of higher education in the GDR and demanded the abandonment of traditional modes of scholarly work.

During his years at Jena, Buchda was the doctoral adviser for eight doctoral theses with an emphasis on legal history. Despite Buchda's personal and academic CV during the Nazi regime, it is worthwhile studying whether his work and the theses of his students at Jena were contrary to socialist legal historiography or not, or whether Buchda and his students formed a scientific circle where pre-Second World War methods and topics were kept alive. We will start with a brief definition of what socialist (legal) history in the GDR entailed, as well as examining Buchda's own publications. This is followed by a discussion of the work of Buchda's students.

Socialist legal history in a nutshell

In the GDR, the significance and place of legal historiography was always ambiguous: One could ask why have legal history at all as a subject in socialist education (and in courses for law students)? Officially, the legal system of the GDR did not have (and could not have) any historical dimension, nor was it based on any tradition. As this study proves, it took years to develop a genuine socialist legal historiography in the law schools situated in the GDR

(Berlin, Leipzig, Halle and Jena). Moreover, the birth and the coming of age of the new socialist state—under the leadership of the working class and its political 'vanguard,' the communist party—and its law had to be emphasized as something completely new, as revolutionary, as different from all that had been before. A researcher or a teacher who would try to constitute the principles of socialist law as disconnected to the socialist revolution was thinking and working against the basic rules of the development of mankind and society.

To overcome this dilemma and to get closer to understanding the standing of socialist legal history in the GDR, we (again) do not refer to Gerhard Haney and his post-GDR assessments but to Gottfried Härtel (born in 1925) and Elemér Pólay (1915–1988). In 1987 they noted concerning Roman Law and Roman legal history that the recognition of Roman law was indispensable for lawyers whose science refers to comparison and history and was of eminent practical importance for understanding legal events in the past and present (Härtel and Pólay, 1987, p. 9); which as such shows commitment to a socialist history of law in the late 1980s. They stressed that 'a Marxist presentation of (legal) history is characterized by the recognition of the fact that any change in the socio-economic base is a source of the process of the development of law' (Härtel and Pólay, 1987, p. 10). Here you find the classic Marxist position of base and superstructure and one of the basic suppositions of historical and dialectic materialism (here: 'histMat' and 'diaMat'). 'DiaMat' supposes that every epoch in the history of humankind is characterized by so-called 'basic' or 'antagonistic contradictions.' Once these contradictions—necessarily class contradictions aroused by the property conditions of the means of production—quantitatively mount up to a point of intolerability, inevitably erupting into a revolutionary situation that creates a new quality of human relations. Accordingly, a Marxist legal historian will describe institutions, principles, institutes of law, law-making and law-makers of any historical period correctly only if he or she derives them from the then given socio-economic preconditions and will preferably refer to revolutionary situations. This is due to Karl Marx's (1818–1883) and Friedrich Engels' (1820–1895) keynote that the property conditions of the means of production shape all social relations. Marx and Engels, who remained classic references for socialist and communist interpretations of social relations and changes in East Germany until the end of the 1980s, studied one revolutionary situation as a fundamental example, namely, the French Revolution in 1789. Hence, the French Revolution remained a central point of interest and necessarily a benchmark for (legal) historians inspired by Marx and Engels. In other words: If you come across the works of a lawyer in one of the Eastern bloc countries that deal with legal problems or legal consequences of revolutions, namely, the French or the Russian revolution in a historical perspective, you will most probably at the same time find some genuine 'socialist' legal historiography. Proof of this are Hermann Klenners' (born 1926) ideas on French revolutionary terror as a matter of legality (Klenner, 1953, p. 14f.). With these basic statements in mind, let us now turn to Gerhard Buchda and then to his scholarly followers and successors at Jena.

Buchda's work as a historiographer of law

Immanuel Kant's civil law, 1929

Buchda's doctoral thesis is a small paper of 95 pages. Buchda compares Kant's (1724–1804) *Metaphysik der Sitten* (1797) to the works of some predecessors, especially to Gottfried Achenwall's (1719–1772) *Prolegomena Iuris Naturalis* (1758) and *Ius Naturae in usus auditorum* (Achenwall, 1755)—books used by Kant for his own lectures. Buchda's thesis is a descriptive account, offering relations, receptions and differences between Kant's positions and those of contemporary scholars of natural law. The 28-year-old Buchda explains, arranges, points out and underlines, but he does not emerge as a critic. Hence there is little originality in Buchda's paper, though he does at least point out that Kant's natural law has some similarity to a 'nowadays aprioristic theory of law' (Buchda, 1929, p. 83). Here Buchda gains critical distance from his pattern of presenting a single position, noting that Kant's positions on donation are contradictory (Buchda, 1929, p. 88). Buchda's first paper affected only his own future work, for there is no sign of a response from the scientific community.

History and critics of the German 'Gesamthandsgemeinschaft,' 1936

Buchda's second book is of special interest due to the special scientific spirit of the age in jurisprudence in the 1930s. The problem Buchda chose, 'joint ownership' (*Gesamthand*), was a classic problem of legal historians who followed the German or Germanic branch of legal history. It is raised by the *Sachsenspiegel* 'law of the region' (*Landrecht*) in chapter I, section 12, and many scholars since the 16th century have tried to elucidate a theory of *Gesamthand*. Discussion about it still continues (cf. BGHZ 146, 341 = NJW 2001, 1056). German legal historians are trying to work out a theory that could explain problems concerning the community of heirs, matrimonial property, non-trading, general partnership and so on. It is of interest whether Buchda was influenced by attempts of the younger generation of lawyers and legal scientists to design new and National Socialist theories of law in 1933. It is said that Buchda did not make any concessions to Nazi ideology; certainly, none of his publications show clear Nazi influences (Lieberwirth, 1977, p. 13).

What we can assume is that Buchda tried to evolve a theory of 'the intelligence of a thing's nature' or 'insight into the nature of things,' and hence his references to Kant (cf. Buchda, 1936, p. 235). In his own words, he wanted 'a nowadays aspired holistic consideration' that was 'urgently needed, not only in biology but also in legal sciences' (Buchda, 1936, p. 234). The task was first 'to study the special structure,' the 'proper legality of every entity' (Buchda, 1936, p. 234f.). Thus jurisprudence had to 'recognize' (especially if there was a legal entity) (Buchda, 1936, p. 255), but it was not the jurisprudence's responsibility to create or design legal entities. As Buchda said, '[I]deal legal subjects' were things that could be thought, but this would not refer to 'our view of life today'

('*Das würde nicht unserer heutigen Lebensauffassung entsprechen,*' Buchda, 1936, p. 255). Reality first was Buchda's headline; thinking (including legal examining) had to follow certain given conditions (cf. Buchda, 1936, p. 255).

The second question, whether an existing entity had subjective rights, 'was a question of interpretation, of exegesis within the legal regime given' (Buchda, 1936, p. 256). From the author's point of view, this could refer to Edmund Husserl's (1859–1938) so-called 'intuition of essences and essential structures' (*Wesensschau*) and could be related to the 'concrete-order thinking' (or more accurately: precise thinking in real regimes) offered by Carl Schmitt (1888–1985; cf. Schmitt, 1934, pp. 17–20, 43), though Buchda did not in fact quote Schmitt or Husserl. This examination becomes even more convincing when we consider that Buchda's critique uses terms like 'sound German attitude to life' (Buchda, 1936, p. 260), appeals to 'demonic religious forces in the sacred leagues of the Germans' to emphasize the 'spiritual community' inside human corporations (Buchda, 1936, p. 261, Fn. 8) and finds that 'leader and loyalty' were 'connected with love and fidelity, with trust and believe, with responsibility and obedience' (Buchda, 1936, p. 234). Was this a concession to Nazi ideology? We rather think that the young Gerhard Buchda drifted with the tide. However, he did not hesitate to quote such Jewish colleagues as Konrad Engländer (1880–1933).

In the conclusion of his paper, he finally proves he was a follower of Otto v. Gierke's (1841–1921) suppositions but not of his conclusions: 'Joint ownership is not an institute but a principle of law; but it is (among other things) only a principle of acting, especially of legal transaction. Wherever human beings act together this represents what joint ownership is' (Buchda, 1936, p. 265f.). But acting does not necessarily reveal what is behind it (Buchda, 1936, p. 270). What was 'behind' the 'acting entity' then was a question of positive law (and of interpretation and exegesis). Once the law gives a claim, a competence, a power to two or more humans as an entity, then this entity was a legal body, a corporate body, a 'juristic person' as far as the power was given (Buchda, 1936, p. 293).

In the 1940s, Buchda set aside his work on the history of dogma in jurisprudence and on the principles, institutions or institutes of civil law. By this time, he only wrote and published on legal history, and all his upcoming legal works focused on one major topic, namely, the jurisdiction of corporations in the Middle Ages and the Early Modern age.

The medieval Pössneck collection of jurymen's votes

Through this work, Buchda has gained an established position among German legal historians. In cooperation with the historians Reinhold Grosch and Willy Flach (1903–1958), he carried out extensive research on the jurisdiction of municipal, jurymen's and University courts from the 13th to the 19th century. He examined votes, sentences, decisions and expert opinions or arbitraments given by Saxon and Thuringian corporations. One of his projects was dedicated to the jurisdiction of the Faculty of Law in Halle (Buchda, 1942a, pp. 210–294; Buchda, 1943, pp. 251–318; Buchda, 1944, pp. 223–347; Buchda, 1954), another to the jurisdiction of the municipal court of Pössneck, a small Thuringian town near Stadtroda and Jena (Grosch et al., 1957–1972). Grosch, Flach and Buchda found 355 jurymen's votes, sentences and arbitraments from Magdeburg, Leipzig and Pössneck itself from the 14th and the 15th century. Buchda ran this project throughout his years at Jena. The project resulted in a book of four volumes, published by Böhlau's in Weimar from 1957 to 1972. Buchda was responsible for volumes 3 and 4. Herein he examined the importance of the votes and sentences for a 'general history of law.' His indexes (on subjects and on persons) are in actual fact not indexes but a full commentary on *Sachsenspiegel* law as executed by the Magdeburg and Leipzig chairs of 'jurymen' (*Schöffenstühle*). The result stands comparison with Guido Kisch's (1889–1985) *Leipziger Schöffenspruchsammlung* (Kisch, 1919) and complements it, with Adalbert Erler's (1904–1992) *Der Oberhof zu Neustadt an der Weinstraße* (Erler, 1968) and with Friedrich Ebel's (1944–2005) Magdeburg editions (Ebel, 1983). To this day, scholars can use it to check medieval and Early Modern corpora of law and legislation against the reality of jurisdiction. This is of significant relevance for comparative approaches to the *Sachsenspiegel* law.

Buchda wrote numerous articles for the journal *Zeitschrift der Savigny-Stiftung für Rechtsgeschichte*, and the Halle project was published there (cf. Buchda, 1936, p. 261, fn. 8). Buchda also published smaller works to achieve a better understanding of medieval and especially *Sachsenspiegel* law (Buchda, 1937, pp. 468–474; Buchda, 1939, pp. 194–207; Buchda, 1941, pp. 257–265; Buchda, 1942b, pp. 353–355; Buchda, 1942c, pp. 355–358; Buchda, 1950, pp. 416–440; Buchda, 1952, pp. 385–399; Buchda, 1955, pp. 205–215; Buchda, 1958; Buchda, 1961, pp. 64–92 and (posthum) Buchda, 1974, pp. 90–116). Another paper was published in the *Vorträge und Forschungen* of the *Konstanzer Arbeitskreis für mittelalterliche Geschichte* (Buchda, 1964, pp. 7–24). We have found theses from 1937 to 1974, and altogether nine theses were printed during Buchda's Jena years. None of these theses broached the issue whether medieval law is an aspect of class conflicts or to what extent it is influenced by the propriety conditions of the means of production. His texts do not refer to 'diaMat' at all, and is it not surprising to read Buchda's own short conclusion about his focus as a scholar in 1966 shortly before he retired: 'Litigation of the chairs of lay assessors, high courts and legal faculties from the 13th to the 19th century in connection with the history of judicature, the law of procedure and the substantive law' (*Spruchtätigkeit der Schöffenstühle, Oberhöfe und Juristenfakultäten vom 13. bis zum 19. Jh. in Verbindung mit der Geschichte der Gerichtsverfassung, des Prozeßrechts und des materiellen Rechts.*). This is truly his legacy and it is worth questioning whether it influenced the work of his graduated students.

The influence of Buchda's work on legal historiography

The Faculty of Law

We now turn to Buchda's influence on legal historiography. First, there is new information on the elder Buchda as a teacher. Rolf Henrich, one of the founders of the NEUES FORUM in 1989 and one of the most profound inside critics of socialist law, who was a student of law at Jena from 1964 to 1967, mentions Buchda's lectures in his recently published memoirs (Henrich, 2019, p. 54f.). Henrich certifies that Buchda had been a voice of courage and honesty who did not refer to the class struggle (Henrich, 2019, p. 54). Buchda's *Sachsenspiegel* lecture was—according to Henrich—far away from any wisenheimery and provided the (very few) students with an understanding of normativity that any scholar had to ascertain for himself due to the fact that it referred to an understanding of law whose presuppositions modern people did not share (Henrich, 2019, p. 55). Finally, Henrich notes that the *Sachsenspiegel* understanding of law ('God is justice himself, that is why justice is beloved by him' [*'got is selve recht, dar umme is em recht lef'*]—*Sachsenspiegel* prologue) appeared to him as a law student to be an antidote against Leninist legal nihilism (Henrich, 2019, p. 55). A strong comment, for sure—but are there echoes of this personally toned attitude in some contemporary scientific elaborations?

Second: Between 1948 and 1967, the Jena Faculty of Law awarded seven scholars the doctorate of law with Buchda as doctoral supervisor (of course there were more doctorates at Jena in this period—but not focused on legal history). In 1969 Buchda once more acted as doctoral supervisor *emeritus.* Two cases show a collaboration with Gertrud Schubart-Fikentscher (1896–1985) from Halle as the second reviewer; one thesis indicates that Rolf Lieberwirth (1920–2019) from Halle was the second reviewer. None of the seven Buchda scholars had ever published more than this one paper as a legal historian, and none of them had ever given their own lecture course on the history of law. This proves that a Buchda doctorate was in no case the take-off for an academic career as a legal historian in the GDR. But let us now take a closer look at these theses. Before starting, one should consider that the East German law of higher education did not obligate candidates to print doctoral theses with the help of a professional publisher. Consequently, doctoral theses did not circulate among libraries. One might say that they were not written for scientific discussion. Moreover, the papers were written on typed paper and are today in a very bad condition.

1 The first thesis under the aegis of Buchda was written by Christian Hopf from Halle. It was disputed in 1951 and deals with 'The utilization of forests and forest management within the limits of Thuringian sources of law from the 16th to the 18th century' (Hopf, 1952). After a short introduction and a description of the sources, Hopf discusses historic forest management. We found no reference to Marxism and cannot estimate whether Hopf followed a special Buchda interest. Anyway, he dealt with Thuringian history of law and thus chose both a traditional approach and method for his doctoral thesis.
2 Gottfried Werner from Weimar was Buchda's second doctoral candidate. He graduated in 1952. His thesis is about 'The Constitution and municipal law of Arnstadt' (Werner, 1952). This relatively brief paper of only 89 pages provides some information on local constitutional history and reports in chapter 1 on Arnstadt as a settlement and marketplace by the end of the 12th century. Chapter 2 is about Arnstadt as a civic corporation by

1850. This paper contains descriptions rather than assessments. It is of interest for the local history of Arnstadt only and is in no way influenced by Marxist theory.

3 In 1952 another scholar, Hermann Wolf from Greiz, graduated with a doctoral thesis entitled 'The development of judicature, especially of penal jurisdiction in the former principality of junior branch *Reuß*' (Wolf, 1952). Wolf's paper is dedicated to the judicature of the smallest territory of German nationality in the Holy Roman Empire that ever existed. It offers a description of the courts' constitutional history. The methodological approach is traditional. The chapters follow epochs as described by traditional historiography (e.g., offspring, the reception of Roman law, the fall of the Holy Roman Empire, the civil revolution of 1848, the foundation of the 'Second Reich,' etc.) and did not refer to 'histMat' stepping stones of social development. Wolf like Hopf and Werner did not publish any further articles.

4 In 1955 Buchda's fourth candidate was Witho Holland from Schmalkalden, a Thuringian town for toolmakers since the Middle Ages. Holland dealt with local Schmalkalden craftsmen's guilds and their law (Holland, 1955). His thesis offers a sketch of how craftsmanship in Schmalkalden had developed, describing the guilds' certificates and the constitution of the Schmalkalden guilds, including the law of the apprentices, journeymen and master craftsmen. He comments on the guilds' courts and their penal law. Unlike Hopf, Werner and Wolf, Holland continued to write on legal matters and became active in legal affairs: later he worked as an in-house lawyer for the local, then the regional and finally the national 'Konsum' cooperative society, which was one of the two national players of trade in East Germany. In 2008 he published a paper about the legal and economic development of the 'Konsum' cooperatives in the GDR (Holland, 2008). It is noteworthy that Holland (like Buchda), a former member of the NSDAP joined the LDPD in 1946, was elected to the Volkskammer from 1963 to 1990 and took part in the central 'Round Table' Discussions in Berlin in autumn and winter 1989–1990.

Holland's doctoral thesis under Buchda's supervision can to a certain extent be described as innovative: It dealt with the legal history of corporations that had an impact on the economy, and Holland as an in-house expert may have used it to design a socialist law for cooperative societies. But to this day, we do not know more about Holland's contributions to law-making. It would be useful to have a biography of Witho Holland.

5 Gerhard Günther from Greiz was a graduate student of Buchda who worked as his tutor's assistant for three years. Whilst his retirement was in process in 1967, Buchda planned to make Günther his successor as chairman of his Institute for State and Legal History (Lingelbach, 1997, p. 42f.). However, the plan failed and Günther did not become Buchda's successor. Günther's doctoral thesis from 1956 was about how Roman civil law was received in Thuringia by 1350 (Günther, 1956). His topic is up to date: it is an examination of canon jurisdiction and lawyers as pace-makers of 'early

reception' (*Frührezeption*) and would be in keeping with modern efforts to examine expert cultures. Probably in accordance with Buchda's empirical research, Günther focuses on whether and to what extent 'legal instruments' (*Urkunden*) prove the application of *Jus Commune* already in the 13th and 14th century. If this thesis had been produced in Göttingen or Freiburg, for example, Günter's academic career may well have taken off. We did not find echoes of Marx's and Engels's positions in his work.

6 Buchda's next doctoral candidate proves that Buchda's own work on municipal courts and jurymen's votes may well have influenced others. Jörgen Haalck, born in Potsdam, graduated in 1957 with a thesis on the responses and sentences of the Rostock Faculty of Law (Haalck, 1957). He describes the process of the normative basis of responding and deciding for courts abroad (*Aktenversendung*) (Carolina, RPolO, Bützower Privileg 1762), the process inside the Rostock Faculty (*Rotulationsverfahren*), the Rostock Faculty of Law as an authority for decisions in penal inquisitions and the content of the Rostock archive. Moreover, he examines how the faculty as a sentencing authority was organized internally and deals with the intensity and effect of the faculty's activity concerning territories and the law itself. What Buchda did concerning Halle, Haalck did concerning Rostock.

7 The last Jena scholar who Buchda actively and successfully supervised was Gerhard Haas from Chomutov/Komotau (Haas, 1967a). He returned to what Buchda's second graduate, Gottfried Werner, did 15 years prior and worked on the constitution and on the municipal law of Arnstadt, though Haas included a few more Thuringian municipalities: Königsee, Saalfeld and Stadtilm. This thesis is remarkable due to the fact that Haas was not a graduated lawyer but nevertheless was awarded the 'doctor iuris.' Haas studied law from 1951 to 1955, did not graduate as a lawyer, studied history and education science and worked as a schoolteacher (cf. Haas' CV; Haas, 1967b, appendix). His thesis is purely a presentation of municipal history, the constitution, courts, municipal iura regalia and municipal law. The focus is on the Middle Ages and Early Modern times. He gives, for example, only one page to the history of Arnstadt from the 17th to the end of the 19th century (Haas, 1967a, p. 64). Haas states that the 1543 statutes had remained the basis for 'legal relations' in Arnstadt by the 19th century and that they had not been critically worked over or emended since then. Only regulations on firefighting had been revised. Some decrees or edicts had been given by the Earls of Schwarzburg-Rudolstadt on guard service, on land surveys, on marriage, on mills and on public bookkeeping. And that is it—nothing whatsoever on socio-economic drivers of changes and developments in law. We find the same method concerning the municipal constitution of Arnstadt (Haas, 1967a, pp. 36–39): Haas lists, what the municipal council in the 19th century was, by whom it was elected, what the council was expected to do, and which authority supervised the execution of various matters.

8 An eighth graduated student, who started with a (now) typical Buchda-topic in Jena, did not finish his work on 'The constitution and the law of the

municipality of Gera in their historical development by the 17th century' in the GDR. The author, Lothar Krahner, member of the CDU since 1949, left the GDR westbound and was—with this work (Krahner, 1965)—successfully awarded the legal doctorate at the Faculty of Law of the Goethe-University Frankfurt/M. in 1965 under the supervision of Adalbert Erler. We suppose correspondence or at least contact between Buchda and Erler according that case. Due to the fact that Krahner's paper was not finished in Jena, we did not include it to our survey as regards content.

9 Did things change after Buchda's retirement? Yes, they did, especially when the class struggle and revolutionary events were introduced into graduate students' work. In 1969 Hans-Jürgen Ziegler wrote on the influence of the French Revolution concerning the development of German commercial law (Ziegler, 1969). Like Günter, Ziegler worked as an assistant at the Institute for State and Legal History. Buchda and Haney acted as his doctoral reviewers. His thesis describes the condition of German commercial law 'at the eve of the French Revolution,' tries to give a picture of the 'present condition of commercial law' and gives a short history of the 'bourgeois character of commercial law.' He then discusses whether French commercial law was affected by the French Revolution (here a definition of class conflict and revolution is given; Ziegler, 1969, p. 73) and whether the French Revolution was a creative power for German commercial law. Ziegler uses 'diaMat' schemes: 'The essential aspects of the socio-economic fabric of feudalism, respectively the municipality, the inner fabric, are decisive for explaining and assessing their politico-legal, external manifestations' (Ziegler, 1969, p. 42). Moreover, Ziegler criticizes bourgeois legal historiography in detail—and this critique is like a door opener for socialist legal historiography. His point is that the 'cosmopolitism of trade,' as 'bourgeois' legal historians argued, made the development of commercial law 'universal.' Ziegler's contradiction is as follows. By that argument (commercial law was universal) an aspect of bourgeois legal historiography that (generally) marked legal positivism came to light: that is to say 'shortening of legal history to the history of the legal form only' (Ziegler, 1969, p. 50f.). Economic history and political history would thus, if taken into consideration at all, only be marginal (Ziegler, 1969, p. 51). Hence, scientists who only referred to the continuity of a form without considering the discontinuity of its functions would be forced into error (Ziegler, 1969, p. 51). Ultimately, Ziegler's job, as he saw it, was to identify law-making both as an agent and as a result of revolutionary class conflicts: the '*Code de commerce*,' for instance, 'accomplished the revolutionary creation of legal unity concerning commercial law. It maintained the revolutionary principle of civil equality and eliminated commercial law as a burgher's privilege' (Ziegler, 1969, p. 119). Ziegler then focuses on how the *Code de commerce* was received in Germany. Buchda had never himself taken this 'class conflict' perspective.

The Faculty of Philosophy and the Faculty of Economics

Buchda held a position as a reviewer of doctoral theses for the Faculty of Philosophy on three occasions. He cooperated with Friedrich Schneider (1887–1962), who held the chair for Medieval History at the FSU Jena from 1947 to 1956. Schneider was a Dante Alighieri expert (Schneider, 1960) and it has been said that he was a 'bourgeois historian' (Heimpel, 1963, p. 249). In 1946 he became a member of the LDPD (like Buchda and his student Hoffmann). The three Schneider graduate students worked on topics related to Thuringian history and matters of law. Their methods and results can be compared with those of the Buchda scholars, Werner, Wolf and Günther.

Gregor Richter (1927–2002) from Weimar dealt with the public policies of the Dukes of Sachsen-Weimar (Richter, 1956) from 1446 to 1589. Unlike Buchda's students, Richter argued in 1956 that these policies were of class nature. Regulations on luxury, for example, marked the differences between noblemen, patricians, peasants and craftsmen (Richter, 1956, p. 4). One could say, however, that this was a badly chosen example and merely Marxist lip service. Helmut Roob (1924–2017) from Gotha, later regionally known as an archivist and historian of the city, wrote on the constitution of Gotha from the 13th to the 19th century and especially focused on the Duchy of Sachsen-Gotha and Veit Ludwig von Seckendorff (Roob, 1958). Ruth Böckel (biographical data could not be found yet) presented a study on the relations between the University of Jena, the council of Jena and the Duchy of Sachsen-Weimar during the 18th century (Böckel, 1958). Her thesis is about student misrule, clashes with soldiers, expulsions (from the University), debt, illegitimate pregnancies and censorship, though with no echoes of 'histMat' or 'diaMat.' Buchda finally was second reviewer for theses written for the Faculty of Economics on two occasions, though these theses made no reference to legal history (Hädrich, 1950; Kopp, 1950).

Post-Buchda years

After Buchda's retirement, some more doctoral theses on legal history were written at Jena. Did they refer back to Buchda's interests or are they examples of a new, socialist legal historiography like Ziegler's thesis?

In 1978 Gerhard Lingelbach from Greiz graduated with a doctoral thesis on the relation of German jurisprudence towards the French Revolution between 1789 and 1820 (Lingelbach, 1978). This thesis originated under the aegis of Gerhard Haney, and ideological echoes can be heard: 'Feudal nobility fought for the primacy of feudal ideology in jurisprudence' (Lingelbach, 1978, p. 41), or 'The bourgeois state and bourgeois law are instruments of domination to maintain the power of a minority over the majority of the masses (…). The oppression of the exploited is the principal duty of the feudal and of the bourgeois state and government' (Lingelbach, 1978, p. 41). Referring to the role of jurisprudence, Lingelbach writes:

> Due to the fact that the bourgeois consciousness of law on the eve of the French Revolution was only weakly evolved and hung behind the material conditions of the second half of the 18th century, sciences and especially jurisprudence were ideological institutions that played an important role in protecting the power of feudal nobility. Hence the nobility tried to control it [the law]. (Lingelbach, 1978, p. 43)

Lingelbach's work refers to a 'histMat' and 'diaMat' scheme to assess German jurisprudence around 1800, and he used this scheme to measure whether a scholar was progressive or reactionary. Progressiveness around 1800 was credited to lawyers which spoke up for 'bourgeois' rights and liberties (e.g., civil equality), 'bourgeois' law codes and the 'bourgeois' government of the state. This indicates that historical science on bourgeois lawyers and their work (here on the historical school of German jurisprudence) in a socialist setting was possible once researchers dressed their topic in 'diaMat' clothing and showed an interest in dealing with classic topics of 'histMat' such as the French Revolution. In this way, researchers could in fact preserve historical knowledge and could even (courageously or 'under cover') emphasize liberal attitudes in a scientific world ruled over by a socialist ideology that intrinsically rejected such attitudes. Hence, Lingelbach's paper is an example of historical science in a totalitarian setting, though contemporary readers may well have to read between the lines to discern the implicit and explicit meanings of the text.

Lingelbach's second thesis from 1985 about the change of the accused's position in overcoming the feudal inquisitional procedure mirrored by German jurisprudence (Lingelbach, 1985) again under the aegis of Gerhard Haney, also uses the 'diaMat' scheme continuously. Such matters as penal law in general, procedure, 'man price' or 'blood money' (*wergeld*) penalties, torture, the position of a person charged with an offense following 'objective circumstances,' 'the processes of material appropriation,' protected and guaranteed the property conditions, ruled conflicts 'objectively' occurring—all these issues, it was argued, reflected economic and political structures, and gained new dimensions on account of and after revolutionary events (for all quotations cf. Lingelbach, 1985, pp. 5–46, 74f.). Concerning to Lingelbach, the inquisitional procedure in particular was a product of a period that saw the decay of feudalism (Lingelbach, 1985, p. 29). He stated that the procedural position of the individual followed the individual's social embedding in feudal society, and property conditions determined socio-economic and legal inequality as well as offering protection (Lingelbach, 1985, pp. 35–40)—truly an up-front appreciation. Again one can say that Lingelbach made an attempt to understand the social and legal relations reigned by fiefdom and vassalage in a non-unidimensional way. In his willingness to abstract from details (Lingelbach, 1985, p. 48, p. 85f., p. 99) he showed an affinity for the new 'diaMat' approach yet remained open-minded about legal historiography. These comments also apply to Sigurd Leitel's doctoral thesis from 1989 (Leitel, 1989). Haney and Lingelbach were Leitel's reviewers.

Conclusion

Traditional history of law at Jena died quickly within the 'Buchda years.' The former Institute for State and Legal History (*Institut für Staats- und Rechtsgeschichte*) collapsed with the third Higher Education Reform (*Hochschulreform*) in 1969. The temporal coincidence between Buchda's retirement and the collapse of his institute was not accidental. Buchda and seven of his scholarly followers did not succeed in offering any topic or any perspective on socialist legal historiography—or perhaps they did not want to offer such an approach. In fact, their works (which were carried out in quick chronology in the 1950s) did not refer to Marxist 'diaMat' at all. Neither Buchda nor his seven followers chose topics to do with socialist legal historiography, such as 'the revolution and the law,' 'the legal history of the working class movement' or 'capitalism or imperialism and the law,' and instead they stuck to traditional topics. We assume that Buchda has supervised research with regional, sometimes local perspectives and has directed his students into the Middle Ages and Early Modern times. The legacy of Buchda's own research apparently lived on in some of the theses he supervised (e.g., Günter and Haalck) but definitely not in the last one he supervised (Ziegler). All in all, this can be seen as a researcher's and a teacher's escape, a getaway from educational politics driven by the SED, from building a new socialist society, education and from establishing a new socialist (legal) historiography. Buchda had the chance to be more political in his teaching—expressions like 'reality first' and 'contemporary attitude towards life' were not mere rhetoric to him—but he chose not to.

The first doctoral candidate with a topic of legal history who referred to 'diaMat' (Ziegler) graduated in 1969, with Gerhard Haney as the second reviewer. This cannot have been an accident. We did not find solid proof that Haney dictated the choice of topic and method for the candidate, and we do not know to what extent Buchda was the real spin doctor behind the last doctoral thesis under his aegis. Nevertheless, our review shows the possibility of pursuing legal history without using Marxist-Leninist theory in universities in East Germany during the 1950s and 1960s. 'The Third Higher Education Reform' of 1969, however, changed matters quickly and completely. Both the GDR system of higher education and the GDR legal system had no need for research that resembled Gerhard Buchda's work—disconnected from the contemporary debates on the fundaments of socialist law and/or legality (cf. Klenner, 1953). Buchda stood alone on 'Last Standing Hill.' After a quick step in 1969 (Ziegler), it took the Jena law school 10 years to establish a new 'diaMat' affine legal historiography (Lingelbach).

Acknowledgments

The authors would like to thank Anna Pischulti for her translations from the German and Mark Shackleton for his critical review of the manuscript. Both are responsible for essential improvements of the text. Gerhard Lingelbach provided useful information to better understanding the system of and the cycles in higher education in the GDR.

References

Achenwall, G. (1755) *Ius naturae in usum auditorium*, Göttingen: Bossiegel.

Achenwall, G. (1758) *Prolegomena Iuris Naturalis*, Göttingen: Bossiegel.

Buchda, G. (1929) *Das Privatrecht Immanuel Kants*, Jena: Frommann.

Buchda, G. (1936) *Geschichte und Kritik der deutschen Gesamthandlehre*, Marburg: Elwert'sche Verlagsbuchhandlung.

Buchda, G. (1937) 'Untertanenpflicht, Frauenschwurgebärde und ein paar ältere Rechtswörter in einem Meusebacher Gerichtsbuch', in *Zeitschrift für Rechtsgeschichte Germanistische Abteilung*, 57, 468–474.

Buchda, G. (1939) 'Dursal (dursal eigen)', in *Zeitschrift für Rechtsgeschichte Germanistische Abteilung*, 59, 194–207.

Buchda, G. (1941) 'Schöffenstuhlsiegel', in *Zeitschrift für Rechtsgeschichte Germanistische Abteilung*, 61, 257–265.

Buchda, G. (1942a) 'Die Spruchtätigkeit der hallischen Juristenfakultät in ihrem äußeren Verlauf, I. Teil', in *Zeitschrift für Rechtsgeschichte Germanistische Abteilung*, 62, 210–294.

Buchda, G. (1942b) 'Eine Bemerkung zu Sachsenspiegel II Artikel 55', in *Zeitschrift für Rechtsgeschichte Germanistische Abteilung*, 62, 353–355.

Buchda, G. (1942c) 'Hegung und Aufhebung des Vogtgerichts zu Kindleben', in *Zeitschrift für Rechtsgeschichte Germanistische Abteilung*, 62, 355–358.

Buchda, G. (1943) 'Die Spruchtätigkeit der hallischen Juristenfakultät in ihrem äußeren Verlauf II. Teil', in *Zeitschrift für Rechtsgeschichte Germanistische Abteilung*, 63, 251–318.

Buchda, G. (1944) 'Die Spruchtätigkeit der hallischen Juristenfakultät in ihrem äußeren Verlauf III. Teil' in *Zeitschrift für Rechtsgeschichte Germanistische Abteilung*, 64, 223–275.

Buchda, G. (1950) 'Zur Geschichte des hallischen Schöppenstuhls', in *Zeitschrift für Rechtsgeschichte Germanistische Abteilung*, 67, 416–440.

Buchda, G. (1952) 'Über die verlorenen hallischen Konstitutionen zum Landrecht der Kurmark Brandenburg (1714)', in *Zeitschrift für Rechtsgeschichte Germanistische Abteilung*, 69, 385–399.

Buchda, G. (1954) 'Die Spruchtätigkeit der hallischen Juristenfakultät in ihrem äußeren Verlauf. Nachtrag', in *Zeitschrift für Rechtsgeschichte Germanistische Abteilung*, 71, 308–347.

Buchda, G. (1955) 'Archäologisches zum Sachsenspiegel', in *Zeitschrift für Rechtsgeschichte Germanistische Abteilung*, 72, 205–215.

Buchda, G. (1958) 'Die Rechtsmittel im sächsischen Prozeß', in *Zeitschrift für Rechtsgeschichte Germanistische Abteilung*, 75, 274–348.

Buchda, G. (1961)' "Gewohnheiten", in der Pößnecker Schöffenspruchsammlung', in *Zeitschrift für Rechtsgeschichte Germanistische Abteilung*, 78, 64–92.

Buchda, G. (1964) 'Die Dorfgemeinde im Sachsenspiegel', in *Konstanzer Arbeitskreis für mittelalterliche Geschichte* (ed), *Die Anfänge der Landgemeinde und ihr Wesen, Vorträge und Forschungen*, vol. 8, Konstanz: Thorbecke, 7–24.

Buchda, G. (1974) 'Über die "Vorrede" im sächsischen Prozeß des 15. Jahrhunderts', in *Zeitschrift für Rechtsgeschichte Germanistische Abteilung*, 91, 90–116.

Böckel, R. (1958) *Die rechtlichen Beziehungen zwischen der Universität Jena, dem Rat der Stadt und der Landesregierung von Sachsen-Weimar(-Eisenach) als*

Ausdruck der gesellschaftlichen Verhältnisse des 18. Jahrhunderts; 321 s., Jena: Dissertation in Thuringia University and State Library, ThULB-Sign, U 59.4111.

Ebel, F. (1983–1995) *Magdeburger Recht*, vol. 1–3, Köln, Weimar, Wien: Böhlau.

Erler, A. (1968–1971) *Der Oberhof zu Neustadt an der Weinstraße*, vol. 1, 2, Frankfurt A/M: Klostermann.

Grosch, R., Flach, W., Buchda, G. and Lauter, K. (1957–1972) *Die Schöffenspruchsammlung der Stadt Pössneck*, vol. 1–4, Jena: Böhlau.

Günther, G. (1956) *Die Anfänge der Rezeption des mittelalterlichen römischen Zivilrechts in Thüringen bis zur Mitte des vierzehnten Jahrhunderts*; Mitberichterstatter Gertrud Schubart-Fikentscher, 320 s., Jena: Dissertation in Thuringia University and State Library, ThULB-Sign. 4. Hist. lit. VI, 10002/11 (1).

Haalck, J. (1957) *Die Gutachter- und Urteilstätigkeit der Rostocker Juristenfakultät in ihrem äußeren Verlauf*; Referent Gertrud Schubart-Fikentscher, 192 s., Jena: Dissertation in Thuringia University and State Library, ThULB-Sign. 4 Hist. lit. VI, 10002/10 (3); 2.

Haas, G. (1967a) *Verfassung und Recht der Städte Arnstadt, Königsee, Saalfeld und Stadtilm von den Anfängen bis ins 19. Jahrhundert*, vol. 1; Mitberichterstatter Rolf Lieberwirth, 244 s., Jena: Dissertation in Thuringia University and State Library, ThULB-Sign. 68 J 43:1.

Haas, G. (1967b) *Verfassung und Recht der Städte Arnstadt, Königsee, Saalfeld und Stadtilm von den Anfängen bis ins 19. Jahrhundert*, vol. 2; Mitberichterstatter Rolf Lieberwirth, 109 s., Jena: Dissertation in Thuringia University and State Library, ThULB-Sign. 68 J 43:2.

Hädrich, C. (1950) *Die Rolle der Entwertung in der Buchführung und Selbstkostenrechnung (Zur Entwicklung des Problems in Schrifttum und Wirtschaftspraxis)*, Jena: Dissertation in Thuringia University and State Library, ThULB-Sign.: 4. Hist. lit. VI, 10002/3 (3) .

Haney, G. (1961) *Der kapitalistische Zivilprozeß und die imperialistische Theorie vom Rechtsschutzbedürfnis in ihrer Funktion der Zerstörung der bürgerlichen Gesetzlichkeit*, Jena: Friedrich-Schiller-Universität Jena.

Haney, G. (1964a) *Die Rechtsstellung des Bürgers*, Jena: Friedrich-Schiller-Universität Jena.

Haney, G. (1964b) *Maunz im Dienste des Faschismus und der CSU. Initiator faschistischen Unrechts, prominenter Politiker und Hochschullehrer in Westdeutschland. Eine Dokumentation*, Jena: Rechtswissenschaftliche Fakultät der Friedrich-Schiller-Universität.

Haney, G. (1967) *Sozialistisches Recht und Persönlichkeit*, Berlin: Staatsverlag der Deutschen Demokratischen Republik.

Haney, G. (1989) *Vom Privilegium zum Recht. Rechtsphilosophie und Revolution 1789–1989*, Siegen: R. Voigt Verlag.

Härtel, G. and Pólay, E. (1987) *Römisches Recht und römische Rechtsgeschichte*, Weimar: Böhlau.

Heimpel, H. (1963) 'Nachruf Friedrich Schneider', in *Historische Zeitschrift*, 196, 249–251.

Henrich, R. (2019) *Ausbruch aus der Vormundschaft. Erinnerungen*, Berlin: Ch. Links Verlag.

Holland, W. (1955) *Die schmalkaldischen Handwerkerzünfte und ihr Recht bis zur Mitte des 19. Jahrhunderts, dargestellt hauptsächlich nach ihren Zunftbriefen*;

Zweitgutachter Martin Posch, 90 s., Jena: Dissertation in Thuringia University and State Library, ThULB-Sign. 4 Hist. lit. VI, 10002/10 (4I) .

Holland, W. (2008) *Die Konsumgenossenschaften in der DDR: rechtliche und wirtschaftliche Entwicklung*, Marburg: Inst. für Genossenschaftswesen.

Hopf, C. (1952) *Waldnutzung und Waldwirtschaft im Spiegel thüringischer Rechtsquellen des 16. bis 18. Jahrhunderts*; Zweitgutachter n.n. Steffen; 181 s., Jena: Dissertation in Thuringia University and State Library, ThULB-Sign. 4. Hist. lit. VI, 10002/5 (2).

Kaiser, T. (2010) 'Hochschule im Sozialismus. Die so genannte "Dritte Hochschulreform" 1968 in der DDR', in Walther, G. (ed), *Wendepunkte in viereinhalb Jahrhunderten Jenaer Universitätsgeschichte*, Jena: Verlag IKS Garamond, 139–158.

Kant, I. (1986) [1797], 'Die Metaphysik der Sitten. Metaphysische Anfangsgründe der Rechtslehre', in *Kants Werke. Akademie Textausgabe*, vol. 6, Berlin: De Gruyter.

Kisch, G. (1919), *Leipziger Schöffenspruch-Sammlung*, Leipzig: Hirzel.

Klenner, H. (1953) *Formen und Bedeutung der Gesetzlichkeit als einer Methode in der Führung des Klassenkampfes*, Berlin: Deutscher Zentralverlag.

Kopp, G. (1950) *Die betriebliche Planung. Analyse der auf eine betriebliche Planung einwirkenden Kräfte*, Jena: Dissertation in Thuringia University and State Library, ThULB-Sign.: 4. Hist. lit. VI, 10002/3 (4), Jena.

Krahner, L. (1965) *Die Verfassung und das Recht der Stadt Gera in ihrer geschichtlichen Entwicklung bis zum 17. Jahrhundert*, Frankfurt A/M*: Rechtswissenschaftliche Fakultät Goethe-Universität Frankfurt am Main.*

Leitel, S. (1989) *Zur Herausbildung der bürgerlichen Rechtsperson unter besonderer Berücksichtigung der Entwicklung des sächsischen Territorialstaates*, 142 s., Jena: Dissertation in Thuringia University and State Library, ThULB Sign. 89 J 87.

Lieberwirth, R. (1997) *'Gerhard Buchda, 22.10.1901–20.12.1977. Ein Nachruf'*, in *Krahner, L. and Lingelbach, G. (eds), Gedächtnisschrift für Gerhard Buchda (22. Oktober 1901–20. Dezember 1977)*, Jena: Friedrich-Schiller-Universität Jena, 11–16.

Lingelbach, G. (1978) *Das Verhältnis der deutschen Rechtswissenschaft, insbesondere der Juristenfakultät der Universität Jena, zur Französischen Revolution zwischen 1789 und 1820*, 244 s., Jena: Dissertation in Thuringia University and State Library, ThULB Sign. 78 J 74.

Lingelbach, G. (1985) *Änderung der Beschuldigtenstellung bei der Überwindung des feudalen Inquisitionsprozesses im Spiegel der deutschen Rechtswissenschaft*, ThULB Sign. 85 J 29. 227 S., Jena.

Lingelbach, G. (1997) *'Das Institut für Staats- und Rechtsgeschichte der Rechtswissenschaftlichen Fakultät zu Jena (1951–1967)'*, in *Krahner, L. and Lingelbach, G. (eds), Gedächtnisschrift für Gerhard Buchda (22. Oktober 1901–20. Dezember 1977), Jena: Friedrich-Schiller-Universität Jena*, 33–55.

Richter, G. (1956) *Die ernestinischen Landesordnungen mit besonderer Berücksichtigung der Entwicklung im Herzogtum Sachsen-Weimar*, 125 s., Jena: Dissertation in Thuringia University and State Library, ThULB-Sign. 56.4562.

Roob, H. (1958) *Verfassungsgeschichte Gothas von den Anfängen im 13. Jh. bis zur Bildung des Landes Thüringen am 1. Mai 1920*; 251 s., Jena: Dissertation in Thuringia University and State Library, ThULB-Sign. U 58.4170:1.

Schmitt, C. (1934) *Über die drei Arten des rechtswissenschaftlichen Denkens*, Hamburg: Hanseatische Verlagsanstalt.

Schneider, F. (1960) *Dante. Sein Leben und sein Werk*, 5th ed., Weimar: Böhlau.

Werner, G. (1952) *Verfassung und Stadtrecht von Arnstadt*; Mitberichterstatter n.n. Harle; 89 s., Jena: Dissertation in Thuringia University and State Library, ThULB-Sign. 4. Hist. lit. VI, 10002/5 (6.).

Wolf, H. (1952) *Die Entwicklung des Gerichtswesens, insbesondere der Strafgerichtsbarkeit im Gebiet des ehemaligen Fürstentums Reuß älterer Linie*; Mitberichterstatter Friedrich Schneider, 152 s., Jena: Dissertation in Thuringia University and State Library, ThULB-Sign. 4. Hist. lit. VI, 10002/5 (7.).

Ziegler, H. (1969) *Einfluss der Französischen Revolution auf die Entwicklung des deutschen Handelsrechts*; Zweitgutachter Gerhard Haney; 305 s., Jena: Dissertation in Thuringia University and State Library, ThULB-Sign. 74 J 9.

9 Roman law and socialism

Life and work of a Hungarian scholar, Elemér Pólay

Éva Jakab

Introduction

A human being, as Aristotle emphasised, is a social being (*zoon politikon*). His life and work can be realised within the framework of a particular social system; in the 20th century in Europe, this meant enormous challenges for many legal historians. Elemér Pólay, the most significant Hungarian Romanist in the 20th century (also my teacher and 'Doktorvater') suffered a turbulent fate—but tried to remain human (and professional) in a cruel and inhuman world.[1]

Over 1915–1988, the beginning and the end of a scholar's life. The 73 years cover a bloody period: the traumas of two world wars, the Soviet-type revolution of 1919, the Treaty of Trianon and the subsequent general depression, the communist dictatorship of the 1950s, the uprising of 1956, and the 'goulash communism' of the 1960s. Elemér Pólay's life and work evolved in this socio-political environment, and he was forced to be a part of this world. His person and his internationally significant professional aspirations must be examined in this context to gain a true picture of him.

Early life, National Socialism and the communist takeover

Elemér Pólay was born on August 23, 1915 in Sombor, in South Hungary (Délvidék, today in Serbia). His father was a high school teacher who was forced to flee with his family after the Treaty of Trianon (a treaty that cut off two-thirds of the territory of Hungary after World War I) (Molnár, 1999, p. 184). They settled in Miskolc; Pólay became a pupil at the renowned Royal Catholic György Fráter Gymnasium.[2] At the end of each school year, the high school published a bulletin and old copies testify to students' performances. Almost every year, Pólay was among the best, decorated with awards and closing the school year as top in several subjects (reading, grammar, literature, translation, geography, drawing, and even physics). In addition, his final report in algebra underlined that Pólay was a model of accuracy.

A note from the 1931–1932 school year reveals that he was also involved in the activities of youth associations. He was a member of the *Vörösmarty* self-education group, where he regularly read from his literary work. In his last school year, he won prizes for his dissertations on history and Hungarian literature in the self-education competition. He was one of three students who graduated with honours from the class.

Pólay completed the high school curriculum with excellent results in all subjects, but his personal interest focused mostly on Latin and history. However, he chose law (persuaded by his family) rather than humanities, and in 1933 he enrolled at the Miskolc Law Academy.[3] Once there, Zoltán Sztehló's strictly pandectist lectures introduced him to the world of Roman law, which fascinated the young student from the beginning. He therefore decided to write his doctoral thesis on Roman law.

From this time on, newspaper articles and documents from Miskolc testify that Elemér Pólay was also an active member of the National Hungarian Protestant Student Association, which sought to educate its young members in social responsibility. For example, the Dean of the Law School, E. Somos, opened the Student Union's Jubilee Congress at Eastern 1936 and gave a lecture entitled 'Pro liberis' on the plight of the children of poor Hungarian families. Pólay attended the Congress as youth president of the Miskolc Association and also gave a presentation. Perhaps his work in this student association, and the experience he gained there influenced him in the choice of his early research topics on the social role of law (*Datio in solutum*, 1938, and *Relationship Between Land Ownership, Population Density and Population Growth*, 1938) (Pólay, 1938a; Pólay, 1938b).

At that time, the Miskolc Law Academy could only grant a diploma (graduation certificate), while the doctoral degree had to be obtained at the Law Faculty of one of the Hungarian universities by passing the *rigorosum*. Pólay chose Pécs and applied for both doctoral examinations at Erzsébet University: in 1937 he obtained his doctorate in law and in 1938 in political science.[4]

Two scholarships to the Law Academy of Miskolc, rewarding his outstanding student performance, proved to be decisive for his entire life and career. First, he received a two-month scholarship to Berlin and then another for a whole year, 1938, for Roman law studies at the Friedrich Wilhelm University[5] His teacher was Paul Koschaker, a highly educated professor of Austrian descent who had graduated in law from Graz and was also promoted there (*sub auspiciis Imperatoris*) (Beggio, 2018, pp. 33–49). He initially taught in Innsbruck and Prague and later received a university chair in Leipzig. He was appointed to Berlin in 1936, where, besides Roman private law and Roman legal history, he became an expert in cuneiform law and early Eastern legal cultures. Koschaker was the father of 'ancient legal history' who pointed out many Eastern influences in Greek and Roman law (Ries, 1980, p. 608). Koschaker's personality and research had a profound effect on Zoltán Sztehló, professor of Roman law at the Law Academy in Miskolc and also on Pólay, his pupil. This fertilising effect is reflected, for example, in the choice of topics in Pólay's scientific articles from 1936, which dealt with criminal law in Hammurabi's Law collection (*Miskolci Jogászélet* (MJ) XII 1936, pp. 3–4, pp. 53–58) and the irrigation culture of ancient Egypt (*A Földgömb* VII, 1936, 6, pp. 218–223).

The illuminating year in Berlin along with the influence of Koschaker's ideas led to a long study with the initially confusing title 'The German Nationalist Socialist Conception of Law and Roman Law' (*A német nemzeti szocialista jogfelfogás és a római jog*, 1938). But already the first few lines emphasize the author's true creed:

> 'National socialism,' says Wilhelm Coblitz, the leader of the German *Reichsrechtsamt*, 'sees it as a historic task and a primary duty to give the German people a German law.' This sentence sheds light on why the question of the status of Roman law is topical in the National Socialist German Empire. (Pólay 1939, p. 125)

It is surely not a mere coincidence that Paul Koschaker published in 1938 an 86-page monograph under the title *Die Krise des römischen Rechts und die romanistische Rechtswissenschaft*. His 'pamphlet' (*Kampfschrift*) was the first volume of the series *Schriften der Akademie für Deutsches Recht* (edited by Dr. Frank, the president of the *Akademie für Deutsches Recht*); it contained an expanded version of Koschaker's lecture at the Berlin Academy in December 1937 (Beggio, 2018, p. 173ff., esp. pp. 181–186). At that time in Germany, the lectures of many renowned legal historians were suspended or outright banned, and many renowned professors were dismissed, often prompting them to leave the country as soon as possible (it suffices to refer to the fate of Fritz Schulz, whose unfortunate encounters with the Nazi administration have been documented in detail by Ernst 2004, pp. 105–203). Roman law, in the eyes of National Socialist politics, embodied a liberal, non-national civil law—which they wanted to replace with a truly 'national' law based on Germanic folk customs. Many young docents had become advocates of National Socialist ideas, such as Franz Wieacker or Ernst Schönbauer.[6] However, Koschaker consistently stood up for the importance of the Roman legal tradition in European private law systems—and this was the very message that Pólay, his eminent pupil, brought back to Hungary.

After returning from Berlin, Pólay became a trainee lawyer, practising law in several places, and from 1940 on he worked as a court clerk and later as a clerk in Debrecen. In 1942 he was called to be a royal district judge for the Debrecen district (Molnár, 1999, p. 184). The schedule of the councils of the Royal Court of Debrecen for 1942 mentions Elemér Pólay as counsellor in the 1st Civil Council, which was competent to deal with 'matters of inheritance, trust, damages and other obligations, protection and resettlement cases, under the chairmanship of Lajos Oláh.'[7] Between 1945 and 1949, Pólay served as a county court judge in Miskolc and was soon appointed as a counsellor. His involvement in teaching Roman law can be traced from 1945 on: first at the Law Academy of Miskolc as a lecturer, but soon as head of the department of Roman law at Miskolc. In 1946 he graduated from the University of Debrecen with a habilitation and became a private teacher qualified in Roman law (Szabó, 2015, 39–46). His habilitation work, *The Role of the Praetor in the Development of Roman Private Law*, was published in Miskolc in 1944.

In 1949, his dynamic university and judicial career was at risk. In autumn 1949, the law academies were abolished throughout the country (among them also the Law Academy of Miskolc). Furthermore, the Faculty of Law and Political Science of the University of Debrecen was suspended. The professors lost their positions; some of them managed to find positions in the Law Faculties of Budapest, Szeged or Pécs—Géza Marton, for example, a famous professor of Roman law at Debrecen went to Budapest. Others had to change their teaching and research field for political reasons—Lóránd Boleratzky, for example, a professor of Protestant Church Law, was relocated to the Department of International Law in Budapest.

Pólay succeeded in gaining a position as judge and university professor in Szeged. The official documents of his appointment have been preserved in the archives of the Court of Appeal.[8] A note from the Minister of Justice to the President of the Szeged Court of Appeal dated August 6, 1949 states:

> Dr. Elemér Pólay, Judge of Miskolc, was transferred to the Szeged Court at his own request. I hereby notify Mr. President, as a further measure, that I have served him with the transfer document at the same time through the Chairman of the Debrecen Court of Appeal. From the order of the Minister: Dr. György Ruttkai, Public Prosecutor. (*Igazságügyminiszter* ('Minister of Justice'), 14.754/1949.I.M.E.)

A few weeks later, Pólay was already in Szeged and at work, as evidenced by the report of Dr. Dezső Kiss, Judge President, dated 29 August:

> With reference to the order of the Minister of Justice, dated August 6, 1949 [...] and to the decree of the President of the Szeged Court of Justice, dated August 11, 1949, I declare that Dr. Elemér Pólay, judge, appeared before me and began his service today.

At the same time, he was also appointed a lecturer in the Faculty of Law at the University of Szeged in the department of Roman Law. In the archives of the Court of Appeal, four short official papers testify to subsequent developments. A year after his move to Szeged, on September 28, 1950, Dr. Imre Lakatos, President of the Supreme Court, wrote to the President of the County Court:

> Dr. Elemér Pólay, judge of the County Court of Szeged was appointed by the Minister of Religion and Public Education for the Chair at the Faculty of Law and Political Science, University of Szeged, with this in mind the Minister of Justice removed him from the judiciary on the 25th of September of the current year, by resolution No. 26.320/1930.I.M. I call on Mr. President to relieve this judge of his position so far and to report the day of his release to me immediately.[9]

This change took place on September 30, 1950. Elemér Pólay became a full university professor (*ordinarius*) in 1951 as head of the Department of Civil Law.

From then on, after eight years practising as a judge, his career focused solely on university teaching and research. His rich scientific oeuvre was marked by the publication of seven monographs, each of them critically analysing ancient sources and scholarly work in Roman law, and by about 140 studies published in Hungarian and also in several foreign languages. He gave presentations in about 31 international conferences; his work was known and respected by the international community of legal historians. All those who knew him felt the tragedy of his sudden death on November 30, 1988. It is characteristic of his unbroken professional interest that he attended a scientific conference in East Berlin just before his death.

The Faculty of Law in a socialist state and the uprising of 1956

Elemér Pólay's career shows the peculiar ups and downs of a Central European scholarly life, drifted and battered by every storm of the twentieth century—but as the Hungarian poet, Endre Ady, has said, despite his heavy fate he remained 'still victorious, new and Hungarian.'

It is not easy for me to paint an objective picture of him, as my memories date back to my first entry into the Faculty of Law in Szeged. Being admitted to the Department of Roman Law as an undergraduate student, I was assigned to the committee under the chairmanship of Pólay. As a freshman, I diligently attended his lectures: all the students admired, respected, and loved him for his imposing knowledge, his consistent treatment of students, and his general humanity. A few years later, after my graduation, I sat anxiously in the dean's office and listened to his persuasive arguments about the necessity for having a new assistant position for Roman law—for me.

Recently, a colleague of mine, Béla Szabó, reported on Pólay's Debrecen years (see Szabó, 2015, p. 39ff), and his outstanding scientific achievements have been praised in several studies. But what do we know about his achievements in Szeged? What is the relationship between his significant work and its socio-historical context? To what extent does Pólay's teaching and research reflect the external political constraints of the 1950s? After all, Pólay might well have said along with Miklós Radnóti (a famous Hungarian poet of Jewish origin, killed in a concentration camp) that

> I lived upon this earth in such an age
> that idolized the sly police informers,
> whose heroes were the killers, spies, the thieves—
> and the few who held their peace or only failed
> to cheer were loathed like victims of the plague.[10]

Below, I recall a few moments of his rich life on the basis of some accidentally surviving documents I was able to find at the Department of Roman law, in the archives of the faculty, of the university, and the city of Szeged.[11] Turning the dilapidated pages of the Szeged daily newspaper *Délmagyarország*, we find the following small announcement: 'The next lecture of the Soviet law course in Szeged will be held by Dr. Elemér Pólay, university lecturer, 30 May, in the Great hall of the University, Dugonics Square, with the title "The Soviet Family Law."' The date is May 27, 1951. This lecture was jointly organized by the Hungarian Lawyers' Association and the University of Szeged. According to *Délmagyarország*, the 'Soviet law course in Szeged' continued for many years as a hallmark of legal activities in the city. The clear emphasis on Soviet law can be seen in a note from the Hungarian Academy of Sciences, which, even in 1955, strongly emphasized that 'it is the duty of the political and legal sciences to deepen the knowledge of the Soviet state and law, to make it known, and to know, process and utilise the results of Soviet law and legal science.' The writing, preserved purely by chance in the archives, comes from the proposal for the second five-year plan and was signed by Gyula Eörsi.[12]

The 'Journal of Jurisprudence' (*Jogtudományi Közlöny*) regularly informed the legal community about continuing legal education (for lawyers rather a re-education or brainwashing) in major cities across the country. Page 36 of the January 1952 issue of a report on the Second Soviet Law Course of the Szeged Local Group of the Hungarian Lawyers Association underlines that 'the organizers of the Szeged course have emphasised in their circular the utmost importance of thorough knowledge of the Soviet legal institutions for any worker who contributes in any way to the application of our socialist law.' Below it is posted the 1951–1952 schedule of the Soviet law course in Szeged, with names well known at the faculty, among them Pólay. In this academic year, Pólay hosted the first conference of the Civil Law department and gave a lecture on Soviet inheritance law on May 15 (*Jogtudományi Közlöny*, January 1952, p. 37). In April 1953, the official reports of the Hungarian Lawyers' Association recorded that the Szeged local group started, 'in addition to the series of professional training courses, a [new] Soviet law course in co-operation with the Szeged Section of Legal Sciences of the Hungarian-Soviet Society. The course consists of four civil law, criminal law and kolkhoz law lectures.' The opening lecture of the course was given by Pólay with the following remarkable title: 'The Development of Soviet Civil Law in the Light of Comrade Stalin's Teachings on Foundation and Superstructure.' The programme, published in the April 1953 issue of the *Jogtudományi Közlöny*, shows that all senior lecturers and professors were forced to produce lectures on highly political topics. János Martonyi (at that time already 'Candidate' of Law[13] and a full university professor), for example, had to present a paper about 'Issues of Discipline and Control in the 19th Congress of the Communist Party of the Soviet Union.' These lectures were, of course, promoted by the local newspaper, highlighting the contribution of 'the best professionals, many of whom have been awarded the title of Candidate.'

The spirit of the age is well represented in the introduction of the 'Annales' (*Évkönyv*) of the Law Faculty, dated 1953:

> Comrade Stalin teaches that the superstructure, once it has become a powerful actor, will actively contribute to the creation of the basis [...] to do its utmost to help eradicate the old basis and the old social classes. This teaching also sets the course for superstructure-type legal studies. We need to cultivate jurisprudence in such a way as to be a real promoter of the construction of the new order, of the socialist order. (Schultheisz, 1953, p. 3)

Parerga... blinks of light on the frozen air of the 1950s, when cruel pressures settled on civilian life, guiding personal fates with 'cunning fear.' But Elemér Pólay found—even in this fearful world—strength and faith to carry out excellent university teaching and scientific research. There are however ten years of silence in his publication list, no studies being published between 1944 and 1953. His habilitation dissertation (enrolled 1944 but defended 1946 at the University of Debrecen) was published as a monograph in 1944 (Pólay, 1944, p. 175 and Pólay 1943, p. 24), and just prior to that, a comprehensive study on 'Interest in Roman Law.' The next publication, however, was not published until 1953, when Pólay tried to settle at the Faculty of Law in Szeged, after his judicial career had ended abruptly (under political pressure). It is something to respect that, in the oppressive atmosphere of the 1950s, he wrote valuable, enduring studies on Roman law, such as his paper on warranty for latent defects (Pólay, 1953) or on Roman wills (Pólay, 1956).[14] Despite political hardships, he enjoyed notable popularity as a university professor in the city's cultural life. One example of this is that the local daily newspaper published a photo-report on him, examining civil law at the Law Faculty (*Délmagyarország*, January 16, 1954, p. 4).

On the other hand, the boxes of the Csongrád County Archives also contain a 'Report on University Teachers,' dated 1950, where handwritten notes are slipped between typed pages to indicate where and when a professor of the faculty has graduated in law, which languages he or she speaks, and whether the professor in question had ever been abroad. 'Travelling abroad' was divided into two categories: the Soviet Union or Western countries. In this era, the authorities had dangerous biographical data regarding Pólay's studies as a graduate student in Berlin, at the Faculty of Law of the Friedrich Wilhelm University, with Paul Koschaker.[15] Koschaker himself was convinced that the two most important pillars of European culture were Roman law and Christian religion.

In contrast was the cold and tight Hungarian reality, the constant ideological struggle of the 1950s. The work plan of the Methodological Committee of the Szeged Faculty of Law for 1955–1956 aimed at 'improving the moral-political education of students, their ideological training and the struggle to counter bourgeois views.' But even in 1961 (on February 22), a dispute was organised at the faculty on the standard Marxist subject of 'Fighting Bourgeois Nationalism and Cultivating Proletarian Internationalisation.' According to the attendance sheet, the meeting was led by Pólay and attended by all lecturers in the departments of civil law, Roman law, and criminal law. The focus of the ideological struggle was on the nationalist views of 'Hungarian cultural dominance' and 'we are a lawyer nation.'[16]

'Hungarian cultural dominance' was one of the characteristic issues of official Hungarian pre-war politics. The 1961 meeting found that one of the main features of this was the denial of foreign influence on Hungarian legal development. It is obvious that the university teachers were expected to take this issue seriously and reflect deeply on the demands of communist propaganda. The lecturers themselves sought to formulate their reflections on a professionally tolerable level. The lecturers stated that 'the teaching of the department of Roman Law strongly emphasises the fact that Hungarian legal development is far from being solely based on specific national customs, but that the reception of Roman law can be demonstrated in Hungary as well.' The protocol continues in a similar tone; it is typical that the empty headlines dictated by official politics are referred to by the educators with feigned seriousness though responded to with genuine professional arguments. The following note from the meeting interestingly echoes the veiled ideological struggle:

> The nationalist view of the relationship between Hungarian and Soviet law is also implicit in the opinion that 'codification work is superfluous, because, in the end, we are mechanically subsuming Soviet law.' Our departments also regularly fight against this [nationalist] distortion by showing specific regulations that are appropriate to our circumstances, with regard to responsible custody and other institutions in civil law.[17]

At this very meeting, the department of Civil Law was represented by Béla Kemenes, who was one of the leading figures of the (just finished) first codification of Hungarian civil law (Act IV of 1959).[18] This Hungarian Civil Code showed surprisingly little Soviet legal influence.

The uneasy meeting must have been, of course, protocolled, and it had to be forwarded to the leading organs of the university and the Communist Party. This was not of course an exceptional case, but the usual way of faculty life. Faculty councils were obliged to regularly discuss the guidelines of the current congresses of the CPSU (Soviet Communist Party) and the MSZMP (Hungarian Socialist Workers' Party).

On December 16 and 17, 1955, at the enlarged Faculty Council, the leading members of the Law Faculties in Szeged and Budapest, together with the lawyer members of the Hungarian Academy of Sciences, discussed the draft of the nationwide obligatory manual 'Civil Law, Part One, General Rules' written by Miklós Világhy.[19] In addition to the professors, representatives of the Supreme Prosecutor's Office and the Central Arbitration Committee, as well as invited judges and lawyers, also took part in the debate. The article on the event highlights that 'the academic depth and success of the debate was greatly facilitated by Elemér Pólay, in his keynote study "The System of the General Part of the Hungarian Civil Law Textbook."' It is worth quoting some of the professional-scientific arguments and politically coloured opinions: 'Critics have uniformly found that the manual is generally firmly rooted in Marxism-Leninism'; 'there is a consistent Marxist-Leninist view of content and method'; 'the author's position is in line with the party's policy, clearly outlining the perspective of socialist legal development'; 'he puts bourgeois views under creative criticism.' However, Szilbereky (professor of civil procedure) made some harsh criticisms: the role of civil law was not emphasised enough in the development of a socialist society. Nizsalovszky and Beck Salamon (professors in Budapest) accused the author of vulgarising Marxism. These were politically rather dangerous attacks.

One feels somewhat uneasy when browsing through such archival materials. It is miraculous that, in such a class warrior milieu, some of the old professors attached to civic values may have somehow survived. Hidden away from the official worker-peasant revolutionary policy, there was still a strong cohesive force of a well-educated, humanist civil society. One could even teach Roman law, in a pandectist or historical spirit, in an almost ideologically free manner. Literature could be promoted, ordinary people educated—well-educated experts from the old world (if not resistant) were needed. The existence of civil society is well illustrated by a photo from the local newspaper: Pólay is shown in the jury of the Petofi Literary Competition for law students.[20]

Pólay was respected and highly estimated in university and city circles. Between 1955 and 1957, he was deputy rector for science and education at the university of Szeged. In the Csongrád County Archives there are hardly any documents on the university's life in 1956.

These few uninteresting official records for this year suggest that the wind of uprising was not felt until the last minute. There are also only a few reports in the local newspaper *Délmagyarország*, about the university. For example, on March 3, 1956, it records that the 'Free University' (lectures popularising science among lay audience) would resume its lectures after a period of extreme cold; later on, there is a report that Elemér Pólay, Deputy Rector, would give the first presentation titled 'Legal Protection of the Family and the Child.' On March 27, Pólay can be seen in a photo talking to the Soviet delegation on 'The Soviet University Days.'

In the spring of 1956, the National Conference of Law Students was organised in Szeged: on April 26, the conference was opened by Dean I. Kovács and L. Németi, who, although only a young assistant professor, nevertheless held an important position as the secretary of the faculty representatives of the communist party. Pólay as deputy rector acted as a chairman of the Section for Civil Law (see e.g. *Délmagyarország* April 25, 1956, p. 3). October 5, 1956, Pólay presented the work plan of the Scientific Committee to the Faculty—university routine as usual. In the archives, the only datum concerning the actions of the revolution is the announcement on October 22: 'Until the introduction of a new regime for foreign language teaching, students will be exempted from attending Russian language classes.'[21] What the archive does not say is that on October 16th, 1956, the students of the University of Szeged held a great assembly at the

Auditorium Maximum, where they formulated 12 points that were transferred by a delegation to all other universities in the country. On October 23, there were violent demonstrations in Budapest and other big cities—the uprising had broken out (Perbíró, 2002, p. 19).

During these turbulent weeks, there is some correspondence preserved between Rector D. Baróti and the dean of the Law Faculty, E. Schultheisz, for example, on rethinking the teaching of Marxist-Leninist subjects. Unfortunately, most of the documents have been lost and the important events can only be reconstructed from other sources. In fact, as Deputy Rector, Pólay was in a very dangerous position. Even in the summer of 1957,[22] the local newspaper summarised the events at the Law Faculty as follows, including also Pólay's name and his activities:

> At the Faculty of Law, Baróti and Fodor's loyal counter-revolutionary associates, György Bónis and Elemér Pólay, insisted on the removal of certain communists. The Baróti-Fodor group delegated Associate Professor József Perbíró to the City Council to influence the counter-revolutionary movements in the city (*Délmagyarország*, June 25, 1957, p. 3).

Bónis, Perbíró, and his other colleagues lost their jobs or ended up in prison, but Pólay was somehow able to avoid their fate. Furthermore, he remained head of the department for Roman law until he became Professor Emeritus in 1988. Although after 1951 he also headed the Department of Civil Law, he had to give it up, and from 1961 on he headed only the Department of Roman Law. His family and immediate co-workers always felt that he had never lived without fear.

His expertise was, nevertheless, appreciated, and he was allowed to continue his teaching and research. As early as 1958, at the request of the National Museum, he was already working on the *locatio conductio* contracts on waxed tablets from Dacia and soon extended his work to all Latin documents from the Roman Empire found in Transylvania. During the late 1950s, he also explored the relationship between Roman imperial law and local law, enthusiastically writing papers and reaching very high international standards of legal history. However, the atmosphere, the university faculty environment, and the political vulnerability did not change much in the late 1950s or early 1960s. Reports on the ideological development of university teachers continued to be made. Teaching and research work were carried out under strict control of the Communist Party, shadowed by work plans and reports.

Let us take a seemingly politically neutral topic, the expansion of the departmental library. In 1962, the department of Roman law ordered books and journals to a total of HUF 3,332 (800 HUF for domestic literature, 800 HUF for literature from the socialist bloc, and 1,529 HUF for literature from the West).[23] Alongside Pólay's own hand-typed order, there is a disapproving circular from the state's 'Culture Foreign Trade Company':

> When reviewing the orders for foreign papers received in 1962, we found that the order for scientific books and journals of the People's Republics, and especially of the Soviet Union, was, although showing some increase, far from satisfactory. The majority of our clients still prefer Western press products.

It is well known that Pólay regularly published in foreign languages (in German, Italian, English) and tried to stay in the mainstream of international scientific life, for which up-to-date knowledge of the specialised literature would have been essential. It is almost inconceivable how he was able to keep up with international scientific life, despite such limited opportunities.

In 1963, the local newspaper reported on his scientific journey to Italy: 'Dr. Elemér Pólay, Professor at the József Attila University of Szeged, head of the Roman law department, travelled to Italy; he was invited by the University of Bologna. The professor from Szeged is attending scientific sessions on Roman law in Bologna and Florence' (*Délmagyarorszég* October 19, 1963, p. 6). This was without a doubt his first trip to the West and the first international conference he had been allowed to participate in since World War II.

The distorted optics of Hungarian universities is well illustrated by the clearly forced tone of Pólay's proposal for the designation of a new member of the department. On December 6th, 1960, as the head of the department, he commended a 'young meritorious applicant' for the position of assistant professor to the Faculty Council: 'Born in 1935, from a working peasant family [here the original text has been revised]. His father and family were actively involved in the struggles of the Soviet Republic and were therefore severely disadvantaged in the years of the counter-revolution.'[24] How could the former vice-president of the National Protestant Student Association of Miskolc survive and keep in with such people in this twisted world?

There is also an official letter among the old records of the department, dated 1961, signed by János Molnár, Deputy Minister, addressed to György Antalffy, Rector of the University of Szeged, on the aims of education at the Law Faculties. Its emphasized elements are the following:

> The Faculties of State and Law Science need to train communist practitioners who are familiar with the fundamental objective laws of society as revealed by Marxism-Leninism, with the theoretical foundations of state and law [...] and who are able to participate in the enforcement activities of socialist law and legality [...]. Philosophy, political economy, and scientific socialism must be taught in order to establish and consolidate the communist worldview.[25]

Socialist history of Roman Law

The last part of my article deals with two further topics: with the preparation of the famous Hungarian textbook of Roman law (written by Pólay and Brósz) and with Pólay's arduous pursuit of doctoral degree from the Hungarian Academy of Sciences.[26] Rather unexpectedly, these two topics are related.

The Roman law textbook, published jointly by Róbert Brósz and Elemér Pólay, has since its publication become a legend. Even Wikipedia points out that generations of students have been socialised into the world of law and order with the 'yellow book' (decorated with a photo from Accursius' *Glossa ordinaria*). The first edition was published in 1974 under the supervision of the state textbook publisher. The original advertising emphasised that it was a modern work, combining the latest achievements of modern Roman law studies with socialist aims, and it 'presents, from an exciting point of view, the nature and evolution of the Roman legal superstructure and demonstrates the decisive nature of economic life'(Brósz and Pólay, 1974, 1). Under the Marxist 'cover,' however, there was indeed a modern textbook of high quality.

The origins of the textbook date back to the early 1960s. The 30807/1960/III resolution of the Ministry of Culture (including 260 appendices), addressed to all rectors and to the deans of the Law Faculties in all universities, called for proposals for a curriculum reform.[27] The task was to compile and discuss training aims and methods by the Faculty Councils at each Faculty. At that time, educational reforms began directly from the initiative of the resolutions of the Hungarian Revolutionary Worker-Peasant Government.

On February 21, 1961, Pólay submitted three densely typed pages for the planned reform of Roman law education.[28] Among its goals were the break with the pandectist system, the validation of the historical approach, the separation of medieval terms from the original Latin terminology, the rethinking of the chapter on the history of Roman law, and so on. He presented many ideas that were realised in the 1974 edition of the new textbook. Most of the goals listed by Pólay were not particularly socialist programmes but rather followed recent trends in Western legal history. He stressed, for example, the significant views of Wolfgang Kunkel and Dieter Nörr (then professor at Münster).

At that time, Pólay already had a close professional relationship with Dieter Nörr, as evidenced by letters in the department's folders. For example, on October 25, 1971, he wrote to Dieter Nörr:

> Dear Dieter, please allow me to contact you with a request [...]. For a long time, I haven't received any message from you. Unfortunately, there was no possibility for me to take part in the German Legal History conference in Salzburg last year [...]. Most likely, you were in Salzburg. How are you? [...] Now, together with colleague Brósz, we are writing the new textbook on Roman law, and just recently I gave my monograph on the contracts of the Transylvanian wax tablets into print. After five years, finally it will be published [...].[29]

First of all he asked for help, for any possible financial support for a few months' research stay in Germany for his pupil, Imre Molnár. But the very personal, friendly lines quoted above also reveal his sad personal isolation and his continued desire to belong to the community of international scholars.

Finally, a few words about Pólay's rough path to the doctoral title at the Hungarian Academy of Sciences (DSC, Doctor Scientiarum). The annual Plan Completion Report of 1960 of the department of Roman Law emphasized that 'the first draft of a 25-print-sheet monograph' on 'Differentiation Processes in Roman Law' was finished and included by the academic publisher in its 1962 publication plan.[30] The departmental documents provide insight into some details concerning the creation of this immense work. We have, for example, Pólay's report, written in 1961, addressed to the rector, Dr. György Antalffy: 'On July 6, 1961, I applied to Comrade Rector for a 1,000 HUF domestic scholarship to cover the costs of my stay in Budapest for the sake of finishing my doctoral dissertation (bibliography research and consultations with Dr. Világhy Miklós).' With the very poor salary of a university professor, he could hardly afford a week's stay in Budapest. He did in fact receive the amount he applied for, and on January 12, 1962, he announced that he had completed his task.[31] His dissertation was at long last finished and he had signed a contract with the academy publishers.

Perhaps the quotations above, either from the contemporary press or from official papers of the universities and of the faculties, make it quite clear that in the early 1960s, official politics expected scholars to have Marxist-Leninist content and methods in their publications. According to the official order of the deputy ministry, quoted above, the purpose of cultivating legal history was to 'present the most important political and legal institutions in their development, according to Marxist history,' to explain 'the most important elements of the social experience accumulated in public and legal life, and thus contribute to a better understanding of the socialist legal system.'

Completing a doctoral dissertation for the Hungarian Academy of Sciences was a heavy task that led Pólay to inevitably provide a Marxist cover for the history of Roman private law. Indeed, when perusing the typewritten original manuscript (the only one was kept in the department's library), we see that the table of contents indicates this endeavour: 'I. Differentiation of the law of the slaveholder state' and 'II. Production conditions, forms of ownership and class struggle in the slaveholder society of Rome.' The titles of the chapters are in line with the 'customs of the age,' and certainly when reading the work, the first 50 pages are clearly marked by Marxist-Leninist historiography.

The Marxist-Leninist reinterpretation of world history was a combative research programme, strictly conducted from Moscow. This is reflected, for example, in the organisation of an extensive international project in which Pólay was invited to contribute. On November 14, 1962, he wrote the following letter to the Department of Social and Historical Sciences of the Hungarian Academy of Sciences:

> I received the attached letter from the Executive Director of the Institute of Ancient Science of the German Academy of Sciences (GDR) inviting me to

> participate in the publishing committee of a volume entitled 'Society and Law in Greek-Roman Antiquity.' Besides myself, the committee members would be a Polish and a Bulgarian professor, and the presiding Professor Irmscher. The purpose of this volume is to prove that ancient science is developing well in the socialist states. In my response to the letter of invitation, I expressed my willingness to be a member of the committee. I sincerely ask you to take note of my announcement.[32]

With permission, Pólay also asked whether several colleagues in other departments could write studies for this volume.

It is well known that Joseph Vogt, a member of the Mainz Academy of Sciences, started a large-scale scientific project in the Federal Republic of Germany in 1950 with the support of the DFG to combat Marxist historiography (*Forschungen zur antiken Sklaverei*).[33] Ownership of slaves and the socio-economic integration of slaves into ancient societies had become one of the cornerstones of the ideological struggle in Hungary and beyond the Iron Curtain.[34] In the light of all this, it is less surprising that Pólay (in consultation with Miklós Világhy) wrote the first 50 pages of his doctoral dissertation for the Academy in a class warrior spirit, based mainly on Soviet historiography: 'Production conditions, forms of ownership, class struggle in slaveholder Rome.'[35] To illustrate the obligatory spirit of this age, I will provide just a few typical phrases:

> The fundamental aim of our work is to show […] what changes in the superstructure have resulted in changes in the base and how the development of the superstructure has affected the base. […] The law of the slaveholder society […] is focused on a single legal institution, on the property on slaves (Pólay, Diss., pp. 3–4, 6). […] It can be stated that there are two forms of ownership in Rome, namely ownership of slaves and common ownership. […] The class struggle was carried out not only between slaves and freemen, but also between freemen. Differences in property as well as differences of origin and nationality were also strongly reflected in the inequality of rights in the area of law. (Pólay, Diss., pp. 49–50)

These first 50 pages, based strongly on Marxist ideas, represent about 10% of the 531-page dissertation. The following chapter discusses the separation of law from other social norms in ancient Rome (*ius, fas, mos, ius fetiale* and *ius gentium*) as the law of peace and war (Pólay, Diss. 53–154). The author then analyses the heyday of Roman law in the chapter 'Developing the perfect law for simple production of goods.' The author touches on the delicate balance and layered formation of the *ius civile*, *ius Latii*, foreign rights, *ius strictum*, *ius aequum*, *ius naturale*, and *ius praetorium* in the latent legislative process of law enforcement. A separate subchapter deals with the slow and gradual separation of the norms of *ius publicum* and *ius privatum* and the codification of the late 6th-century Emperor Justinian (Pólay, Diss. pp. 344–401, pp. 402–446.)

Concluding remarks

Turning over the yellowed pages of Pólay's archived dissertation for the Hungarian Academy of Sciences, with corrections in Pólay's own hand, the reader feels appreciation and respect: it is a thoughtful, well-grounded work that reflects on the results of contemporary international science. They show a sincere commitment to scientific research, a passionate desire for knowledge, and an infinite power to radiate knowledge from the pale pages. The 'internal emigration' of the creative mind: a distinguished lawyer, a dedicated university professor, and a well-educated European scholar seeking and finding refuge in the relatively small, secluded, elegant, and exclusive world of Roman law, seeking protection against historical storms, injustice, humiliation, inhumanity.

The manuscript of Pólay's dissertation for the academy was never published in Hungarian as a book.[36] Why? The authorities no doubt judged that there was too much 'bourgeois literature,' and it seems likely that despite the first 50 Marxist-Leninist pages, he delivered a too honest piece of professional work.

But his manuscript did at least meet the expectations of the Hungarian Academy Sciences: in 1964 Pólay was awarded the degree of DSc.[37] But afterwards, as the years went by, certain circles blocked his further career, not considering him worthy of a membership in the academy. Seven monographs, 140 scientific studies, and an international reputation were not considered sufficient for a membership in the Hungarian Academy of Sciences. Perhaps the shadow of the deputy rector's post of 1956 was never forgiven, nor his bourgeois origins and Western education.

This is also indicated by the fact that the Agitation and Propaganda Committee of the Central Committee of the MSZMP (Hungarian Socialist Workers' Party) even dealt with Pólay at its November 1986 meeting (just two years before the collapse of the communist world). Evaluating the initial experiences of OTKA (Hungarian Research Funds), Pólay's research was discussed extensively (his project on 'The Advancement of Roman Legal Thinking'). It is ironic to discover his name on the agenda as the main topic of the meeting was to reflect on and consider ways to take more decisive actions against democratic opposition![38]

Notes

1 Pólay was the most prominent Hungarian scholar of Roman law after the Second World War, both nationally and internationally. Of his generation of Roman law professors Pólay was the only one who, with great difficulty, obtained all (also the newly introduced Soviet-type) scientific degrees and titles and was constantly present also in international discussions. It is worth to mention, that at that time the significance of Roman law extended far beyond the boundaries of the discipline—it conveyed the dogmatics of private law to generations of lawyers at a time when civil law education was rather manipulated through Soviet patterns.

2 Most of the students were Roman Catholic; but the report states that Lutheran, Greek Catholic, or Israeli boys were admitted to the high school as well.

3 On the structure, teaching, and scientific achievements of such law academies, see Stipta, 2019, p. 203–244.
4 According to contemporaries, Lutheran students mostly chose Pécs to take doctoral examinations.
5 A detailed analysis of Pólay's life is also given in Molnár (1999), pp. 7–12.
6 For the life and academic work of renowned Roman lawyers in dictatorships, see the work of the research group led by Kaius Tuori, 'Reinventing the Foundations of European Legal Culture 1934–1964.' See also Tuori, 2017.
7 Igazságügyi Közlöny (Justice Bulletin), 1942, Személyi hírek (Personal news).
8 My thanks to my colleague, Tamás Antal, for the copy.
9 Ibid.; in 1950 the Hungarian courts were reestablished, and filled with trustworthy communists.
10 Radnóti Miklós, Töredék (Fragment), dated May 19, 1944, shortly before he was killed in a concentration camp.
11 Henceforth Arc. Dprt. Roman L. Szeged., Arc. Fac. L. Szeged, and Arc. C. Csongrád. For an overview on Roman law in the so-called socialist countries, see the chapter by Adrian Schmidt-Recla in this volume.
12 Arc. C. Csongrád. There is not a great deal of material, only six boxes or so about the Faculty of Law. Until 1951, Eörsi served as Chief Justice of the Ministry of Justice, first in the private law and then in the law-making department. In 1951 he was appointed consul for New York and Washington. He returned home in 1952 and became head of the Legislative Preparatory Department of the Ministry of Justice, leading the department until 1957.
13 An academic degree, introduced by the communist government, following the Soviet model.
14 Pólay (1953), p. 21; he deals with the same topic in his thesis for his 'candidate' degree at the Hungarian Academy of Sciences (see Pólay, 1955). At the same time, he was also occupied with the law of succession; see Pólay, 1956, p. 3.
15 New colleagues, recruited from the worker class, usually spoke no foreign languages and had never visited a Western country. One can imagine their attitude towards Pólay.
16 Arc. Fac. L. Szeged.
17 Ibid.
18 For the development of Hungarian civil law, see the chapter by A. Földi in this volume.
19 Arc. Fac. L. Szeged; teaching and textbooks were regulated and strictly controlled by the ministry, and the universities had no autonomy to purchase teaching material on their own.
20 Report in the local newspaper Délmagyarország, with a photo of Wagner Márton.
21 Arc. Fac. L. Szeged.
22 It is well known, and the revolution was soon suppressed. On November 4, 1956 the Soviet troops started their invasion of Budapest.
23 Arc. Fac. L. Szeged.
24 Arc. Fac. L. Szeged; the report refers to the Soviet-type revolution of 1919 in Hungary, which stayed in force for 133 days—and was admired by the communist government of Hungary. On the Horthy government, see Romsich, 2018.
25 Arc. Fac. L. Szeged.
26 At that time, scientific degrees were only granted by the Hungarian Academy of Sciences. The universities had no autonomy and the academy controlled, according Soviet patterns, all higher education and scientific research in the country.
27 Arc. Fac. L. Szeged.

28 Ibid.
29 'Lieber Dieter, sei es mir gestattet mit einer Bitte an dich zu wenden [...]. Seit langem habe ich von Dir keine Nachricht bekommen. Leider es gab mir keine Möglichkeit voriges Jahr an dem Deutschen Rechtshistorikertag in Salzburg teilnehmen zu können [...]. Aller Wahrscheinlichkeit nach warst Du in Salzburg. Wie geht es Dir? [...] Jetzt schreiben wir mit Kollege Brósz das neue Lehrbuch des röm. Rechts und eben in diesen Tagen habe ich meine Monographie über die Verträge der siebenbürgischen Wachstafeln in Druck gegeben. Nach fünf Jahren wird es doch endlich erscheinen [...].'
30 Arc. Dprt. Roman L. Szeged; the book was actually published in 1964, but only in German.
31 Arc. Dprt. Roman L. Szeged.
32 Ibid.
33 See www.sklaven.adwmainz.de for further information.
34 See the article by Rudokvas and Erkkilä in this volume.
35 The main sources of Marxism-Leninism were Maskin (1951) and Maskin (1953).
36 A German translation was published in Hungary; see Pólay (1964a).
37 For the contemporary scientific qualification system; see Pólay (1964b), pp. 586–590.
38 I would like to thank my colleague Béla Révész for this information.

References

Antal T. (2015) *A Szegedi Királyi Ítélőtábla története 1914 és 1921 között (The history of the Royal Court Szeged)*, Szeged: Országos Bírósági Hivatal Magyar Igazságügyi Akadémia Tudományszervezési és Dokumentációs Osztálya; Szegedi Ítélőtábla.

Beggio, T. (2018) *Paul Koschaker (1879–1951). Rediscovering the Roman Foundations of European Legal Tradition*, 2nd ed., Heidelberg: Universitätsverlag Winter.

Brósz, R. and Pólay, E. (1974), *Római jog*, Budapest: Tankönyvkiadó.

Ernst, W. (2004) 'Fritz Schulz (1879–1957)', in Beatson, J. and Zimmermann, R. (eds), *Jurists Uprooted. German-speaking Émigré Lawyers in Twentieth-century Britain*, Oxford: Oxford University Press, 105–203. DOI: 10.1093/acprof:oso/9780199270583.001.0001.

Homicskó, Á., Nánási, L., Stipta, I. and Törö, C. (eds) (2019) *A kecskeméti Református Jogakadémia története 1875–1949 (The History of the Calvinist Law Academy of Kecskemét)*, Budapest: KGRE ÁJK.

Jakab, É. (2015) *Tudós és kora: Pólay Elemér életútjáról, Acta Facultatis Politico-Iuridicae Universitatis Scientiarum Budapestiensis de Rolando Eötvös nominatae, tom. LII (2015)*, Budapest: Eötvös Roland University, 17–32.

Koschaker, P. (1938) *Die Krise des römischen Rechts und die romanistische Rechtswissenschaft (Schriften der Akademie für Deutsches Recht Nr. 1)*, München, Berlin: Beck.

Maskin, N. A. (1951) *Az ókori Róma története (The History of Ancient Rome)*, Budapest: Tankönyvkiadó.

Maskin, N. A. (1953) *Augustus principatusa (The Principate of Augustus)*, Budapest: Akadémiai Kiadó.

Molnár, I. (1999) 'Pólay Elemér', in Hamza, G. (ed) *Magyar Jogtudósok I (Hungarian Legal Scientists)*, Budapest: Nemzeti Tankönyvkiadó.

Molnár, I. (1999) *A római jog professzorai a szegedi egyetemen (The Professors of Roman Law at the University of Szeged)*, Acta Jur. et Pol. Szeged. 1999, Szeged: University of Szeged, 7–12.

Perbíró, J. (2002) *1956 Szegeden emlékeimben (1956 in Szeged in my Memories)*, Szeged: Belvedere Meridionale.

Pólay, E. (1938a) *Datio in solutum*, Miskolc: Ludwig István Könyvnyomdája.

Pólay, E. (1938b) *A földbirtokmegoszlás, népsűrűség és népszaporodás kapcsolata*, Miskolc: Ludwig István Könyvnyomdája.

Pólay, E. (1939) *A német nemzeti szocialista jogfelfogás és a római jog (The German National Socialist Concept of Law and Roman Law)*, Miskolc: Ludwig István Könyvnyomdája.

Pólay, E. (1943) *Kamat a római jogban (Interest in Roman Law)*, Miskolc: Ludwig István Könyvnyomdája.

Pólay, E. (1944) *A praetor szerepe a római magánjog fejlődésében (The role of the praetor in the development of Roman private law)*, Miskolc: Ludwig István Könyvnyomdája.

Pólay, E. (1953) *Az eladói kellékszavatosság szabályozásának első megjelenése a római jogban (The first traces of ruling the warranty for latent defects in Roman law), A Szegedi Tudományegyetem Állam- és Jogtudományi Karának Évkönyve (Yearbook of the Faculty of Law and State Science of the University of Szeged)*, Budapest: Tankönyvkiadó Vállalat.

Pólay, E. (1955) *Az eladói kellékszavatosság szabályozása a római árutermelő rabszolgaság korszakának fejlődő szakaszában (The first traces of ruling the warranty for latent defects in Roman law)*, Budapest: Manuscript in Eötvös Loránd University Library.

Pólay, E. (1956) *A római végrendelet eredete (The origin of the Roman will)*, Acta Universitatis Szegediensis, tom. II., Szeged.

Pólay, E. (1962) *A társadalmi normák differenciálódása az ókori Rómában (Differentiation of Social Norms in Ancient Rome)*Szeged: Manuscript in Szeged University Library.

Pólay, E. (1964a) *Differenzierung der Gesellschaftsnormen im antiken Rom*, Budapest: Akadémiai Kiadó.

Pólay, E. (1964b) *Wissenschaftliche Grade in der Ungarischen Volksrepublik. Das Hochschulwesen (DDR-Berlin), 7–8*, 1964, 586–590.

Révész, B. (2013) 'Állambiztonsági célcsoport 1989-ben: az Ellenzéki Kerekasztal', *Forum: Acta Juridica et Politica*, 4:1, Szeged, 169–219.

Révész, B. (2014) 'A pártállami idöszak ismeretlen hatalmi testülete: a Koordinációs Bizottság (1975–1988) (The unknown authority of the period of the party-state)', in Jakab, E., Pozsonyi, N. (eds) *Fschr. Molnár, Tanulmányok Molnár Imre egyetemi tanár 70 születésnapjára*, Szeged: Szegedi Tudományegyetem Állam- és Jogtudományi Karának, 387–399.

Ries, G. (1980) *'Koschaker, Paul.', Neue Deutsche Biographie (NDB)*, 12. Band, Berlin: Duncker & Humblot.

Romsich, I. (2018) *A Horthy-korszak (The Horthy Era)*, Budapest: Helikon Kiadó.

Schultheisz, E. (1953) 'Elöszó (Preface)', in *A Szegedi Tudományegyetem Állam- és Jogtudományi Karának Évkönyve (Yearbook of the Faculty of Law and State Science of the University of Szeged)*, Budapest: Tankönyvkiadó Vállalat, 3.

Stipta, I., (2019) 'A Jogakadémia tanári Karánk tudományos munkássága (The Scientific Work of the Teachers of the Law Academy)', in Homicskó, Á., Nánási, L.,

Stipta, I., Törö, Cs. (eds) *A kecskeméti Református Jogakadémia története 1875–1949 (The History of the Calvinist Law Academy of Kecskemét)*, Budapest: Károli Gáspár Református Egyetem, Állam- és Jogtudományi Kar, 203–243.

Szabó, B. (2015) *'A Debreceni Tudományegyetem Jogi Karának szerepe Brósz Róbert és Pólay Elemér pályakezdésében (The Role of the Law Faculty of Debrecen in Starting the Career of Róbert Brósz and Elemér Pólay)'*, in *Acta Facultatis Politico-iuridicae Universitatis Scientiarum Budapestinensis de Rolando Eötvös nominatae, tom. LII*, 33–46.

Tuori, K. and Björklund, H., (2019) *Roman Law and the Idea of Europe*, London, Oxford: Bloomsbury, DOI: 10.5040/9781350058767.

Index